# CHILDREN and ADOLESCENTS IN NEED

# CHILDREN and ADOLESCENTS IN NEED

*A Legal Primer
for the Helping
Professional*

## Virginia G. Weisz

**SAGE** Publications
*International Educational and Professional Publisher*
Thousand Oaks   London   New Delhi

*For information address*:

 SAGE Publications, Inc.
2455 Teller Road
Thousand Oaks, California 91320

SAGE Publications Ltd.
6 Bonhill Street
London EC2A 4PU
United Kingdom

SAGE Publications India Pvt. Ltd.
M-32 Market
Greater Kailash I
New Delhi 110 048 India

Printed in the United States of America

**Library of Congress Cataloging-in-Publication Data**

Weisz, Virginia G.
    Children and adolescents in need: A legal primer for the helping professional / author, Virginia G. Weisz.
        p. cm.
    Includes bibliographical references and index.
    ISBN 0-8039-4659-7 (cl). — ISBN 0-8039-4660-0 (pb)
    1. Social work with children—Law and legislation—United States.
2. Children—Legal status, laws, etc.—United States. 3. Child welfare workers—Handbooks, manuals, etc.—United States. I. Title.
KF3735.Z9W45 1995
344.73′0327—dc20
[347.304327]                                                    94-31050

95  96  97  98  99  10  9  8  7  6  5  4  3  2  1

Sage Production Editor: Yvonne Könneker

# Contents

# Acknowledgments

I wish to thank the volunteer and attorney guardians ad litem in Los Angeles and North Carolina for providing me with real frontline crises faced by children they represented. Undergraduate and graduate students at the University of California at Los Angeles (UCLA) and University of Southern California (USC) provided questions, comments, and encouragement. My students in the UCLA Interdisciplinary Graduate Training Program in Child Abuse and Neglect and my fellow faculty, Sue Edelstein and Robert Goldstein, reviewed many of the chapters and made helpful suggestions. My colleagues at Public Counsel were most supportive.

Judith Eastman, Jill Waterman, Richard Cook, Barbara Bergstein, Mara Ziegler, Michele Sartell, Inez Hope, Sue Slager, and Kathleen Murphy Mallinger provided specific comments on different chapters in the manuscript. I especially want to thank Frances Greiff, a volunteer social worker at the Children's Rights Project, who has reviewed and edited each chapter with such care and expertise that come from a professional life dedicated to vulnerable children. Thanks to C. Terry Hendrix at Sage Publications who challenged me to provide a practical legal primer for the professional who works with children and adolescents every day.

    I am grateful also to my daughters, Dawn and Allison, and to my husband, John, who has provided professional consultation and emotional support as we stretched the walls of our home study to accommodate endless hours of writing.

Virginia G. (Jenny) Weisz

# Introduction

*To the doctor, the child is a typhoid patient;*
*To the playground supervisor, a first baseman,*
*To the teacher, a learner of arithmetic.*
*At different times, he may be different things to each of these specialists,*
*But rarely is he a whole child to any of them.*

White House Conference on
Children and Youth, 1930

The conscience of a society is reflected in its children, all its children. But what happens to the unfortunate ones who are failed by their parents, the persons most intimately responsible for their well-being? How those children and others with special developmental needs are served legally by public and private agencies is the subject of this book. In looking at community systems to shelter children, to meet their physical and mental health needs, to educate, to confront child abuse and neglect, and to meet other critical needs, this book examines legal principles, statutes, and case law that shape the decisions so influential in the lives of children and adolescents, in some instances even before birth.

In subsequent chapters, case studies will be cited to illustrate legal foundations of children's law that come into focus when family breakdown or other circumstances place the child within the sphere of one or more community legal systems. It will be seen that although community intervention usually goes hand in hand with good intentions, there can be agency blundering with tragic results.

Throughout this discussion, it will be recognized that very often one aspect of children's law creates a major dilemma for those striving to make just and lasting decisions. That dilemma arises when the behavior or objectives of parents come into direct conflict with what appears to be in the child's best interests. In those situations, whose rights are paramount? Is it the constitutional rights of the parents or the more recently evolving rights based on the best interests of the child?

What are the basic needs of every child? What special considerations should be given to children who are emotionally fragile, who are physically dependent by age or medical condition, who have suffered physical or emotional damage from those responsible for protecting them, and who are especially vulnerable for other reasons and who may have had sorry treatment as a result of poorly coordinated community services?

For those children and for children and adolescents who have been abandoned, have run away, or have been removed from their biological parents, this book looks at what the community provides as a substitute for "the good parent" to remedy the past and to prevent further trauma. I have divided different facets of laws concerning children into separate chapters. The separation is only for the sake of clarity. Many children have complex needs that transcend chapter categories. Several case studies are included that bring a picture of the whole child into focus so that professionals educating the child will become aware of the legal demands of the social worker who is working with the child's family, the mental health professional who is treating the child, and the eligibility worker who is determining whether that family qualifies for Supplemental Security Income (SSI), food stamps, and housing. In order to be truly helpful, each professional must work with the child, the family, and other agencies to ensure a positive impact on the whole child.

For whatever reasons, some parents are caught up in such troubled family dynamics that they, too, are entitled by law to have community agencies make reasonable efforts to help them achieve a state of readiness to take back parental responsibility and reunify the family in a safe home. The book also discusses how termination of parental rights can give children other alternatives when parents fail and reasonable efforts are ineffective or inadequate.

No matter what measures are employed, we often will be left in today's world with a crucial unresolved question. During times of crisis, who in the community has the ultimate power to make certain that children and adolescents, with or without parents, will have the resources they need to anticipate a future with hope and confidence? This is the challenge for children's law and for all professionals who serve children.

This book applies selected legal principles to the problems faced each day by professionals who work with children and adolescents. It is hoped that this legal framework will help the professional contribute to a more cohesive structure of service when working with other disciplines in behalf of vulnerable children and adolescents. The case studies highlight the complexity of coordinating multidisciplinary services to achieve long-term positive results for children. Cases based on published legal decisions carry the legal citation and case name. Although the other case studies are based on actual problems of children I have worked with, I have changed names and some circumstances to keep identity confidential. This book is not intended to be a legal treatise but rather an easily understood and practical handbook for professionals and trained volunteer child advocates working with children and adolescents, who have legal rights that must be protected. Unless specified otherwise, *children* will be used to refer to infants, children, and adolescents.

# I

# Who Is Responsible for Children?

# 1

# The Best Interests of the Child

*And looky here—you drop that school, you hear? I'll learn people to bring up a boy to put on airs over his own father and let on to be better 'n what he is.*

Mark Twain, *The Adventures
of Huckleberry Finn*, 1884

The custody of a young girl was in question in an 1881 Kansas case. She was an infant when her mother died. Her mother's sister took the infant into her own home on a farm where work and love abounded. The child's father was a drifter. Five years after the child's birth the father and his wealthy parents decided they wanted her to live in the grandparents' home.

The judge observed the loving aunt and uncle who had cared for the child for over 5 years and wanted her to continue to be in their family. The paternal grandparents, on the other hand, promised a governess, a higher education, and superior opportunities for cultural enrichment. The judge recognized the strong bond of love between the child and the only parents she had ever known, her maternal aunt and uncle. His decision was easy to make. Basing it on the best interests of the child, he determined that the girl was doing well where she was and should remain in that loving home (*Chapsky v. Wood*, 1881).

The interests of the child, the parent, and the state balance delicately. The natural rights of parents have a constitutional basis in American law and cover such areas as control over religious training, medical decisions, mental health treatment, and discipline. Parental rights are not absolute. The child's interests are protected by the state through the *parens patriae* power. The state is not the ideal parent because of the limitations on the assistance it can provide to children and the difficulty of coordinating the services of many agencies to fulfill the needs of one child. The state uses guardians ad litem and special child advocates to protect many children whose parents' rights are questioned. The basic rights and interests of the parent, the child, and the state that are presented here will be elaborated on in subsequent chapters.

## Balancing Parents' Rights
## Against Children's Best Interests

Who in these final few years of the 20th century has the power, by law and by custom, to decide how children should live their lives? Is it their biological parents? Is it agents of local, state, or federal government? Is it political power groups? Is it the ancient cultural and family codes brought to these shores from all parts of the globe and modified throughout the last 300 years? With increasing momentum during the past century, a growing body of children's law has evolved to protect children and redress wrongs. A Kansas judge first used the best interests of the child standard in the custody decision *Chapsky v. Wood* (1881). Since the 1960s the U.S. Supreme Court has recognized that children have many of the same basic constitutional rights adults enjoy (*In re Gault*, 1967; *Tinker v. Des Moines Independent Community School District*, 1969).

Becoming a parent confers both legal rights and legal duties. At every point of encounter between parent and child, the law is behind the scenes to safeguard both the parent's rights and the child's best interests. This chapter shows how those legal safeguards work, not only in the home but in the community in which children encounter the other major determinants that shape their lives.

Two significant legal resources, to be discussed in more detail, are frequently relied on to help ensure that the child's best interests are considered. One is the early English common law concept of *parens patriae*, the power of the state to intervene for the protection of the child. The other comes from the recently developed body of nonaligned champions of the child: the guardian ad litem (GAL) or court-appointed special advocate (CASA). Each child advocate is appointed individually to act, often in a volunteer capacity, to represent children in court or to make recommendations to the court that are in the best interests of the child.

The "best interests of the child" standard is the basic guideline governing civil cases involving children. In broad terms, it means that a court must operate in such a manner as to further justice while at the same time promoting the welfare and well-being of a child. The best interests standard is used in a variety of situations: mental health commitments; delinquency hearings; abuse, neglect, or dependency hearings; and custody determinations following a divorce. In each case, the parents' rights and responsibilities are balanced against the child's best interests. Above all other considerations, the child's interests, in the eyes of the judge, are paramount. But to enforce the rights of the child above those of the parents, the parents' rights first must be overcome.

## Defining Parental Rights

The parent has the responsibility of guiding, protecting, and supporting a child until the child is no longer a minor. During the child's early years of relative helplessness and immaturity, parents logically are entrusted with making decisions and safeguarding the well-being of their children. Bonds of affection between parents and child usually ensure the parents' willing acceptance of the legal duties and myriad responsibilities involved with child rearing. Most parents act to benefit their children. Providing food, clothing, shelter, love, education, self-respect, and security are among the tangible and intangible ways a parent demonstrates concern and natural affection for a child. The parent-child relationship normally is free from interference by the state precisely because most parents do not harm or fail their children.

Both parents have a legal duty to protect and provide for their minor children and may be held criminally liable for failure to take reasonable actions to keep them from harm. The state can enforce the parents' duty to support their children within their means to avoid having them become public charges. If parents fail to fulfill their legal obligations, their parental rights may be terminated.

*Natural and constitutional rights.* Parents have a natural right to custody of their children. In 1923 the U.S. Supreme Court decided that the 14th Amendment protects an individual's right to marry, establish a home, and bring up children (*Meyer v. Nebraska*, 1923). More recent Supreme Court decisions make it clear that the parents' right to the companionship, care, custody, and management of their children is a firmly entrenched, legally protected interest. The parental right to custody is protected against state interference unless the child is being harmed substantially. Under early common law, the child, regarded as a chattel, was in the primary custody of the father; today both parents share an equal right to custody and equal responsibility toward the care of their child.

*Right to control education.* Parents' rights extend to controlling the education of their child, including the decision to send a child to a public or a private school. Parents have the right to guide the child's education, to help prepare the child for additional obligations of adulthood, and to give the child an education suitable to the family's station in life (*Meyer v. Nebraska,* 1923; *Pierce v. Society of Sisters,* 1925). In no way, however, should the parental right to control a child's education be interpreted to mean a parent completely can forgo providing an educational program for a child. Compulsory school attendance laws must be obeyed. The U.S. Supreme Court balanced the rights of Amish parents to withdraw their children from public schools against the rights of the children to a formal education when the Court reaffirmed the power of the state to require education to age 16 in a public or private school that meets state standards (*Wisconsin v. Yoder,* 1972).

In another case a state court of appeals rejected a father's claim of a fundamental right to educate his son, who had mild mental retardation, at home in his "School of Universal Studys [*sic*] and Understanding," which met all statutory criteria for nonpublic schools. The court determined that this particular father could not give his developmentally delayed son the quality of specialized care and training offered by the public school's special education classes (*In re Devone,* 1987).

*Right to provide religious training.* As part of the law's deference to parental control, a parent is allowed to decide what religious training a child will experience. This right is limited when specific religious practices conflict with public policy or morality. In *Wisconsin v. Yoder* (1972), the Supreme Court decision mentioned previously, the parental right to guide the religious upbringing of a child was interpreted to mean that Amish parents could limit their children's exposure to public education because of historical Amish religious beliefs.

In an earlier case, the Supreme Court decided a parent's control over religious matters concerning a child was curtailed by the state's power to establish laws against child labor. In this case, the custodian of the children used them to sell copies of religious leaflets on public street corners. Massachusetts criminal statutes did not allow children to engage in the public sale of printed material. Thus through its criminal statute, the state exercised authority over the custodian's religious practice to protect the physical and mental health of the children until they reached an age of discretion. The state may use the *parens patriae* power to restrict parental control by requiring school attendance, by regulating or prohibiting a child's labor, and in many other ways (*Prince v. Massachusetts*, 1944).

*Right to make medical decisions.* Parents are accorded the right to make decisions regarding medical treatment of their children because the law assumes that parents act to further the child's welfare and that children are incapable of rational, informed decisions. The law assumes further that the parent will pay for the medical services. For these reasons, parental consent usually is required before medical services can be rendered.

Apart from parental consent, the right to control medical treatment of a child may be limited by economic factors. The parent may want medical treatment for the child but be unable to afford it. Many working parents do not receive insurance coverage as a job benefit. When their income exceeds the maximum for medicaid eligibility, the parent often must choose between needed medical care and basic living expenses. If a parent should refuse to allow essential medical service for a child, the state may intervene to protect the physical welfare of the child by taking custody of the child. Some parents have been driven to voluntarily relinquish custody to the county to qualify the child for medicaid. The parental consent doctrine may be abrogated in emergency situations whenever a delay in obtaining parental consent threatens the child's life. In most states, a mature minor has the right to seek medical and mental health care. This is discussed in more detail in Chapter 2.

*Right to make decisions regarding mental health treatment.* In 1979 the Supreme Court decided that traditional parental control over a child's physical and mental health treatment should not be absolute in a decision for voluntary commitment of a child to a state mental institution. The court concluded that an independent examination by a neutral fact finder was a necessary check to ensure that the child met the admissions criteria for institutionalization (*Parham v. J. R.*, 1979). In extreme cases, unfettered parental authority can lead to inappropriate hospitalization for children or adolescents whose behavior is so taxing that the parents want them confined out of the home. The problem of overhospitalization, the *Parham* decision on commitment procedures, and the general mental health treatment of children are discussed in detail in Chapter 14.

> *Case study.* The control the parent has over determining treatment for the child and the position in which this puts the child and the therapist can be illustrated by the following case: Two college professors have three children. The mother so hates her son that even though he has threatened suicide, she continues to tell him in overt ways that she hates him. She currently is looking for a place to hospitalize the boy. His therapist believes it is the mother who needs to be hospitalized, not the boy. The mother drops out of therapy with anyone who remotely threatens to confront her. Unless the court appoints a guardian ad litem to represent the boy in advance of the admissions hearing, he is at great risk of being committed if his mother can convince a doctor to admit him.

> *Case study.* In another case, a developmentally delayed preschooler has treatment needs that are being ignored by the parents. This child can qualify for special therapeutic day care designed to stimulate early development. Although the child has significant delay, the parents refuse to utilize the available free program. Should these parents be considered as candidates for forceful government intrusion? If the parents are found to have neglected the child, the juvenile court could fashion a benevolent order by keeping the child with the parents only if they immediately enroll the child in the structured therapeutic day care.

*Right to discipline.* For control of a child, the parent possesses the right to discipline. A parent's ability to enforce obedience through discipline is subject to standards of reasonableness. When disciplinary measures exceed what is considered reasonably necessary, as with severe corporal punishment, the parent may become liable for abuse. The topic of physical abuse and corporal punishment is discussed in Chapter 3.

## The *Parens Patriae* Power Defined

Under early English common law, the father was entitled to the custody of his children for the purposes of protecting both their person and his property interest. On the father's death or because of parental impoverishment, the control of the child was left to the lord of the manor or to the local governing power. This practice introduced the doctrine of *parens patriae*, or ultimate parent, which gives the state the power to intervene in a variety of actions to protect both the child and the interests of society. The court has the power to determine who will have custody of the child. A judge using the *parens patriae* power should act as a wise, affectionate, and careful parent in doing what is best for the child (*Finlay v. Finlay*, 1925). The *parens patriae* power gives the court the authority to make decisions regarding the custody of children.

Although scholars have criticized judicial custody decision making as often reflecting personal values and prejudices, states have made the judge the final arbiter in determining custody disputes. Specific factors for judges to consider are embedded in the case law and statutes of the states. The mental health professional can provide valuable testimony that emphasizes critical factors the court should consider in a specific case. The following discussion is based on factors considered significant by most state courts.

## Factors for Determining
## Custody in the Best Interests of the Child

The difficulty of making decisions to promote the best interests of a particular child cannot be overstated. Useful factors to consider have included the child's behavior, the child's mental and physical health, the child's sex and age, the parent's love and affection for the child, the parent's past conduct in meeting the child's needs, and the state's goal of preserving a family unit (Oster, 1965). Although the long-term needs of the child also should influence a court's determination of what is in the child's best interest, this broad point of view is not always included.

*The law of human experience.* A decision may be based on only one's individual experience as stated in the *Chapsky* opinion written over a century ago:

> What the future of the child will be is a question of probability. No one is wise enough to forecast, or determine absolutely what would or what would not be best for [the child]; yet [the court must] act upon these probabilities, . . . guided by the ordinary law of human experience. (*Chapsky v. Wood*, 1881, p. 655)

*Social and developmental needs.*  In a series of books, Joseph Goldstein, Anna Freud, and Albert Solnit have sparked discussion of the best interests standard, giving special attention to standards for custody decisions. Making a strong case in their first volume for continuity with "the psychological parent," identified as the adult with whom the child is bonded most strongly, they modified their view to acknowledge the biological parent's primary right to custody unless that parent seriously has failed the child. Only then would the psychological parent be considered as preferential custodian in a nonmarital dispute. In most cases, of course, a biological parent is the psychological parent of the child.

The Goldstein, Freud, and Solnit proposals focus on the array of psychological issues that should be considered when custody decisions are made. They include the child's need for continuity with the psychological parent; the need to recognize the child's sense of time, which is much shorter than the adult's; the law's limited ability to intervene based on a prediction of long-term behavior; the court's lack of capacity to supervise interpersonal relationships; the principle that the well-being of the child, not the parent, family, or agency, must determine placement; and finally, the principle that the least detrimental placement alternative is best for safeguarding a child's growth and development. These principles give judges better tools than mere "experience" for making most custody decisions and can guide other professionals when they evaluate children and parents to make custody recommendations to the court.

Two basic themes emerge from their work as guidelines for safeguarding the best interest of a child: (a) minimum state intervention into an existing biological or psychological family and (b) making the child's interests paramount. These two themes are symbiotic in application until the family fails in its function, at which point the child's interests become a matter for state intrusion (Goldstein, Freud, & Solnit, 1978).

*Least detrimental alternative.*  To guide placement decisions, Goldstein, Freud, Solnit, and Goldstein (1986) introduced the least detrimental alternative standard:

> Specific placement and procedure for placement which maximizes, in accord with the child's sense of time and on the basis of short-term predictions given the limitations of knowledge, his or her opportunity for being wanted and

for maintaining on a continuous basis a relationship with at least one adult who is or will become his (or her) psychological parent. (p. 5)

Goldstein, Freud, and Solnit (1973) suggested substituting the "least detrimental alternative" test for the best interests of the child standard

> to remind decisionmakers that their task is to salvage as much as possible out of an unsatisfactory situation and reduce the likelihood of their becoming enmeshed in the hope and magic associated with "best" which often mistakenly leads them into believing that they have greater power for doing good than bad. (p. 63)

Although these principles give judges tools they need to make most custody decisions, professionals serving children recognize increasingly that the custody decision, even when carefully made, cannot guarantee to meet all the child's needs. This is true particularly when the state is awarded custody.

## The State as Parent

Although parents have the right to rear their children free from state interference, some are unable to exercise the concomitant responsibilities. Without removing custody, the state can provide assistance to those families and children as a preferred alternative to separating the children from their parents. But the historical role of the parent as protector of the child must yield to the *parens patriae* power of the state if the health and education or safety of the child are jeopardized because of actions or inactions of the parent. Once the state exercises its power of control over the child, the best interests of the child are governed by the rules and regulations of bureaucratic benevolence, subject to certain procedural statutory guarantees (see Rodham, 1973).

What responsibility does the state have to children in its custody? The system of state-provided services is so complex that the social worker assigned to a family often cannot begin matching the children's pressing needs with the most appropriate basic services. The child protective services worker, as the primary community agent charged with providing child protection, is stymied too often by tight budgets and inadequate family services and is powerless to ensure that other community services play a vital role in protecting vulnerable children.

Thus, the investigative social worker has three basic problems: (a) lack of control over services outside the immediate child protective services unit; (b) lack of control over such economic safety net services in the department as Aid to Families With Dependent Children (AFDC), food stamps, and the Special Supplemental Food Program for Women, Infants, and Children (WIC nutrition program); and (c) lack of control over supportive and treatment agencies such as mental health, child support, education, and drug and alcohol rehabilitation. Inadequate funding of public service agencies, turf boundaries that narrowly define the area of children's needs served, and office hours unmanageable for many targeted families make the process of providing services to families so burdensome that protection agencies often are pushed into the path of least resistance and remove the children from the home (Weisz, 1990).

*Services available.* When the state does intervene to provide protection for the child, it has an array of public services that should be available for families and children: public schools, day care centers, public hospitals, local and state mental health centers, social services, alcohol and drug rehabilitation programs, public health services, public housing and low-rent maintenance, parks and recreation facilities, and juvenile detention homes. Integrating these and other public services into a cohesive network to support families and children is a challenge to providers as well as consumers. A conglomeration of rules and regulations overlie the statutes, legal principles, and standards that are applied variously by agencies and courts of law.

*Coordinating multiagency service delivery.* When working together cooperatively, these public service agencies can do more than benefit a family. What is more critical, they can help to keep the child in the home. The costly foster care system, easily accessible to the child protective services worker, may be an unfortunate response to failures in agency coordination. Other professionals in the community share a responsibility to meet the needs of children in their care. A teacher who sees that a child is distraught over the unexplained disappearance of a parent should refer the child for counseling. Otherwise, the child's emotional state may deteriorate and the child's ability to function adequately in the classroom and in the community becomes affected seriously. But community mental health services for children are not available for all who need them. Children in state custody have special mental health

needs. These will be discussed more fully in subsequent chapters. The
following case study illustrates the importance of agency coordination.

> *Case study.* Sam was born into a poor family in New England. He is malnour-
> ished and lives in an unheated apartment with his parents and four older
> siblings. He develops an ear infection that goes untreated until the child has
> convulsions. The hospital emergency room doctor prescribes medication that
> treats the illness but does not prevent it from recurring. Frequent ear infections
> lead to hearing loss that goes undetected. Sam's illness is aggravated by his
> exposure to an unheated home. Although penicillin cures this ear infection,
> only adequate heat and improved nutrition will strengthen Sam's ability to
> resist further infections. No one at the hospital is authorized to send a family
> social worker to Sam's home to help his parents apply for food stamps or
> to Sam's landlord to make sure the heat is paid for and turned on.

Although Sam's parents have the right to custody of their children,
they cannot fulfill their responsibilities. They are hampered by poverty,
a lack of clout with the landlord in enforcing basic housing standards,
and a lack of sophistication about applying for urgently needed food
stamps and school lunch programs. It is not in Sam's best interest to
continue to be malnourished or to suffer recurring ear infections that can
diminish his hearing; nor is it in his best interest to be removed from
his parents and siblings who are the foundation of his emotional
well-being.

The least detrimental alternative for Sam would be to remain with
his family in their apartment with adequate winter heat. Regular visits
from a public health nurse and food stamps would be much less costly
than placement of Sam and perhaps his four brothers and sisters in foster
homes. Unless the emotional dynamics in the family are found to be
extremely poor—and there is no indication of that—the children's health
would be affected detrimentally more by removal from the home than
by the provision of support services in the home to strengthen the
family's viability.

The state has the power to intervene under the *parens patriae* doctrine
and can wield that power most beneficially by providing support services
for the intact family, turning to removal of the children only as a last
resort. Without public intervention, the future for Sam and his family
does not look bright. Continued malnourishment and illness make his
chances bleak to attend school regularly and to learn while there. Precious family resources needed for food, rent, or heat may be diverted

to emergency medical treatment. Thus, instead of being able to escape poverty, the family can be drawn more tightly into its grasp. If Sam's parents are petitioned into court for child neglect, the court may be able to fashion an order to make the social worker responsible for providing services the family needs.

## The Court-Appointed Advocate for the Child

To fill the need for a representative who independently will determine and protect the child's best interests, many state statutes mandate the appointment of a guardian ad litem, also called a court-appointed special advocate. Guardian ad litem appointments can be made for cases of delinquency, child abuse or neglect, termination of parental rights, divorce/custody, visitation, guardianship, and adoption matters. Although some states mandate appointment of a GAL, CASA, or attorney in all such cases, a court is always open to a motion to appoint a child advocate when the case warrants it. The appointment usually lasts from the time the petition is filed until the custody issue is resolved by the court and the child's custody is returned to a parent or the child is adopted (Weisz, 1987).

The Child Abuse Prevention and Treatment Act of 1974 mandated that any state receiving federal child abuse funds must provide a GAL to represent any child petitioned into court for abuse or neglect. Every state now requires the appointment of a GAL who often is, by statute, appointed to represent the best interests of the child. In many states programs have been developed using trained volunteers who work directly with the attorney to represent the child or are appointed separately as the GAL or the CASA. In 1991 over 91,000 children were served by 28,000 trained volunteer GALs/CASAs who provided countless hours of information gathering and advocacy and presented "best interests" recommendations to the court (National CASA Association, 1991). The GAL/CASA receives a minimum of 25 hours of thorough training and is supervised by professional staff usually under the arm of the juvenile court. The trained volunteer makes reports to court and keeps in contact with agencies responsible for working with the child and family. Chief Judge Poitrast of Boston Juvenile Court spoke highly of the volunteer GAL/CASA when he said, "They can irritate the hell out of the standard participants in the case. They have nothing to lose; they tell the absolute truth" (Golden, 1992).

The *Boston Globe Magazine* exposed the poor record of many highly paid state-appointed GALs who were attorneys, social workers, or mental health professionals who had little training in representing children and little concern for making thorough, independent investigations. Bias, conflict of interests, and incompetence were major problems that judges reported with many of the paid GALs (Golden, 1992). The paid attorney may work with a trained GAL/CASA volunteer. This partnership representation of the child provides strong investigative and legal advocacy that is cost effective, unbiased, and idealistic (Weisz, 1990).

The child advocate plays the following roles: fact finder/investigator; legal representative; case monitor; mediator; and critical consumer of information (Duquette, 1990). The child advocate has access to confidential agency records. If a GAL or CASA represents an abused child whose mental health assessment indicates that the child needs treatment, the therapist can convey that recommendation directly to the court or by way of the GAL, CASA, or attorney appointed to represent the child. In every state an attorney must be appointed to represent any child alleged to be a delinquent. The role of the attorney is to zealously defend the youth against the delinquency charges. This role is different from that of the guardian ad litem who presents to the court what is in the best interest of the child. The mental health professional who recognizes this distinction will understand better how to work with the child advocate in presenting evidence of mental health evaluations, treatment, and recommendations.

## Conclusion

The parent, the judge, the child's attorney, and the guardian ad litem or court-appointed special advocate are held accountable for protecting the child's interests. The court determines who has custody and what services should be ordered to safeguard the child whose parents have not exercised their rights in a capable manner. Other professionals provide these services to help make the child safe outside the courtroom. At times the responsibilities of these professionals may conflict with parental authority. Professional duty to children will be explored in Chapter 2.

# 2

# Professional Responsibility for Children

*Everyone who receives the protection of society owes a return for the benefit, and . . . each should be bound to observe a certain line of conduct towards the rest.*

John Stuart Mill,
*On Liberty*, 1857

A therapist treating parents of two adopted children was criminally charged for failure to report abuse. The parents, who operated a preschool, had been seeing the therapist for several months regarding what the therapist called "time-outs," which were used to discipline their adopted children. Their 9-year-old boy was confined regularly to a small, unfinished, damp basement cubicle, large enough to hold only a sleeping bag and with a light bulb dangling from the ceiling. When not in school, the child was required to spend all his time confined to his basement room. He could leave only to go upstairs to the bathroom. His younger sister, who was enuretic, had been confined for months to the kitchen where she slept on the floor in a sleeping bag. The couple's two biological children had their own room and complete run of the house.

Although the therapist argued that the parents were doing fine in treatment, he heard only their side of the story. The children had no one to protect them from the gross neglect and abuse to which they were subjected chronically. Only when school personnel finally reported the parents were the children able to get the help and protection they desperately needed. The boy had been so emotionally traumatized that he had to be admitted later to a state mental hospital.

Professionals who serve children act under basic principles embedded in law, professional codes of ethics, state regulations, and specific rules of the agency employing them. This chapter will consider how the

16

professional can balance the needs of the child against the rights of the parent and at the same time maintain professional, ethical, and legal standards.

Because children are dependent, they are vulnerable to the actions of adults whose intervention can, at times, be overreaching. From their earliest years, children are taught to do as adults tell them, trusting the adult authority to know what is best. Of all professionals, those in the mental health field are in key positions to know when their child clients are being abused, neglected, or exploited. Although most professionals would take action to protect the children in Jim Jones's cult before he exploited them and eventually orchestrated their deaths, many would pause before intervening when a distressed parent commits a daughter to a mental hospital because she has started experimenting with marijuana. Where does the mental health professional strike a balance between serving the parent or guardian who consents to treatment (and pays the bill) and serving and protecting the child who is the client?

A young child rarely seeks mental health services without the help of an adult, usually a parent. Young children are not able to provide consent for treatment, although in many states adolescents have that right. Most children should not be expected to understand the need to investigate the possible consequences of treatment before agreeing to proceed. Therefore, the therapist of the young child must obtain the consent of the parent or guardian before beginning an evaluation or providing treatment. In the area of confidentiality, the professional must place the parent's desire to know what the child says in therapy against the child's need to be in a confidential and trusting therapeutic relationship. If, before evaluation or therapy begins, the therapist explains the rules of confidentiality to both parent and child, the effectiveness of the therapy will be enhanced. Informed consent and confidentiality in relation to child therapy are complicated by a unique consideration: the need to break confidentiality to warn victims or to make mandated child abuse and neglect reports. These issues will be discussed further in both this chapter and in subsequent chapters.

## The Doctrine of Informed Consent

Certain principles of the doctrine of informed consent need to be understood when the doctrine is applied to the treatment of children.

The professional always has the duty to disclose relevant information to a patient seeking treatment. The patient must consent willingly to the proposed treatment or therapy. When the child is the patient, parental consent must be obtained. In some states, assent by the child is necessary also in specific kinds of situations.

Legally effective informed consent requires legal competence of the patient to make a decision, the provision of sufficient information to allow the patient to make a knowledgeable choice, and the lack of coercion of the patient, allowing freedom of choice (Merz & Fischoff, 1990). Thus the elements of consent are capacity, relevant information, and voluntariness.

*Capacity.* Decision-making capacity requires to a variable degree possession of a set of values and goals, the ability to communicate and to understand information, and the ability to reason and to deliberate about one's choices (President's Commission, 1982). Capacity is expressed usually in terms of mental capability to know and understand the nature and consequences of personal action. A person who lacks capacity for one purpose does not necessarily lack it for other purposes. Thus a 7-year-old child might not be able to sign a contract to build a grocery store but would be able to buy a candy bar.

Parents are considered to have the capacity to consent to treatment of their children based on the assumption that parents seek what is best for their children. Parental consent usually is necessary also when the child will be a research subject. The interest of parents in making important decisions regarding the welfare of their children normally overrides the child's competency or right to decide (Buchanan & Brock, 1990).

*Relevant information.* After considering capacity to give consent, the therapist must consider the element of relevant information. Consent is ineffective unless information is communicated clearly in relation to the subject matter for which the consent has been sought and in terms the patient can understand. The information must encompass everything material and relevant for a knowledgeable decision. This includes the advantages and dangers inherently and potentially involved in a medical treatment or a type of therapy. Physical, social, psychological, legal, and long- and short-term benefits and risks should be explained and alternate courses of therapy discussed as well as the patient's right to give, withhold, and withdraw consent without reprisals. When the explanation of the risks poses a detrimental threat to the health of the patient, the professional is permitted to be excused for failing to disclose. This is called the therapeutic exception. The professional's duty to disclose relevant information is measured objectively by the standard of a reasonable person in the patient's position. The test would be the level of significance that a reasonable person would attach to the risks and advantages of the proposed therapy (*Canterbury v. Spence*, 1972).

Psychiatrist Charles Popper (1987) discussed the problem of prescribing psychotropic medications for children in the face of uncertainty. He added the concept of emotional consent, a clinical concept that he believes is crucial for clinical care. It allows the parents to emotionally "come to terms" with the nature of the child's illness and treatment recommendations and adds a clinical ethic to the legally mandated requirements for informed consent by the family and assent by the child.

*Voluntariness.* The third and final element of the informed consent principle is that of voluntariness. The professional must not use coercion, duress, rewards, or punishments in order to obtain consent. Special caution must be taken in restrictive settings such as public hospitals and state institutions, in which the patient is most likely to do what is asked or expected. It is significant especially that the sole fact of a child or adolescent being institutionalized does not mean that the young person loses the right to be informed and to give assent. Under a typical state statute, consent can be invalidated by "any element of force, fraud, deceit, duress, coercion, or undue influence" (California Health and Safety Code sec. 24173[e]).

Obtaining the consent of the parent who has legal custody is necessary in many states unless a court orders otherwise. The professional who treats or does research with a child without the custodial parent's consent could be subject to professional discipline (*White v. North Carolina State Board of Examiners of Practicing Psychologists*, 1990).

## Parental Consent Exceptions

Several exceptions to the legal requirement of parental consent are recognized: emergency situations endangering a child's health, treatment of emancipated or mature minors, and instances in which parents unreasonably refuse to consent to treatment. The following case study illustrates the need for the emergency exception to the consent rule.

> *Case study.* Nick, age 16, began hallucinating and acting violent on a transcontinental flight to his mother's home after a visit with his father. When the plane touched down on its first stop, police removed the boy from the plane and booked him at the local jail. When the severity of his emotional condition became apparent, he was transferred to a mental hospital. The hospital was not able to contact either parent for consent until after he was admitted to the hospital. The capacity of the youth was limited because of his age and mental condition. Only Nick knew how to contact his parents. Thus, neither Nick nor his parents were capable of giving consent for treatment.

The professionals treating Nick had to make a judgment as to whether the condition was severe enough to endanger the minor's life or if left untreated would threaten permanent impairment. The law assumes parental consent would be granted in such emergencies and makes the parents financially responsible for emergency care provided for their children.

*Emancipated or mature minors.* Minors who have been emancipated legally have the capacity to consent to their own medical treatment. In most states minors must be at least 14 and able to prove to the court that they can provide their own support and make mature decisions before the court will emancipate them. Once emancipated, the adolescent has the right to make legal decisions and enter into contracts in the same way as an adult.

Other adolescents who have reached the minimum age defined in state laws and who have the maturity required for making important decisions are allowed to seek certain types of treatment without parental consent. Many states give adolescents the capacity to seek treatment for such problems related to substance abuse, pregnancy, communicable disease, mental illness, or obtaining contraceptives. Virtually every state has legislation allowing minors to consent to treatment for venereal disease (Horowitz & Davidson, 1984).

A Supreme Court decision upheld the Pennsylvania statute that required parental consent for women under the age of 18 who seek an abortion (*Planned Parenthood v. Casey*, 1992). Evaluating whether a minor is mature enough to make an abortion decision with court approval but without parental consent is a matter of current debate. Some professionals believe that judging the maturity of a pregnant teenager is not within the realm of the mental health professional's expertise (Melton & Pliner, 1986); others propose that such an evaluation can be made if it is based on the girl's capability of appreciating the nature, extent, and probable consequences of proposed treatment alternatives (Carter & St. Lawrence, 1985).

Another Supreme Court decision raises the issue of the competence of a minor to decide to have an abortion (*Ohio v. Akron Center for Reproductive Health*, 1990). In some states the mature minor rule allows an adolescent to bypass the need for parental consent by submitting evidence of her maturity to a judge who then rules if the minor is mature and therefore competent to make her own decision regarding abortion. A professional evaluation is required to give the judge the clear and convincing evidence needed to make a judicial determination (Quinn, 1991).

Other states give to a child age 12 or older who is deemed to be a mature minor by the attending physician the capacity to consent to mental health treatment or counseling on an outpatient basis if the child presents a risk of serious physical or mental harm to himself or others without such treatment or is the alleged victim of incest or child abuse (California Civil Code sec. 25.9(a), for example). States may remove the risk of liability for breach of confidentiality by allowing therapists to notify parents that the minor is in therapy in situations in which parental notification would benefit the child's treatment. California requires parental notification and participation for therapy with violent or abused minors unless the therapist documents reasons why that would be inappropriate (California Civil Code sec. 25.9(a) (Suppl.), 1991).

*Parents unreasonably refuse to consent to treatment.* Children may need treatment that the parents oppose. The opposition may be based on religious conviction against immunization or blood transfusions or for other personal or financial reasons. Professionals rarely proceed with treatment in opposition to the parent unless the foregoing exceptions can be applied or a petition can be brought against the parents alleging medical neglect. The professional will want the court to determine not only whether it is reasonable for the child to receive treatment but also who will be financially responsible for the treatment. Although the parent has the capacity, the professional can turn to the judge to exercise that capacity when the parent's refusal is unreasonable.

## Assent of the Child

Assent of the child requires the professional to give attention to the child, provide the child with information, and offer the child the opportunity to express feelings about the treatment. Assent is advised to begin at age 7 when most children have reached the Piagetian stage of concrete operations, can discuss their motivations, and can conceptualize long-term consequences. Clients or research subjects deemed capable of providing assent, generally those older than 7 years of age, should agree affirmatively to participate. The age, maturity, and psychological state of the child are factors to consider in determining whether to proceed with therapy or research without a child's assent (DeKraai & Sales, 1991).

## Types of Consent

Two types of consent are used. The first type is active. It requires the signature of the patient or the parent before intervention may begin. Active consent is used for medical and psychological treatment and therapy. It is required also in most legal, educational, social service, and business settings. Passive consent is used sometimes in research settings. Complete information is sent to the parent or authority whose consent is needed. The person is asked to consent passively (no written signature required) or to sign a refusal to participate. If nothing in writing is received from the person whose consent is sought, the professional then assumes that consent is given and proceeds with the research or intervention. Before deciding to waive active informed consent, psychologists planning archival research or the study of anonymous naturalistic observations should consult with American Psychological Association, federal, and state guidelines or human subject review committees at the university level. Consider the following case study:

*Case study.* Twenty-year-old Kim went to the prenatal clinic for her regular checkup. While waiting for the usual blood test, physical exam, and her physician's battery of questions about her health, she was given a printed questionnaire.

"Part of the routine of the clinic," the receptionist said. "We ask all expectant mothers to fill it out."

The title on the sheet was innocent enough: "Differences in Bringing Up Children." She thought it probably was used in a research project at the university connected to the clinic. The questions were designed generally to measure self-awareness, self-control, attitudes about upbringing, and perceptions about how much help or support the mother could expect from family members, friends, and neighbors. What Kim did not know was that the interpretation of her responses might result in labeling her a potential child abuser.

Negative implications from Kim's answers might lead to the conclusion that she was at high risk of being an abusive or neglectful parent based on a comparison of her responses to those of known abusing mothers. As such screening is intended to prevent abuse and neglect, mothers labeled as "high risk" would be offered the kinds of services and supports normally targeted for abusing parents. Does the well-meaning intention of preventing possible abuse give the state the right to try to protect an unborn child by invading the parent's right to privacy? A test that correctly or incorrectly labels a person a "potential child abuser" has a powerful capacity to stigmatize. If the test interpretation is false, the negative consequences could be severe. Psychiatrist R. D. Laing (1967), for one, has called attention to the power of diagnosis in molding people's behavior, leading them to "act as they are called" (p. 139). A mother falsely labeled in that fashion might have a major emotional hurdle to overcome in bonding with her child and feeling secure in her role as parent.

Although the signing of consent forms prior to treatment is routine in public clinics, our legal system requires such consent to be fully informed and voluntary. Kim has the right to be informed that the test is used to identify potentially abusing mothers and that the test results are used as a basis of intervention with services. More important, Kim should be told that no known screening test can identify accurately a distinct group of parents who will physically abuse or seriously neglect their children (Helfer, 1976). If such tests are administered only to families that cannot afford private care, they discriminate on the basis of social class; maltreatment occurs in families at all levels of society. Kim's consent must be truly voluntary. It cannot be won when she is under exceptional stress or under an implied threat to have her needed care withheld if she fails to "volunteer" (Weisz, 1978).

What would you advise Kim if you knew the questionnaire was designed to label potential child abusers? If you, as a professional, knew the questionnaire would mislabel at least 20% of the mothers, would you administer it? If the questionnaire inquired about drug or alcohol use and if you were Kim and you had a history of substance abuse, how would you answer those questions? If you were asked to complete the questionnaire in the office of your private obstetrician, would your actions be any different than Kim's? If you were seeking Kim's informed consent, what would you tell her before handing her the questionnaire? What elements of coercion can be found in this scenario? Should Kim be treated any differently if she is a teenager? Mental health professionals, especially when involved in research, must answer these questions every day.

## Confidentiality

The ethic of confidentiality protects the patient or client from any unauthorized disclosure of information. The content of information that passes between the professional and the patient or client is held in confidence. Even the fact that the person is being seen by the professional is confidential. The justification for confidentiality is based on several factors. Highly personal information is revealed in therapy. The release of this information would invade the patient's right to privacy. Secrecy in therapy is required to encourage people to be fully open to the therapist. A guarantee of secrecy is required before some people will choose to enter therapy. This secrecy is an essential basis for the development of a trusting relationship between the therapist and the patient (Smith & Meyer, 1984). The tongue-wagging practitioner could lose a professional license for willful and unauthorized communication of information received in professional confidence. But legitimate instances do arise when protection of the client or safety of members of the community may require the professional to breach confidentiality. A therapist has the duty to warn the intended victim if a client threatens harm. A physician or a therapist is mandated to report any reasonable suspicion of child abuse or neglect.

### Reporting Threatened Harm

The *Tarasoff v. Regents of the University of California* decision (1976) established the legal principle that the therapist owes a legal duty not only to his patient but also to his patient's would-be victim and is subject in both respects to scrutiny by judge and jury. The *Tarasoff* case provides fertile ground for exploring the limits of confidentiality.

> *Case study.* On October 27, 1969, Prosenjit Poddar, a former psychiatric patient, killed Tatiana Tarasoff. Two months before the murder, Poddar confided to his therapist his intention to kill Tatiana when she returned home after spending the summer in Brazil. On the therapist's request to hold Poddar for hospital commitment, the campus police briefly detained Poddar but released him when he appeared rational and promised to stay away from Tatiana. The director of the department of psychiatry concurred that no action should be taken to hospitalize Poddar. When Poddar was released from custody, the hospital staff failed to notify the parents of Tatiana that their daughter was in danger. Subsequently, Poddar persuaded Tatiana's brother to share an apartment with him near Tatiana's residence. Shortly after Tatiana returned from Brazil, Poddar went to her residence and killed her. The court decided that the therapist and his supervisor could not escape liability merely because Tatiana herself was not their patient and concluded that when a patient presents a serious danger of violence to another, the therapist incurs an obligation to use reasonable care to protect the intended victim.

Following a discussion on the essential quality of free and open communication in psychotherapy, the court concluded that "the public policy favoring protection of the confidential character of patient-psychotherapist communications must yield to the extent to which disclosure is essential to avert danger to others. The protective privilege ends where the public peril begins" (*Tarasoff v. Regents of the University of California*, 1976, pp. 442, 27, 347).

How does the Tarasoff opinion apply to a practice with children and adolescents? Consider a case brought against a county. A youth known to have extremely assaultive behavior was released from county custody into the community. The youth later killed a 5-year-old child in the neighborhood. Should the county be held liable for its failure to notify the youth's mother of his potential for violent acts or to notify the local police? If a therapist had evaluated the youth prior to his release and was aware of his violent behavior, the therapist would at least have the duty to warn his mother. The duty to warn the mother would include an additional mandated breach in confidentiality if the youth's behavior had been suicidal while he was in county custody.

*Court proceedings.* If the judge orders the evaluation of a child or parent, the client knows from the outset that the psychological report will go

to the judge and attorneys; thus the formal psychologist-client privilege would not apply. If a party to a court hearing deliberately makes
his mental condition an issue in a lawsuit, information from the therapist also may be presented to the court. Therapists should seek legal
advice for breaching confidentiality in such situations, especially when
abuse is alleged by the county or in a divorce proceeding (Myers, 1992).

### Reporting Child Abuse

The next exception to the rule of confidentiality is the legal mandate
to report reasonable suspicions of child abuse. This portion of the
chapter will discuss this legal but professionally controversial obligation to report. Consider the following scenario.

> *Case study.* A father in therapy for severe depression reveals to his thera-
> pist that he has been masturbating as he peeks through a crack in the bathroom
> door to watch his 12-year-old daughter bathe. The following week he in-
> dicates that he has been fondling her breasts. Aware that the child could be
> removed from the home and placed in an institutional county shelter or in a
> foster home, the psychologist is concerned that the progress the father could
> make in therapy would be reversed if the therapist breaches confidentiality
> by reporting this suspicion of sexual abuse. He also fears that the father never
> again would be able to trust a therapist. However, the duty to warn compels
> the therapist to break the confidentiality by warning the mother to protect
> her child. Under child abuse and neglect reporting laws, the therapist is
> required also to report the father's action to the department of children's
> services (DCS). The therapist is not required to tell the parent that a report
> is being made; however, advising the parent or even making the report in
> the presence of the parent is more therapeutic than being secretive. If the
> parent is psychotic, has poor impulse control, or has an alcohol or drug
> problem, informing the parent may not be appropriate (Peterson & Urquiza,
> 1993).

Statutory reporting laws in each state clarify the duty of the professional to report this suspicion of abuse. In 1974 the passage of the Child
Abuse Prevention and Treatment Act set in motion a comprehensive system of child protection (42 U.S.C.A. sec. 5103). All states now have
mandatory reporting laws based on a reasonable suspicion of current
abuse or neglect. These reporting laws abrogate the statutory profes-
sional-client privilege. Mandatory reporters in most states include

licensed mental health professionals as well as physicians, teachers, day care workers, and others who have professional contact with children. In some states, all persons, professional or not, have a mandatory duty to report any reasonable suspicion of abuse or neglect. Some statutes require reporting if the professional has direct contact with the child; statutes of other states do not require actual observation of the abuse or receipt of the abuse disclosure (*Krikorian v. Barry*, 1987). Under those laws, therapists treating adult abusers must report their clients. Mandatory reporters are protected from civil or criminal liability for any report made in good faith. In many states this immunity extends to participation in judicial proceedings arising from the reports.

The types of abuse that must be reported include physical and emotional abuse and neglect, sexual abuse, and exploitation. The basis of a mandated report may be harm already suffered by the child or threatened harm. A determination should be made as to whether the abuse occurred in the past. If the abuse happened long ago and the abuser no longer constitutes a threat to children by being present in a capacity such as grandparent, scout leader, or child care provider, the professional may determine not to report. Such a decision should be considered carefully as the propensity and the opportunity to abuse children rarely disappear with time.

*Case study.* An army officer told his therapist he had been abused by his high school counselor more than 10 years earlier. The therapist felt compelled to contact the high school and follow up with a report to that county's child protective services (CPS) agency. Although the counselor had transferred to a different school district, the state reporting network was able to make the referral to the appropriate county and report the counselor.

*Failure to report.* Tort liability could be a possible sanction for professionals who fail to report as in the *Landeros v. Flood* (1976) case. In that situation a doctor failed to diagnose and report as abused a child who had the classic battered child syndrome. Dr. Flood was open to a $2 million civil liability suit because he failed to exercise due care in diagnosing and reporting. In a more recent case a therapist who reported to the noncustodial parent who had brought the child for a sexual abuse evaluation was open to tort liability for reporting to the father instead of to the state child protective service (*Searcy v. Auerbach*, 1992).

*Factors influencing the decision to report.* In a study of professional adherence to mandatory child abuse reporting laws, it was found that male mental health professionals were more blaming of the father, and their female counterparts were more blaming of the mother. The study found that factors affecting the decision to report included concerns over confidentiality, possible disruptions to treatment, characteristics of the family, and the abusive situation itself (Kalichman, Craig, & Follingstad, 1990). In a study of pediatric psychologists, other factors that influenced the reporting of sexual abuse included the presence of highly specific sexual abuse symptoms, the anticipation of discontinued contact with the child, or a direct statement of abuse from the child. The psychologists were more likely to suspect abuse than report it at every level of symptom presentation (Finlayson & Koocher, 1991).

*Mandatory reporting by adult therapists.* The reporting of disclosures of child sexual abuse has not been well accepted by therapists, especially those who treat adult abusers. Smith and Meyer (1984) suggested that any action that can discourage voluntary treatment for abuse is counterproductive. They proposed modifying reporting statutes to require reporting only when there is a threat of serious, permanent physical harm to the child or cases in which therapy is not continuing and the threat of child abuse continues. Other therapists who oppose reporting found that the rate of pedophile self-referrals for sexual abuse occurring prior to treatment dropped from seven per year to zero when sexual abuse reporting became mandatory in Maryland. They concluded that mandatory reporting reduced the number of identified child abuse victims to zero but failed to mention that before Maryland law mandated reporting, the number of children they identified to a protective authority was also zero (Berlin, Malin, & Dean, 1991).

Other professionals argue with the reluctance to report by therapists who treat adults. Lawrence Wessow (1990) in his volume *Child Advocacy for the Clinician* wrote that a full guarantee of confidentiality serves only the sex offender's interest to continue the abuse undetected. Therefore, he concluded, the therapist must take a clear stance that the abuse is wrong and must be punished. Wessow further believes that successful treatment for the sex offender rarely is completed voluntarily. This supports the argument for mandated reporting to ensure that treatment is ordered. To encourage treatment, qualified immunity from prosecution could be considered for abusers who voluntarily seek

psychotherapy. The state of Maine still mandates reports from therapists but now requires the child protective services to consult with the
therapist and consider the abuser's willingness to seek treatment
before determining how to proceed (Maine, *Revised Statutes*, 1988).

How can children be protected if not through mandated reporting?
Certainly since the advent of the mandatory reporting laws, the large
number of children identified as suffering physical, sexual, and emotional abuse has surprised and shocked mental health professionals.
Reporting can result from a therapist's personal or professional standards completely apart from legal mandates. A therapist's responsibility
to protect potential victims has been seen as an ethical professional
obligation as well as a matter of personal ethics for most mental health
professionals (Givelbar, Bowers, & Blitch, 1984).

*Beneficial effects of reporting.* When they examined the impact on parents making a report, Harper and Irwin (1985) found that reporting
can have a beneficial effect on the therapeutic process. Strong positive
outcomes for parental alliance and for child well-being led them to
contend that it is possible to "ally with the healthy part" of the abusive
parents and to use child abuse reporting as part of the therapeutically
desirable "limit-setting" function of inpatient treatment (p. 554). They
found that reporting not only was free of risk but contributed to the
healing process. Reporting can help both parties relate more clearly to
reality and avoid both wishful thinking and denial with regard to a
major threat to the child. Testing the above findings in an outpatient
clinic, Watson and Levine (1989) found support for the view that the
therapeutic relationship can survive and occasionally benefit from the
action of a therapist confronting and reporting abusive behavior. The
assumption made by many therapists that the reporting breaches
confidentiality and leads to a flight from therapy is challenged by their
data that shows that relatively few clients actually terminate therapy
shortly after the filing of a report.

Besides encouraging parental improvement, the reporting requirements could trigger child protection agency intervention that would
require that the parents remain in therapy to maintain custody or to be
reunited with their children who have been placed in foster care.
Services that the family needs could be provided or mandated by court
also (Weisz, 1992). An informal system between CPS workers and expert
mandated reporters allows staff to take reports of abuse that are not

too serious but not act on them, with the understanding that the expert making the report will monitor the case. This informal arrangement satisfies the reporting requirement but relies heavily on personal judgments and relationships that should be formalized into a system that would not be required to immediately investigate every report (Zellman, 1991).

*Negative results of reporting.* A major reporting pitfall occurs when the report triggers an investigation that can disrupt family dynamics and become a new source of trauma for the family. An estimated 700,000 reports made annually are not substantiated. The professional who does not understand clearly the definition of abuse or neglect or know how to gauge reasonable suspicions could be contributing to the flood of unfounded reports that overwhelms the limited resources of child protective agencies (Besharov, 1990b).

Reporting by therapists can lead to involved and time- consuming investigations and evaluations as well as court appearances. Although many children are served well through child protective services, the child's health or stability can deteriorate in the course of multiple and prolonged placements in emergency shelters, foster homes, or group homes; meanwhile the parents must work toward rehabilitation with limited access to treatment and other resources. In reality the public child welfare system might neglect to meet the child's individual needs more seriously than did the parents. No therapist wants the family to fall into this abyss. The lack of appropriate services to respond adequately to the needs of both child and parents encourages some ill-advised therapists to attempt to take sole responsibility for treating the abuse and neglect, assuming that by failing to report, at least the parents will receive the ongoing treatment they need (Weisz, 1992).

*Professional duties beyond reporting.* Professionals who do report should not stop their advocacy with the phone call. Rather, they should maximize the opportunity for the child to recover fully by advocating for a safe and caring permanent home, adequate educational opportunities, medical care, and mental health therapy. This advocacy can keep many children from falling through the cracks in a system that is unable to plan, coordinate, and provide services to meet the complex needs of these vulnerable children (Jellinek, Murphy, Bishop, Poitrast, & Quinn, 1990).

Major deficits must be acknowledged in the often overwhelmed and uncoordinated programs of services for children and families and for those who abuse children. Against these deficits, the rights of the children must be balanced. Who is there to protect the child? Who really knows whether the child is staying in a nice room in the basement, as the parents imply, or confined to a damp concrete block cubicle with a dangling light bulb? Who is to say if the father has quit sexually abusing his little girl since he started therapy?

The law regarding reporting is clear. A professional who reasonably suspects abuse must make a report. By understanding the definition of abuse, the signs to look for before making a report, and the choice society has made to protect the child rather than patient confidentiality, the therapist who reports can contribute to the protection of children and work to increase the provision of quality care and treatment to these victims and their families.

## Confidentiality of Child Abuse Reports

The Child Abuse Prevention and Treatment Act of 1974 requires confidentiality of child abuse and neglect records to protect the rights of the parents and the child in civil but not in criminal proceedings. Federal funding statutes require states to make the unauthorized disclosure of such reports a criminal offense. States are permitted to except the following types of disclosures:

1. Agencies or organizations that generally accept reports. This allows sharing of information with multidisciplinary teams including child protection, law enforcement, education, mental health, and medical professionals.
2. Courts. Subpoenas may be issued for records and records may be made available in some restricted cases.
3. Grand juries.
4. Legally designated agencies or teams in process of investigating or providing services (including foster parents).
5. Physicians. Medical doctors have access to otherwise confidential child protective service records 24 hours a day.
6. Anyone legally authorized to place a child in protective custody.
7. Agencies with authority to diagnose or treat a reported child.
8. Anyone who is the subject of a report. The identity of the reporter cannot be revealed if to disclose would endanger the life of the reporter. Most states protect this confidential disclosure.

9. The child and the attorney or guardian ad litem for the child.

10. State or local officials responsible for administration or state legislators.

11. Persons, agencies, or organizations doing bona fide research, with no identifying information made available.

12. The original reporter may be given feedback or a summary of the outcome of the report.

13. Representatives of the U.S. Department of Health and Human Services and the General Accounting Office.

14. Child protective information can be provided to agencies or persons doing background screening for employment in child care programs or to be foster parents, and so forth. (45 C.F.R. 1340.14)

*Confidentiality in criminal cases.* The exception to confidentiality in criminal cases is illustrated in a case in which the accused sought to gain access to the child victim's mental health records. The U.S. Supreme Court allowed the judge in the case to review the records in judicial chambers, and only records tending to prove innocence could be turned over (*Pennsylvania v. Ritchie,* 1987). A majority of states have enacted statutes that allow statements made out of court by child abuse victims to be entered into evidence in court. Professionals receiving requests from attorneys prior to a trial do not have a legal obligation to share confidential information. They are not at liberty to release such information without permission from the client or person in a position of authority. The professional who receives a subpoena for a client's records must bring such records to court, but privilege will keep the records out of evidence unless the judge rules otherwise (Myers, 1992). When the parent is charged with abusing or neglecting the child and the parent refuses to authorize the release of the professional's therapy sessions with the child, the judge may authorize someone such as an appointed guardian ad litem for the child to make decisions about release of confidential information (*In re D. K.,* 1976).

## Conclusion

If concerns for client confidentiality are superseded both legally and ethically by child protection issues, the mental health professional can increase the likelihood of a positive outcome for the child not only by reporting but by continuing to provide therapeutic support to the child.

# When Harm Comes to Children

# 3

# Physical Abuse

*A loving parent's hands should be as soft as feathers and not cast iron and not break bones.*

African (Ghana) proverb

Joshua DeShaney was born in 1979. When his parents divorced in 1980, his father, Randy, was awarded custody. By 1982, when Randy had remarried and was divorcing his second wife, she complained to the police that "he hit the boy, causing marks, and was a prime case for child abuse." A year later Joshua, now 4, was admitted to the hospital with multiple bruises and abrasions but was returned to his father following a department of social services (DSS) investigation. A month later Joshua was back in the hospital for injuries considered of suspicious origin. The social worker making monthly visits to the home observed similar injuries on Joshua's head but took no action.

In November 1983 the emergency room notified DSS that Joshua was treated once again for injuries they believed were caused by child abuse. On the social worker's next two visits to the home, she was told Joshua was too ill to see her. In March 1984 Randy DeShaney beat 4-year-old Joshua so severely that he fell into a life-threatening coma. Emergency brain surgery revealed a series of hemorrhages caused by traumatic injuries inflicted to the head over a long period of time. Although Joshua survived, he suffered brain damage so severe that he was expected to spend the rest of his life in an institution for profoundly retarded persons. His father was convicted of child abuse. The department of social services, on a case that went to the U.S. Supreme Court, was not found liable to Joshua because DSS did not owe the boy any duty as long as he was in the custody of his father (*DeShaney v. Winnebago*, 1989).

The DeShaney case raises a critical question: What right does a child have to be protected from abuse by a parent? Although, traditionally, parents exercise the right to govern their child without state intervention, the state may intervene through its *parens patriae* power to protect the child. More recently, as the awareness of child abuse increases, the law is beginning to abridge general parental controls over a child by imposing criminal liability on those parents or caretakers who prove to be abusive. The state may prosecute a parent or guardian for abuse under the criminal code as was done finally in the case of Randy DeShaney, or the state may attempt to strengthen the parent-child relationship through appropriate support and protective services provided under the civil dependency code.

In 1992 over 2.9 million children were reported to be victims of child abuse and neglect (McCurdy & Daro, 1993). These children can be subject to one or more kinds of abuse: physical, sexual, substance, and emotional abuse and neglect. Characteristics of each type overlap as do long-term consequences, both social and emotional. This chapter will focus on physical abuse. Subsequent chapters will discuss other types of abuse and neglect.

The term *physical abuse* is defined in different ways within the medical, social welfare, psychological, and legal professions. Each definition reflects the major concern of that profession; even within each profession there is discussion on how to define physical abuse. To understand best how to recognize symptoms, when to report suspicions to authorities, and what treatment is best for the child victim, the professional must be familiar with each specialist's definition.

The medical professional focuses on the injury, its severity, and its cause. The social worker is concerned with adequacy of the family to provide for the basic needs of the child and the family's willingness to accept protective services that will minimize risks for future abuse. The psychologist examines individual pathology and environmental stressors that could cause the abuse and uses a spectrum of therapy techniques to ameliorate both the negative family dynamics and the long-term emotional impact of abuse on the child. The legal world wants to balance the constitutional rights of the parents and the children against the due process right to know precisely what behavior is prohibited and to make certain that state intervention occurs only when evidence is presented to warrant it. There must be precision in definition and in court orders to protect the legal rights of both the child and the parents and to provide a legal framework for family treatment and either reunification or permanent out-of-family placement.

Abuse reports are made by professionals who serve children as well as by concerned members of the public. Public and professional definitions of abuse generally are broader than those used by protective services workers who investigate the report. The court's working definition may be more restrictive. Thus of the nearly 3 million children reported annually, about 60% of the families investigated are subjects of unfounded reports (McCurdy & Daro, 1993). Of the substantiated reports, fewer still are brought to court and adjudicated to constitute neglect or abuse (Besharov, 1990a).

The spanking of a 1-year-old child in the supermarket might be reported by a bystander who suspects abuse. On investigation the next morning, the social worker might find no physical signs of spanking or suspicious bruising on that child. This would result in an unsubstantiated report. On the contrary, the social worker may observe red marks. If the parent admits to the spanking but agrees to accept help to reduce the impact of stressors in the family situation that cause the parent to react abusively to the child's behavior, a court petition would not have to be filed.

At the other end of the spectrum is the infant who is brought to the hospital in a coma with bruises and lacerations caused by being beaten and thrown across the room. All professionals agree that this child is a victim of physical abuse. The physician refers the case to the child protective service. The caseworker substantiates the report and immediately files an emergency petition in court to remove the child from the care of the parental abuser. The court listens to the facts and approves removal of the child. Referral to criminal court would be in order.

Turf battles between professionals can create barriers to success. In such battles, when resulting from sole acceptance of a partisan definition of abuse, there may be failure to acknowledge other professional viewpoints that together must form the conceptual basis of multidisciplinary services the child and family need. A clear understanding of distinctions used by child-serving professions will contribute to a more broad-based treatment approach.

## Medical Indicators

Over 30 years have passed since the medical profession first alerted society to the epidemic of child abuse. Dr. C. Henry Kempe and his colleagues in their groundbreaking article "The Battered Child Syndrome" (Kempe, Silverman, Steele, Droegemuller, & Silver, 1962) defined child abuse as a condition with diagnosable medical and physical symptoms found in those who have been injured deliberately by a physical assault. This medical definition is limited to those acts of physical violence that produce a diagnosable injury.

Since the Kempe article was published, the medical profession has produced research and literature that identifies symptoms indicative of physical child abuse. Such evidence is divided into medically descriptive categories:

*Bruises and abrasions.* Bruises and abrasions on the skin are called cutaneous manifestations of abuse. In determining whether abuse caused the skin condition, the doctor, nurse, and/or other medical personnel must obtain a detailed, concise history of how and when the injury occurred. In dating bruises the location, size, and color of the bruise is important. Loose skin not supported by bony structures is bruised more easily. Thus the blood vessels of the eyelids and genitalia are predisposed to burst even on slight impact. The color of the bruise helps to indicate the age of the injury. To determine whether the injury is accidental or caused by abuse, the physician also considers the site of the injury. One bruise on a single surface may indicate a fall, whereas injuries on many areas of the body raise the suspicion of abuse. Common indicators of abuse are belt, strap, or loop marks from an extension cord; bite or hand marks; circumferential marks from tying or gag marks; and pinch marks.

*Abuse by burns.* Burns are involved in 6% to 16% of child abuse cases with the peak age occurring between 2 and 3 years of age. Accidental burns are found usually on the front of the head or neck, trunk, or arms. Suspicious burns occur on the back of the head, neck, chest, extremities, and genitalia. Immersion burns are caused by placing a child in water with a temperature above 125 degrees. A stocking pattern on the hands or feet or doughnut hole pattern on the buttocks usually indicates a nonaccidental burn. A scald burn results from a hot liquid being thrown or poured onto the child. Contact burns are made by cigarettes, hot combs, cigarette lighters, heater grates, irons, or branding by heated keys or other metal objects (Feldman, 1987).

*Abusive fractures.* Transverse or spiral fractures of the extremities, caused by twisting of the long bones, account for most fractures of abused children. Infants under 2 years are more likely to suffer rib fractures and chip fractures at the ends of long bones. Vertebral fractures are caused by hyperflexion, a forced bending of the spine. In nonambulatory infants under 12 months of age, fractures are indicators of nonaccidental injury. Evidence of multiple healing fractures also can indicate abuse.

*Injuries to head, eyes, and mouth.* Vessels between the brain and skull are damaged easily when the head is shaken. This "shaken baby impact syndrome" results in a subdural hematoma that is a common cause of morbidity and fatal injury. The shaking usually is accompanied by sudden impact as when the infant is thrown forcefully into a crib or on a sofa. Retinal hemorrhages in the eyes are caused by an abrupt increase of pressure on the head or by chest pressure. Retinal hemorrhages accompany 50% to 70% of subdural hematoma. The prognosis for the shaken impact baby is ominous: 30% die and 30% are disabled (Bruce & Zimmerman, 1989). Common injuries to the mouth include bruises or lacerations often caused by a blow to the face or the jamming of a spoon or bottle into a resistant child's mouth (Smith, Benton, Moore, & Runyon, 1988).

*Internal injuries.* Blunt trauma to the abdomen, lower back, or chest results in internal injuries that require immediate emergency treatment. Although these cases compose less than 2% of child abuse cases, 50% of those children die.

*Poisoning.* Nonaccidental poisoning can be divided into four categories: impulsive acts under stress, bizarre child-rearing practices, neglect, and Munchausen syndrome by proxy. Impulsive acts under stress include forced ingestion of table salt, the most common cause of nonaccidental poisoning. Water intoxication resulting in a condition called hyponatremia can lead to seizures, convulsions, confusion, lethargy, coma, and death. This condition can be caused also by overly diluted baby formula. Household products and drugs are used also in this type

of abuse. Bizarre child-rearing practices can include anything from wash-
ing out the mouth with soap to keep the child from lying to putting a
bitter-tasting and toxic cleaning product on fingernails to prevent nail
biting. Neglect or lack of supervision results in children being left alone
to investigate household cleaning fluids stored behind unlocked doors,
on the floor, or on a counter. Liquid and solid medicines left within reach
can be toxic to children, especially when attractively colored and gulped
or eaten by the handful. Outdated medicines neglectfully administered
to children can cause serious damage, including death. Munchausen
syndrome by proxy is an abusive parenting disorder named after the
18th-century author of wild, exaggerated tales of life. The parent, who
often has had some kind of medical orientation, typically hurts the
child to gain sympathy or attention. The child suffering from pediatric
illness fabrication has such common symptoms as fever, diarrhea,
vomiting, rashes, bleeding, and seizures. The parent may fabricate
symptoms or actually induce symptoms in the child. Either course can
lead to extensive and invasive medical evaluations and treatment. The
elements of Munchausen syndrome by proxy are a parent or care-giver
repeatedly bringing a child for medical care, the perpetrator denying
having knowledge regarding etiology of the illness, and acute symptoms that abate when the child is separated from the parent or caretaker (Smith et al., 1988).

> *Case study.* A report of a highly publicized case concerned a 2-year-old who
> had been hospitalized more than 20 times for pneumonia, mysterious infec-
> tions, and sudden fevers. His mother, a nurse, took his temperature rectally
> every hour and checked his breathing with her stethoscope. A police search
> of the home uncovered syringes and plastic tubes containing sodium chlo-
> ride solution. The mother was charged with a felony, third-degree assault.
> The son has been healthy since his removal from his mother's care ("Parent
> Indiscretion," 1991; see *People v. Phillips*, 1981).

*Suspicious parent and child behavior characteristics.* Certain parent and
child behaviors will cause the physician to suspect that physical abuse
is present. The parent may deny pregnancy, have inappropriate expectations of the child, demonstrate immaturity, be socially isolated, or abuse
drugs or alcohol. A history of injury or neglect of another child would
raise suspicion as would domestic violence or a propensity to react
violently to frustrations.

A low birth weight or premature infant or one with whom the mother had a difficult pregnancy may be vulnerable to abuse. When a child has cognitive deficits or other developmental disabilities, abuse may be more likely to occur (Ammerman, Van Hasselt, & Hersen, 1988). Other stressors that may set the stage for abuse include conditions that interfere with bonding, differences in parent-child temperament, and significant difficulty with achieving early developmental stages.

## Documentation

The potential for court involvement requires the medical professional to keep a detailed written record when physical abuse is suspected. In addition to the physical examination with the injury description and laboratory test results, the history should include the date and time the child is brought to the hospital; the name of any professional or other adults who accompany the child; the informant (parent, child, or both); the date, time, and place of the incident; the parent's verbatim explanation as to how the incident occurred; the precipitating event, if injury was due to punishment; who allegedly injured the child; any known history of past physical abuse obtained from a previous hospital chart; and, finally, a note of any inconsistencies (Berson & Herman-Giddens, 1986). Medical personnel must be listening always for disclosures of abuse. Statements made spontaneously or to members of the medical profession are recorded in the chart so that these out-of-court statements can be submitted into court as evidence. Such statements are exceptions to the rule against hearsay and may be substituted for the child's personal appearance in court.

## Interdisciplinary Child Abuse Team

In many large hospitals a team of professionals meets regularly to screen cases in which abuse or neglect is suspected. The team is composed of physicians, nurses, psychiatrists, psychologists, social workers, public health nurses, attorneys, and other professionals as needed. Consultation, coordination, and guidance are provided by the team to staff throughout the hospital and to outside agencies. The team reviews active cases to ensure that appropriate assessments and treatment plans are in place before the child is released from the hospital (Berson & Herman-Giddens, 1986). The medical response is to treat the particular physical injury and to recommend intensive therapy for the perpetrator. This model is limited when it fails to consider social, family dynamic, and economic pressures that need attention to prevent recurrence of abuse. By working cooperatively with other disciplines, the medical professional is better able to protect the child from further injury.

### Reporting

Medical personnel who suspect physical abuse are required to report to the department of child protection or in some states to the police. The proper authority receives the referral and investigates to determine if the report should be substantiated and, if so, what action should be taken to protect the child.

*Reporters.* Mandated: Every state mandates reporting by certain officials such as physicians, nurses, emergency room personnel, mental health professionals, social workers, school officials, teachers, day care or child care providers, and law enforcement personnel. Any person who suspects: In some states, any person with reason to believe a child is a victim of abuse or neglect must report. Permissive: In all states, anyone may report. Anonymous: All states accept anonymous reports.

## Investigation of
## Report by Social Workers

An individual in the community who suspects abuse makes a referral to the child protective service unit at the department of social services. The CPS worker receiving the call makes a home visit to see the child and the home environment. In order to substantiate the report, the CPS worker looks beyond the child's injury to see whether the parent or caregiver engaged in the particular behavior prohibited by the abuse or neglect statutes. Some of the factors considered for abuse are:

1. Excessive corporal punishment: Although the punishment is admittedly too severe, the child usually acknowledges having done something wrong. The punishment is limited to whipping after the child is old enough to understand parental expectations for behavior (at least

school-age). The injuries are not life threatening and are usually limited to bruises, welts, or minor cuts.

> *Case study.* Fifteen-year-old Dana returned home from a date 20 minutes late. Furious with her, the father took out his anger by beating her with his belt. The wounds on her face, chest, back, and legs were obvious when she appeared at school. The investigative child protective services worker placed Dana in the home of her aunt. A juvenile court judge heard the evidence and found that the father had abused the girl. She was ordered to remain with the aunt until her father completed a program of intensive therapy.

2. Misguided attempts at education: Parents may burn children to teach them to avoid fire or bite them to teach them not to bite. The caretakers generally are surprised that their behavior could be viewed as abusive.

3. The battered child syndrome: The child is usually under the age of 4; the parents are immature emotionally and have unrealistic expectations of the child and of parenting. The parents often are isolated socially and emotionally. A careful history of the injury is essential in diagnosing this dangerous form of abuse.

> *Case study.* On repeated occasions during the first year of her life, Gita was beaten severely by her mother and father. When she was 11 months old, her mother took her to the hospital for treatment of a leg fracture that gave the appearance of having been caused by a twisting force. The mother gave the doctor no explanation for the injury. Gita had bruises over her entire back, as well as superficial abrasions on other parts of her body. She also had a linear fracture of the skull that was in the process of healing. She showed fear and apprehension when approached. The doctor, who allowed the child to return home where she was beaten again, was open to a civil suit for failing to recognize the symptoms and to report her as a victim of battered child syndrome (*Landeros v. Flood*, 1976).

4. The serial batterer: Persons who inflict injuries on more than one infant or child present grave danger because the injuries are often fatal.

> *Case study.* Two young professionals gave birth to three children. The firstborn had died mysteriously in infancy. The second child was doted on by both parents. The third child was brought to the hospital with a crushed skull. An investigation revealed the father could not endure the baby's crying at night when he needed to sleep. Although he insisted the infant had fallen onto the floor, the skull was injured actually by manual crushing.

After the injuries to this child were documented, the authorities reopened the investigation on the cause of death of the firstborn.

5. Sadistic or torturous abuse: Injuries that reflect a deliberate effort to torture, inflict pain, or kill include branding, hanging, pulling out toenails or fingernails, and deliberately starving (Bowdry, 1990).

*Case study.* Patti and Michael, two emotionally disturbed children, were adopted by parents who forced them to perform sexual acts with each other. When they disobeyed their parents, they were beaten, then handcuffed together and hung over the top of the bedroom door. Patti was forced to eat hot peppers, was beaten, then was hung from the door until she died.

**Protective Services:**
**Investigation and Assessment**

Working in an overwhelmed service delivery system, the caseworker with too many reports to investigate may tend to substantiate cases on the basis of available services or on a subjective reaction to the family situation. To avoid subjective decision making, the caseworker can use needs assessment tools when investigating an abuse report. Although still controversial because of efficacy questions, these tools can help in evaluating factors that would interact either to protect or to endanger the child. Coercive intervention should not be justified on the basis of the presence of risk factors alone (Wald & Wolverton, 1990). As a result of the social worker's investigation and evaluation, the child is left in the home with necessary protective services being provided, or the child is removed and placed with a relative or in a foster home. Many children remain in the home without services. One national study found that from 1990 to 1992 the percentage of families with substantiated abuse who received any services at all dropped from 78% to 60% (McCurdy & Daro, 1993).

Factors in the home that indicate a high risk are:

___ The parent is moderately to severely handicapped, has a poor perception of reality, or has unrealistic expectations and perceptions of the child's behavior.
___ The parent has severe incapacity from alcohol or drug intoxication.
___ The parent has poor impulse control, has been violent in the home, or has a criminal record.

— The parent does not believe there is a problem and refuses to cooperate or is disinterested or evasive.

— The parent may provide appropriate physical care, but is unresponsive to the child's needs by failing to respond to crying, using poor eye contact, making infrequent visits, and having inappropriate expectations and criticism of the child (*UCLA Medical Center Protocol*, 1993).

After finding substantial evidence of abuse or neglect, the child protective services worker will make a decision about removing the child or providing services. Specific behaviors and conditions that are potential risk factors for abuse will be identified first and then evaluated in relation to criteria of controllability, immediacy, and severity as well as the estimated vulnerability of the child. After examining the ways in which family strengths, resources, and available services could counteract troublesome behaviors and conditions if the family remains together, the CPS worker will develop an emergency plan to safeguard the child and a safety plan that would keep the family together if possible (DePanfilis & Jones, 1990). This same evaluation is used for children who are neglected or abused sexually or emotionally (see Chapters 4 to 7).

The most severely abused children will not be returned to their homes. Parental rights are terminated, and the children are then free for adoption or are placed in a permanent guardianship or foster home. However, most abused children can remain in the home with protective services or are able to return home after the parents have participated in parenting training, supervised visits with their children, counseling, substance abuse rehabilitation, or other specific treatments. If the parents do not respond to the social services offered within a period of 1 to 2 years, the department of social services will place the children in a permanent home and forgo further reunification efforts. The issues of in-home services, foster care, parental reunification, termination of parental rights, and adoption will be considered in Chapters 8 to 12.

Many abusive parents are required by contract with the social worker or by court order to participate in mental health therapy. Local mental health centers should have staff who are trained especially to evaluate violence-prone families. This enables those therapists to assist the court in determining what has taken place, what intervention is needed, and what type of treatment can help the family. In an effort to keep children safe in their homes after abuse is substantiated, it is critical for mental health professionals to provide immediate treatment to parents who have been violent with their children. Coordinating evaluation, treatment, and progress with the social worker and, where necessary, the court is a responsibility the professional must assume whenever agreeing to work with abusive parents.

## The Mental Health
## Professional's Assessment of the Parent

A profile of an abusive parent is difficult, if not impossible, to draw with accuracy (Wolfe, 1987). Characteristics of both the parent and the child can interact with stressors in the home environment to produce physical abuse. A developmental perspective is necessary to understand the full spectrum of mediators that may affect the child who has been abused. The child's inner experience must be examined as well as behavior and relationships (Briere, 1992). Although the medical professional focuses attention on the injury and the social worker assesses the home environment, factors considered by the mental health professional include psychological disorder in the parents, parental psychological availability, abuse-eliciting characteristics of child, dysfunctional patterns of family interaction, past and present stress-inducing forces and the family's ability to cope, abuse-promoting cultural values, and quality of social networks and supports (Belsky, 1980; Briere, 1992).

Child abuse, in one psychologist's view, is "the product of an interactive process that develops over time, and therefore classification systems that focus primarily on parental characteristics must be sensitive to the other critical variables that impinge upon the parent-child relationship" (Wolfe, 1987, p. 95). Multiple violence-eliciting variables can adversely affect a parent who is not known to be impaired psychologically. One prevalent critical variable is economic stress. Although the stress of poverty can contribute to abuse, parents who abuse their children come from all socioeconomic groups (Bruce & Zimmerman, 1989).

Lack of knowledge about parenting is another factor that must be assessed. Abusive parents often rigidly demand more of their child than should be expected at the child's age level. Significant deficits in child-rearing knowledge and skills can hamper the parent in developing a positive parent-child interaction. Mental illness or retardation are critical variables that are sometimes present. Such disorders include depression, antisocial personality disorder, multiple personality, uncontrolled psychosis, mental retardation, and religious fanaticism (Seagull, 1987). In studies of abusive parents, attempts have been made to classify them by personality type and by parenting style, but little empirical evidence exists to support those theories (see Sloane & Meier, 1983).

## Evaluating the Child

The therapist often is asked to conduct an evaluation in the midst of a crisis that involves physical injury to a child. Safety and trust must be established before the therapist can evaluate the status of the child's mental health and the psychological impact of temporary or permanent disabilities caused by the abuse.

Because of recent U.S. Supreme Court decisions, the therapist must be extremely careful to follow court guidelines to ensure that the evaluation can be offered as evidence at the court hearing. This is especially important in the few states that do not have a medical exception to the hearsay rule. To increase the reliability of the evaluation, the criminal investigator of the case against the parents should not be the same individual who brings the child in for the evaluation. Some feel the professional doing the evaluation should have a clean slate when beginning the evaluation. In the same context, it is controversial as to whether prior to seeing the child the professional should read the child's record and its allegations about the nature of any suspected abuse and the identity of the alleged perpetrator. Although professional standards strongly encourage finding out all that is known about the child prior to the initial interview, prior knowledge of the allegations could bias the professional's line of inquiry and nullify the prospect of a successful criminal proceeding against an abusive parent. Briere's (1992) Child Maltreatment Interview Schedule may be a useful tool for clinical assessment.

The person evaluating the child should not ask leading questions, nor should the evaluation include any indication of prompting or manipulation. Even "training" a child for memory recall, as suggested by some experts in the field, could bring charges of influencing the child's statements. Using cognitive interview techniques increases recall without using leading questions (Saywitz, Geiselman, & Bornstein,

1992). The court reasons that by adhering to the court guidelines the evaluation is more reliable and therefore acceptable into court (*Idaho v. Wright*, 1990).

Speech and language disorders are characteristic of many physically abused children. Besides evaluating the effects of the trauma on the child, the therapist must assess the child's social, emotional, cognitive, and language development in order to discover areas needing future evaluation and treatment (Seagull, 1987). In their book *Working With Violent Families*, Bolton and Bolton (1987) report that victims of family violence generally suffer poor self-concept and low self-esteem, confused dependencies, difficulty in trusting, revictimization, denial, defensiveness, withdrawal, isolation, emotional trauma, psychological difficulty, subsequent deviance, behavior problems, sexual maladjustment, and social and interpersonal problems. After the therapist has evaluated the child and formed an opinion as to the cause of the child's trauma, the therapist may appear in court and, if qualified as an expert witness, may give the causative professional opinion to the court. The therapist also may offer testimony in court as to the effects of the abuse on the child. At the dispositional phase of the hearing, a recommendation may be given regarding the temporary and/or permanent placement of the child.

For the parent who is abusing substances, the therapist must see the parent when the parent has completed substance abuse treatment to evaluate the underlying issue of family violence before a decision is made about returning the child. The therapist will assess the parental functioning level, try to pinpoint the cause of the abuse, and develop a treatment plan that will require parent participation. The therapist also can evaluate others in the home who potentially would be available to protect and care for the children. Before giving a court opinion about a custody decision, the therapist should evaluate each parent and other proposed caregivers separately and with the child. Only then can a reliable and reality-based opinion be provided.

For the child placed outside the home, a case plan that includes ongoing therapy provides a bridge from the abusive environment to the protective placement and supplies emotional support for a healthier adjustment for the child and parents while they attempt visitation and reunification. When removed from the parents, the child may go through a period of grief much like mourning the death of a family member. Foster children can become depressed, commonly thinking they are the cause of the family problems. They might exhibit a high level of anxiety. The therapist needs to keep close watch on affected children and be ready to ask the court to order additional services for the child. To minimize continued trauma, the therapist should work toward coordinating service plans and delivery so that medical, educational, parenting, emotional, and other needs of the child will be met fully.

As a result of physical abuse, the child can suffer also from post-traumatic stress disorder (PTSD). Vulnerability to PTSD is related to several factors: constitutional and personality makeup, developmental status at the time of the traumatizing event, and prior life experience. Memory, school performance, and learning may be affected as well as interpersonal relations, affect, and self-control. The child will feel many distressing emotions: shame, rage, guilt, and sadness and will fear repetition of the abuse. The court should be informed fully when the child suffers from PTSD in order that the child can be protected permanently from the abusive parent and the emotional as well as the physical wounds will have the opportunity to heal (Bolton & Bolton, 1987; Briere, 1992).

## Criminal and Civil Child Abuse

Physical abuse of a child may constitute a felony, particularly when the child is injured fatally. Most criminal statutes define felony abuse as injury to the child that is serious, permanent, and intentionally inflicted. Some states list specific acts or injuries that constitute physical abuse; other states have a vague definition. The purpose of the criminal statute is to punish the perpetrator. Juvenile court will hear cases of civil child abuse for the purpose of protecting the child (see Chapter 9). The present trend is to broaden the scope of child abuse reporting laws. A few states now include infants who are born exposed to or dependent on a dangerous drug and children who are victims of an injury or inadequate care, control, or subsistence because of drug-related activity (Davidson, 1990).

*Corporal punishment.* California includes in the definition of child abuse "willful cruelty or unjustifiable punishment of a child, unlawful corporal punishment or injury" (California Penal Code sec. 11165.6). Parents have the right to discipline their children, but not by the use of excessive force. The parent's infliction of reasonable and moderate punishment on a child generally is tolerated as part of the parent's right and privilege to enforce obedience by the child. The U.S. Supreme Court concluded that corporal punishment, such as paddling a student as a means of maintaining school discipline, does not constitute cruel and unusual punishment in violation of the Eighth Amendment of the Constitution. The dissenting opinion took issue with the majority decision that punishment in the public schools is never limited by the Eighth Amendment. The dissent considered "barbaric, inhumane, or severe corporal punishment" a justification for the Eighth Amendment's protection from cruel and unusual punishment (*Ingraham v. Wright*, 1977, p. 692).

U.S. Supreme Court Justice Brennan outlined the test for cruel and unusual punishment that could apply readily to corporal punishment by parents of children and adolescents when he wrote: "If there is a significantly less severe punishment adequate to achieve the purposes for which the punishment is inflicted, the punishment inflicted is unnecessary and therefore excessive" (*Furman v. Georgia*, 1971, p. 279).

## Long-Term Effects of Abuse

The intergenerational transmission of child abuse, once widely accepted by professionals, has become a controversial issue as professionals have discovered that most adults who were abused as children do not repeat the cycle of abuse with their own children. Although a high percentage of abusive parents were victims of child abuse, one study found that as few as 18% of parents abused as children went on to abuse their own children (Kaufman & Zigler, 1987). A history of abuse interacts with the other factors of stress, social isolation, and poverty to determine whether the parent will abuse the child. The abuse history alone does not determine the negative outcome. Therefore, parents who were abused should not be conditioned to feel that they will abuse their children (Kaufman & Zigler, 1987; Widom, 1989b).

To reduce long-term effects, social factors contributing to abusive behavior must be eliminated or at least reduced. Stresses commonly associated with family violence include unemployment; pregnancy, especially unwanted pregnancy; parenting demands; and sexist cultural patterns. As long as the use of corporal punishment is condoned as an approved societal attitude for solving problems, child abuse will continue to be a problem (Feshbach, 1980).

## Conclusion

To understand the type of severe physical abuse that doctors, social workers, mental health professionals, and lawyers encounter, consider again the case of Joshua DeShaney described in the introduction to this chapter. How much proof did the social worker need to intervene for Joshua's protection? The first visit to the hospital raised suspicion, especially considering the earlier reports. The subsequent home visits with observed bruises as well as the November emergency room treatment certainly would present strong evidence in most courts for a finding of physical abuse. Yet the social worker was reluctant even to ask to see Joshua, much less to file a petition.

A child protection team at the hospital where Joshua was seen at age 3 reviewed his case. This multidisciplinary team recommended that Joshua be enrolled in a preschool program and that his father's girlfriend move out of the home. The father entered into a voluntary agreement in which he promised to cooperate with these recommendations. No one took responsibility for enforcing the plan through presentation in court, incorporation into the court order, and timely follow-up. Perhaps a guardian ad litem or CASA could have ensured protection for Joshua. When the social worker visited the home and found the girlfriend still living there and the child not enrolled in preschool, the father's noncompliance, especially if he had been under court order, would have led to grounds for immediate removal of Joshua from the home.

# 4

## Sexual Abuse

*She was Lo, plain Lo, in the morning, standing four feet ten in one sock. . . .*
*But in my arms she was always Lolita.*

Vladimir Nabokov,
*Lolita,* 1955

Ben Adams had been president of the PTA, a leader in his community and in his church. Today he is in dependency court charged with sexually abusing Susan, his youngest daughter, and his sons, Justin and Kevin. The evidence presented shows a man consumed with the need to control. Ben began sexually abusing Lisa, his oldest daughter, when she was 5 years old and continued throughout her high school years. He arranged several abortions for Lisa before she finally gave birth to a child. By the time Lisa left home, Ben already had begun sexually abusing Sheri, the next daughter, and then Susan, the youngest. The children all feared their father, who used strong disciplinary measures to control them. He doled out privileges only when the children consented to satisfy his sexual demands. When Sheri went away to college and began dating, her father became jealous and demanded that she spend her weekends at home with him. He threatened to cut off her college support if she refused. Sheri had thought her father would leave the younger children alone if she cooperated with him, but during her last visit home, Susan, Kevin, and Justin all told Sheri their father was sexually abusing them. Finally, Sheri reported the sexual abuse to protect her sister and brothers from their father.

Parents do not have the right to use their children to satisfy their own sexual needs. Brothers, stepparents, uncles, and cousins do not have the right to molest the children they live with or care for. Criminal courts deal with sexual abuse in defined crimes: statutory rape, incest, sodomy, molestation, exploitation, and employment of minors in obscene acts. Juvenile courts protect sexually abused children by removing the perpetrator from the home or by placing the child outside the home. During the time the criminal court is prosecuting the mother's boyfriend, the dependency court may be placing the child in foster care because her mother refuses to believe her boyfriend sexually abused the child.

Sexual abuse of children, as in the case of Ben Adams, typically results from a progression of sexually oriented acts directed toward the child. Generally, a preadolescent child, sometimes as young as 3 to 4 years of age, will be molested sexually for a number of years before penetration takes place. A considerable time lapse may occur before the incidents of sexual abuse are reported. This delay causes problems in providing clear physical evidence of sexual abuse. Prompted by "bribes, misrepresentation of morality, affection, threats, parental psychological authority, losing affection or being blamed," a child often will suffer and endure the abuse instead of seeking help (Bulkley, 1984, p. 171).

## Incidence

Although reports of maltreatment increased by 66% from 1980 to 1986, sexual abuse reports more than tripled. One national authority stated that a child is abused sexually every 2 minutes in the United States (Bjerregaard, 1989). Other studies indicate that about one third of all females and one sixth of all males have been abused sexually before the age of 18 (Nuce, 1990). Despite these astonishing statistics, few cases are reported and one study found less than 10% of those filed with police even go to trial (Alcoff & Gray, 1993). The vast majority of sexual abuse is committed by adult males, leading Russell (1986) to assert that males are socialized to sexualize power, intimacy, and affection, and sometimes hatred and contempt. Both Russell (1986) and Finkelhor (1979) stressed the influence of cultural norms that define masculinity and promote and maintain the transference of male sexuality into violence, rape, sexual harassment, and sexual abuse.

The problem of group sexual abuse was publicized widely through the Jordan (Minnesota) cases in the early 1980s, the McMartin Preschool trial in Los Angeles, and in the more recent Little Rascals Preschool trial in North Carolina. Learning from the mistakes made in the Jordan and McMartin cases in questioning, evaluating, and treating, the Little

Rascals prosecution was able to convict on 99 of 100 counts against the man who owned the day care center.

Sexual abuse that takes place out of the home is not the main focus of this chapter. Overwhelmingly, sexual abuse is more likely to occur in the home. Causes, symptoms, evaluation, treatment, and the aftermath for children who are abused sexually must be studied in a different context than for children who are abused physically. The following medical, psychological, social, and legal aspects of abuse have major significance in the lives of youthful victims of sexual abuse.

## Medical Indicators

Many children who are abused sexually display no physical evidence of the abuse (Kerns & Ritter, 1992). Proof of abuse may rest on the testimony of the child and any corroborative evidence that can be collected to support the child. When physical signs of abuse are present, they can include bruises, scratches, and bites; sexually transmitted diseases; blood stains on underwear; bruising or swelling of the genital area; pain in anal, genital, gastrointestinal, and urinary areas; unexplained or inconsistent genital injuries; injury to the labia; grasp marks; enuresis; and head trauma (caused by wedging against bedstead or wall).

The medical examination for sexual abuse involves searching for evidence that can be used in prosecution: sperm recovered from the vagina, genital/rectal region, or mouth; pregnancy; genital or anal injuries or recently healed lacerations in children of both sexes; sexually transmitted diseases or foreign bodies in the vagina, pharynx, urethra, or rectum; and other physical evidence of trauma that supports the child's statements such as rope burns or bite marks (Bays & Chadwick, 1993).

## Psychological Indicators and Theories

The impact of sexual abuse is primarily psychological; therefore, the professional must place paramount importance on the mental health of the child as information is gathered. The professional must be aware of the wide range of possible causes for behavior changes other than sexual abuse (Reece, 1994).

*Behavioral changes.* Some sexual behaviors of children are signals that the child may have been abused sexually. Detailed and age-inappropriate sexual understanding or activity, especially in younger children, is a strong indicator. Unusual inappropriate or aggressive sexual behavior with peers or toys is another indicator (Kendall-Tackett, Williams, & Finkelhor, 1993). Compulsive masturbation can be a symptom, especially during the toddler and early childhood years. For the preteen and young teenager, unusually seductive behavior, promiscuity, and pregnancy are indicators for girls; boys may show excessive concern about homosexuality. It should be noted that inappropriate sexual behavior has been found also in studies of nonsexually abused children (Deblinger, McLeer, Atkins, Ralphe, & Foa, 1989).

Other behaviors to be scrutinized as possible indicators of sexual abuse of the child 5 years or younger include fear of a particular person or place; feelings of strong shame or guilt; physical ailments such as vomiting, feeding problems, bowel disturbances, and sleep problems; regression to earlier forms of behavior such as bed-wetting, stranger anxiety, separation anxiety, thumb sucking, baby talk, whining, and clinging; and failure to thrive. From age 6 to 9 more common symptoms that could indicate sexual abuse are eating disturbances (eating too much or too little), fears, phobias, overly compulsive behavior, nightmares and other sleep disturbances, physical ailments such as abdominal pain or urinary difficulties, school problems, and significant change in attitude or grades.

From age 10 to 12 the sexual abuse victim may withdraw from family and friends, suffer depression, have nightmares, become fearful about falling asleep, or sleep unusually long hours. The preteen may have poor school performance or may demonstrate fear of home life by arriving at school early or leaving late. Use of illegal drugs or alcohol may begin. The child may become self-conscious of his or her body beyond what is expected for this age. Aggression is also common.

The early teen who has been abused sexually may run away from home, suffer severe depression, use illegal drugs or alcohol, exhibit suicidal thoughts or gestures, skip school, perform poorly in school, refuse to dress for physical education, and become fearful of showers or rest rooms. He or she suddenly may acquire money, new clothes, or gifts without a reasonable explanation; cry without provocation; have aggressive or delinquent behavior; grieve over the loss of virginity;

display anger and rage about being forced into a situation beyond one's control; and show poor self-esteem (Hillman & Solek-Tefft, 1988).

*Child sexual abuse accommodation syndrome.* Roland Summit (1983) described a syndrome to explain the adjustment patterns of children caught up in sexual abuse. The accommodation syndrome includes five characteristics: secrecy, helplessness, accommodation, delayed disclosure, and retraction. The syndrome is not meant to be accepted in a court of law as evidence of sexual abuse. It does help clinicians and caregivers understand the child's alienating and prejudicial behavior patterns. Summit's clinical case report was meant not to establish a basis for determining that children had experienced such abuse but rather to elicit improved therapy and effective advocacy for those children who were known to have been abused sexually.

> *Case study.* Kelly and her stepfather have a secret. She is afraid to tell anyone what he does to her because of his threats and her fear that no one will believe her. She doesn't want to cause her family to be torn apart. By the time she is 12 years old, she begins using mutilation and then delinquency to help her survive the sexual abuse. Finally, Kelly runs away from home and reveals she is being abused sexually. Unbelieving, her family says Kelly has mental problems and needs help. Humiliated for disrupting and shaming her family, Kelly recants her accusations of sexual abuse when family pressures overwhelm her with guilt feelings. Untrained professionals see this as an excuse to drop the case.

## Legal Intervention

*Investigation.* Initial disclosure may occur when the child tells a best friend, a family member, or a trusted teacher or school counselor. When the disclosure is made to a mandated reporter, a referral must be made to the department of social services or the police, depending on the laws of the state. A trained criminal investigator, social worker, or mental health professional then carries out an investigation. Chapters 8 and 9 will discuss the investigation and court process.

### Professional Therapy for the Child Victim

A therapist asked to evaluate children for sexual abuse must be fully aware that three roles are played: clinician, evidence gatherer, and protector of the child. The first objective of the clinician is to develop rapport by relating to the child on the child's level, developmentally and physically. Sessions often are conducted with both therapist and child sitting on the floor along with puppets, dolls, and other toys. The clinician uses simple words and sentences and the language of play. The puppets, dolls, and assorted toys can aid greatly in communication with the child, especially with children who have limited verbal skills (Waterman, 1994).

As evidence gatherer, the therapist must be especially careful to avoid asking leading questions. Major criminal actions have been unsuccessful because interviews were filled with leading questions and innuendoes based on preconceived ideas of the mental health professional. Suggestive interviews containing implicit and explicit bribes, threats, stereotypes, and repetition of certain questions result in distorted reports (Ceci & Bruck, 1993). Cognitive questioning techniques include developmentally appropriate interview etiquette and reliable memory retrieval procedures. The professional begins with the broadest questions, then goes to the specifics and takes care never to suggest a specific sexual act or perpetrator (Saywitz et al., 1992). These techniques are detailed in Chapter 9.

As protector of the child, the therapist must avoid emotionally upsetting the child while exploring the sense of security the child feels in the family home or foster home. The clinician stays within a realistic framework of what can be guaranteed, being careful not to give the child false reassurance. As a result of the session, the clinician often is asked to recommend where and with whom the child should be allowed to live. The therapist must provide emotional support to the child, evaluate any immediate danger to the child, and formulate a plan of action on behalf of the child (Perry & Wrightsman, 1991).

### Professional Therapy for the Perpetrator

The number of cases of sexual abuse of children is increasing dramatically as is concern over the lack of positive results from treatment of perpetrators. Most defendants convicted of child sexual abuse are sentenced to probation with mandated therapy related to their sexual orientation toward children. Little consensus exists about what type of treatment works best. The field of treatment for men who molest is in its infancy. A study of the problem found that programs for child sexual abuse offenders are extremely limited in focus and have long waiting lists. Greater numbers of therapists and more alternative therapy settings such as halfway houses, therapy within prison, and therapy within jails were listed as needed. No therapist surveyed would accept a patient who denied sexual conduct with children. Styles used range from holistic support therapy to confrontational therapy. Although behavior modification has been a preferred treatment, it is usually short term. Group therapy helps break down the cloak of secrecy and was found to be much more effective than psychoanalysis. Coordination between the treatment provider and probation personnel became difficult because heavy caseloads reduced the likelihood that the essential coordination would occur. One drawback of a multidisciplinary system was the failure of any one person to assume ultimate responsibility. The final and most critical problem was the lack of long-term success. Most therapists believed that the offenders are at high risk of reoffending as soon as probation is terminated (Smith, Hillenbrand, & Goretsky, 1991). Mandated hospital programs in California were discontinued in the 1980s because they could not prove efficacy and were costly. Therapy can help to control but cannot eradicate the problem.

## Incest

A study at the Kempe National Center for the Prevention and Treatment of Child Abuse and Neglect reached the conclusion that families characterized by incest will tend to support and maintain incestuous behavior. Such families have a rigid family belief system, a dysfunctional parental coalition, parental neglect and emotional unavailability, and failure to nurture autonomy in family members. Family members were found to deny their actual feelings, emotional availability, and ability to resolve conflict. Expressed perceptions of other family members were ridiculed or ignored. This study's conclusions disagree with other literature that characterizes the parental relationship by dominance and submission (Madonna, Van Sroyk, & Jones, 1991).

The attitude of the professionals who work with incest survivors can make a strong impact on the family. Ringwalt and Earp (1988) found that CPS workers they studied were more likely to recommend the father's incarceration in the incest cases in which they attributed more responsibility to the father and daughter than to the mother.

# Long-Term Effects of Sexual Abuse

*Psychological.* Problems thought to be associated with a history of sexual abuse include sexual dysfunction, depression, and low self-esteem. These and other problems could be caused also by a wide range of other traumas. Child sexual abuse expert David Finkelhor proposed analyzing experience of sexual abuse in four traumagenic dynamics:

1. Traumatic sexualization: The child is rewarded for sexual behavior; the perpetrator exchanges attention for sex; sexual activity is conditioned with negative emotions.
2. Stigmatization: This dynamic distorts the child's sense of self-worth.
3. Betrayal: The child learns that someone she loved has harmed her. If the child is disbelieved by the family, blamed, or ostracized, betrayal weighs even heavier on the child.
4. Powerlessness: The child has a distorted sense of personal ability to control his or her own life (Finkelhor & Browne, 1986).

The interaction of the child's developmental capacities with these traumagenic dynamics may compromise the child's ability to develop subsequent age-appropriate competencies, thus placing the child at greater risk for psychopathology.

*Post-traumatic stress disorder.* PTSD may be a response of children who are exposed to trauma including sexual abuse. The mental health professional should be able to identify the many signs and symptoms through clinical interviews of children, parents, and teachers and begin effective therapeutic interventions (Briere, 1992). The suggestion that sexual abuse causes dissociation or borderline pathology is controversial as is the hypothesis that family dysfunction is a causal antecedent to sexual abuse (see Briere & Elliott, 1993; Nash, Hulsey, Sexton, Harralson, & Lambert, 1993).

*Social.* Placement of the child can become a more difficult challenge if the family is disrupted to the extent that the child does not have a supportive parent to provide permanent care. Tenuous placements out of the home leave some children feeling rootless. For others, the out-of-home placement provides protection they always have wanted from abusive family relationships. The goal of permanent placement of the child who has been abused sexually is difficult to accomplish when the perpetrator is still part of the family unit. His return or his continued presence in the community can threaten the child's security. Long-term therapy helps some children resolve their feelings of anger toward the abusive parent and learn ways to cope with new family dynamics. Adjusting to long-term foster care or adoption is particularly difficult for the older child who has a remembered family history that complicates the establishment of trusting relationships with adults. Above all, the sexually abused child must have the promise of a secure home life if the emotional problems resulting from the sexual abuse are to be survived.

*Legal.* The child who has been abused sexually is more likely to be involved in dependency and in criminal proceedings than victims of other types of abuse or neglect (Tjaden & Thoennes, 1992). A recent study showed that if the sexually abused child is removed from the home, she is less likely to be placed in kinship care than victims of other types of abuse or neglect (Dubowitz, Feigelman, & Zuravin, 1993). The court process can cause additional anxiety for the child through inherent delays and numerous hearings and reviews. If the child is placed under the supervision of dependency court or in custody of the county, court reviews are mandated every 6 months. Although the purpose of the court hearings is to make certain that the child's case is not put on the back burner, the reviews may remind the child of her tenuous status and the sexual abuse she is trying so hard to forget. The reviews do help the court ensure that needed services are being provided for the child. Reunification efforts with the parents are encouraged if it appears likely that the child will not be harmed further. If reunification is not possible, the court looks for permanent placement through termination of parental rights and adoption (see Chapters 11 and 12).

Goodman et al. (1989) reported on the emotional reactions of child sexual assault victims to testifying in court. They found that 65% of the children experienced distress of some type from testifying in court. Their most striking finding was the children's negative attitude about confronting the defendant. Recent Supreme Court decisions discussed in Chapter 9 provide protection to children whose statements are necessary to convict the perpetrator of sexual abuse.

## False Accusations and
## False Memories of Sexual Abuse

False accusations do occur sometimes because of malicious accusations made most often during visitation or divorce-custody battles. Although these false accusations may be rare, their effects can be devastating. Children may be removed from families, parents may be denied any contact with their children, and the accused may suffer the substantial stigma of being labeled a child molester. The legal system has constitutional safeguards that provide protection to the defendant in civil and criminal trials such as the right to trial by jury and the right to cross-examination.

False memory of child sexual abuse is a problem that is receiving increased attention. Studies of female patients report histories of child sexual abuse at rates between 36% and 51% (Briere, 1992). Therapists who think every female client's problems have historical roots in a history of sexual abuse, even when the client is unaware of such a history, can ignite a major bombshell on an innocent family's life. The issue of false memory is being addressed by a special committee appointed by the American Psychological Association (*APA Monitor*, 1993).

## Unresolved Questions

For child victims of sexual abuse, the community does not yet have clear guidelines for prevention and remediation. Although great strides have been made in reporting and identification, there has been much less long-term success resulting from intervention with the abuse triad: the child, the perpetrator, and the involved family members. Unfortunately, the child already victimized in the home is at further risk that today's known choices of social and legal interventions may again victimize the child. Which public agency should be responsible for positive outcomes for the child victim of sexual abuse? How can the community provide a continuum of preventive and supportive social and mental health services for the child? If child molesters have shown such a poor prognosis for successful therapy, how can the child victim be protected from sexual attack and continue to be part of an intact family? These questions regarding options for remediation will be discussed more fully in Chapters 8 and 9.

# 5

# Substance Abuse

*The Lord's angel appeared to her and said, "You have never been able to have children, but you will soon be pregnant and have a son. Be sure not to drink any wine or beer."*

Judges 13:3-4

## The Dilemma in Protecting the Unborn

The doctor suspected Karley would be born severely malnourished with a small head and bloated belly, a pathetically typical example of the youngest victims of drug abuse. He knew a cocaine-exposed infant may show signs of withdrawal for several days after birth. When the infant goes home with his mother, he may be inconsolable and cry night and day; shrink from touching; and have vomiting, diarrhea, and muscle cramps. A baby like this is at high risk of abuse by a burned-out mother addicted to drugs who cannot cope with an incessant crier. A husband or other male companion in the home, perhaps also addicted, may compound the dangers to the severely distressed infant. If the mother does not respond positively to the efforts of the visiting nurse and the social worker, court action might remove the infant.

In another courtroom a judge is considering removal of custody from a mother who has been using a legal drug, alcohol, during her pregnancy. Although she claims she limits herself to one drink per day, her doctor has warned her that one daily drink might be enough to induce fetal alcohol syndrome (FAS).

In the third courtroom the substance-abusing parents already have had two children removed for neglect. Their 4-month-old premature daughter, who has difficulty breathing and a cardiac condition, is able finally to leave the hospital. With a history of significant problems with drugs, these parents may not be able to give her the demanding care she needs. Their middle child has been diagnosed with fetal alcohol syndrome. The oldest child has already lived in six placements and is on a waiting list for a residential treatment center. The parents, who are allowed visits with the children, have been able to stay off drugs and alcohol for only the past 2 months. The children's needs are so great that these parents will require comprehensive and well-coordinated support services if the children ever are to be returned to their care.

In up to 80% of the cases heard in juvenile court, drug addiction or alcoholism of the parent is a major factor in the history of neglect or abuse of the child (McCurdy & Daro, 1993). When the money required for food, clothing, and rent to meet the child's needs is diverted to the parent's need for alcohol and drugs, the child may end up in court for neglect or abandonment. At the same time, if drugs or alcohol contribute to making the parent behave with violence, the children may suffer physical abuse. Often the child becomes a target for sexual abuse when drugs or alcohol overcome normal inhibitions and make one more child an innocent victim. This chapter will focus on the child exposed prenatally to harmful substances. Those children who are abused or neglected by substance-abusing parents during their childhood years constitute such a large proportion of the child abuse/neglect population that their specialized needs are addressed in other chapters.

## Incidence

In recent years the use of drugs has had a profound effect on the newborn. The National Association for Perinatal Addiction Research and Education (NAPARE) estimates that 375,000 infants, or 1 in 10 of every newborn in the United States, have been exposed prenatally to drugs (Toufexis, 1991). According to recent estimates, fetal alcohol syndrome occurs in one to three infants per 1,000 live births and in a higher percentage of inner-city and other high-risk populations (Little, Snell, Rosenfeld, Gilstrap, & Gant, 1990). Marijuana, cocaine, and alcohol as well as some prescription medications, tobacco products, or caffeine can present serious threats to pregnancy or fetal development. Are these

threats sufficient to invoke criminal or civil sanctions against the pregnant woman?

*Legal definition.* In many states a fetus is not defined as a minor child or
juvenile, thus precluding child abuse or neglect action. A definition of
a juvenile as "any child from birth to 18" would present legal barriers
to juvenile court jurisdiction. As of 1992, 22 states require the reporting
of drug-exposed infants and 4 states require the reporting of pregnant
substance abusers (McCurdy & Daro, 1993).

## Legal Intervention

Evaluating danger to an unborn child's future welfare is not a simple
task. Infant victims of prenatal substance abuse can be living tragedies.
Tragic family situations can be created also by premature court intervention that creates a barrier between the mother and her unborn child;
that act alone can have a devastating effect on the emotional and physical
welfare as well as the quality of parental bonding for the child. Filling
wards of hospitals with high-risk babies who have been abandoned
because of dire prebirth predictions is not a beneficial option. Can the
state provide better infant care than the mother? An unborn child thrown
into the legal system has urgent needs for which the law is an inadequate and clumsy substitute. A decision to take the pregnant mother into
custody should take into account the specific deficiencies and strengths
of any alternative jurisdiction in providing effective prenatal protection. Jailing a mother-to-be through a criminal action may be the only
way to keep her from the addictive substance and thus protect the fetus.
But in the long run, is that a wise alternative? Lyn Weiner, director of
the Fetal Alcohol Education Program at Boston University School of
Medicine, believes alcoholic women should be educated about the
dangers of alcohol to their unborn babies. Rather than providing jail
cells, she suggests treatment programs willing and equipped to treat
pregnant chemically dependent women (Dorris, 1989).
    Understanding the effects of drugs on the addict is necessary before
planning a workable intervention program. It is recognized univer-
sally that potentially harmful substances are used rarely in isolation.
As a result, the effects of using one drug may be enhanced or otherwise
complicated by interaction with other drugs, legal or illegal.

# Substances of Abuse

## Drugs

*Stimulants: cocaine, methamphetamine.* Originally a drug used mostly by the wealthy, cocaine was in widespread illegal use throughout the United States by 1982. The cocaine cycle produces an immediate sense of power, enhanced self-esteem, decreased fatigue, and an increased sense of sexual prowess. The downside of the cycle leads to hypersomnolence, hyperphagia, irritability, and depression. It is physically addictive, particularly in the high concentration form of crack or rock (Cregler & Mark, 1986).

The most important physical effect of cocaine is powerful constriction of the blood vessels. This causes the uterus to contract, leading to an observed 23% spontaneous abortion rate (Chasnoff, Burns, & Schnoll, 1985). The cocaine-affected baby may be born with high respiratory and heart rates, depressed interactive abilities, poor feeding patterns, tremulousness, startling, stiff muscles, arched back, and irregular sleeping patterns. The cocaine baby has a higher incidence of physical abnormalities, including deformed kidneys and neural tube defects. These babies may have withdrawal symptoms that make them more irritable and resistant to bonding than other babies (Cole, 1990). Cocaine withdrawal symptoms may continue for months longer than symptoms of heroin or methadone withdrawal. Although most cocaine-exposed infants do not suffer serious long-term effects, not all escape. In a 2-year follow-up study, a developmental pediatrician found that some cocaine babies may experience permanent damage to sensory, motor, and cognitive abilities. Howard (1990) stated, "They don't always know where their body is in space. They have trouble planning a motor act, such as climbing steps or getting off a chair to crawl on the floor. And they fear quick movements" (p. 311). She suggested that the mood dysfunction evident in these infants, specifically their inability to express positive feelings, may stem from cocaine's inhibition of maternal dopamine reuptake and may be permanent (Howard, 1989).

Other research indicates that in early childhood some prenatally cocaine-exposed children have serious difficulty relating to their world: socializing, making friends, engaging in normal play, and feeling love for their mothers or other primary caretakers. These young children must have structure and continuity to develop to the maximum of their often limited potential. Accurate and comprehensive information about the long-term effects of cocaine exposure is lacking (Soman, Dunn-Malhotra, & Halfon, 1993).

Methamphetamine is produced locally in stills using simple chemicals, primarily ephedrine. The white powder, called crystal or speed, is taken intranasally with the rapid onset of a "high." A chronic user can develop acute psychosis. Use is associated with diseases of the heart and blood vessels, life-threatening high fevers, and abnormally high blood pressure. Methamphetamine-exposed infants may exhibit poor feeding, poor alertness, and severe physical inactivity. Although most have minor neurological abnormalities, development is usually within normal limits during the first year. Most abnormalities noted after a relatively benign neonatal course suggest frontal lobe dysfunction that could affect school performance outcomes (Dixon, 1989).

*Narcotics: heroin, methadone.* The newborn whose mother used narcotics may have a high-pitched cry, sweating, trembling, and gastrointestinal upset. In addition, heroin-exposed newborns may be at high risk for HIV infection and AIDS from their mothers' intravenous heroin use during and prior to pregnancy.

*Hallucinogens: PCP, LSD, mushrooms.* Prenatal exposure to PCP and amphetamines has been found to cause brain damage. Estimates of the prevalence of prenatal exposure to drugs other than cocaine are inexact. Most current data disregards commonly used drugs that are potentially injurious to fetuses such as alcohol, heroin, amphetamines, methamphetamines, and PCP (Soman et al., 1993).

### Effects

Separating the effects of one drug from another is difficult because of the common practice of using a wide variety of drugs. To further complicate etiology, alcohol often is used to counter the downside of the drug cycle. Identifying the exact cause of problems that develop is complicated further by the concurrent influence of multiple factors such as poverty, inadequate nutrition, abuse or neglect, unstable out-of-home placements, and positive exposure to early intervention and support services. Exposure to alcohol or drugs during the first trimester can affect the formation of major organs. In the second and third trimesters, fetal growth may be poor, leading to miscarriage, low-weight infants, or prematurity. Premature infants are at high risk for respiratory distress syndrome with life-threatening implications and chronic respiratory problems that will need medical attention through childhood. They are more likely to have intracranial hemorrhages that place them at risk for cerebral palsy or to develop subtle motor or cognitive problems.

A positive toxicology screen of the newborn provides direct evidence of drugs in the mother's body within a 72-hour period before birth. An analysis of the infant's meconium (the first bowel movement) reveals drug use in the preceding 3 to 5 months. Positive toxicology screens do not prove the child has been harmed. A cluster of evidence that indicates possible harm to the child includes premature birth at less than 37 weeks, low birth weight, small head circumference, and abnormal neurobehavioral development. The mother's drug test along with poor weight gain, dilated pupils, and physical exhaustion in the infant confirm the evidence of drug exposure but is not sufficient to prove the child will suffer long-term harmful effects.

### Alcohol

Alcohol is a widely used drug that is legal for adults to use except when driving. Although the effects of alcohol on the drinker have been known for ages, the effects on the fetus have been reported only recently. Any amount of alcohol consumed at certain times during pregnancy may produce fetal alcohol syndrome. The American Medical Association, the American Academy of Pediatrics, former Surgeon General Koop, and a number of other experts have concluded that total abstinence is the only way to ensure no ill effect from alcohol consumption during pregnancy (Committee on Substance Abuse, 1993; Council on Scientific Affairs, 1989). One study showed that consuming one to two drinks a day during pregnancy substantially increased the risk of giving birth to a growth-retarded baby (Mills, Graubard, Harley, Rhoads, & Berends, 1984).

Withdrawal symptoms may interfere with the newborn's adaptive behavior (Abel, 1980). The affected infant with full-blown FAS has mental and physical retardation, face and skull malformation, and central nervous system problems. The abnormal facial appearance is characterized by small head, small eyes, snub nose, flattened nasal bridge, narrow upper lip, small chin, low-placed ears, and flat midface. Some infants have a deformed heart or deformed joints. The FAS child has borderline or below normal intelligence and retarded academic achievement. Even those with no physical abnormalities may have cognitive deficiencies, but those with the most physical abnormalities are also the most severely retarded. Impaired fine and gross motor functioning is typical (Ulleland, 1972).

Fetal alcohol effect (FAE) is not as severe as FAS. More difficult to recognize, FAE frequently results in learning or behavioral problems. Many factors other than alcohol consumption can play a role in severely impairing the fetus. Age, diet, metabolism, the number of pregnancies, stress level, and use of other drugs or smoking can affect the unborn. Maternal alcohol consumption may be related to increased rates of attention deficit hyperactivity disorder (ADHD). The director of the fetal alcohol and drug unit at the University of Washington Medical School followed 1,500 women for 7 years after they were pregnant. She found that alcohol use was linked to activity level, attention deficits, and difficulties in organizing tasks (Streissguth, Martin, Barr, Kirchner, & Darby, 1984).

In another Streissguth study of 61 adolescents and adults born with FAS, none of the subjects were supporting themselves, managing their own money, or living independently. Many had dropped out or were expelled from school. Their academic functioning was at the second to fourth grade level. Streissguth reported that the most frequent known cause of mental retardation is alcohol. Every year at least 7,000 more babies are born disabled due to FAS. The pregnant alcoholic has little help available. Although women make up about one third of the 10 million alcoholics in the country, most rehabilitative programs are designed for men. Few provide child care or accept pregnant women (Freiberg, 1991).

*Case study.* Born on an Indian reservation, Adam was adopted by a Native American college professor, who looked for the cause of the boy's significant developmental delays. The search led back to the alcoholic mother and uncovered the heartbreaking intergenerational epidemic of FAS within Native American populations (Dorris, 1989).

## Smoking

Smoking mothers have 28% more miscarriages, stillbirths, and babies who die soon after birth. A mother's smoking appears to have the most profound effects on the fetus during the last trimester, especially in the final weeks when the fetus should be able to gain weight. Carbon monoxide and nicotine in the mother's blood impair fetal development by reducing the amount of oxygen carried by the blood—thus constricting placental vessels and reducing the amounts of oxygen and nutrients reaching the fetus—resulting in lower birth weight. Smoking also can impair brain development, create heart abnormalities, and cause short stature (Sachs, 1985; Streissguth et al., 1984).

## Legal Framework

### Reporting Obligations

An important issue arises in determining if and when prenatal substance exposure should be reported to child protective services. To make such a determination, it is necessary to understand the requirements of mandatory reporting of child abuse and neglect of the state.

*Content of report.* All forms of child maltreatment must be reported. The standard under the federal Child Abuse Prevention and Treatment Act of 1974 is that injury must be sufficiently serious to endanger a child's health or welfare. Without specific legislation parental substance abuse would not be reportable unless there is reason to believe the child will be harmed seriously due to the substance abuse. Threatened harm must be reported also. Reasonable suspicion is all that is required to trigger mandatory reporting requirements. Child protection agencies are then responsible for deciding whether intervention is necessary. This is most difficult when it must be determined if exposing a fetus to harmful substances should be reported. Either explicit laws must be created to deal with this question or the answer must be inferred from existing state child abuse and neglect reporting laws (Besharov, 1990a).

*Reporting of prenatal exposure.* A growing number of states have dealt with the prenatal drug exposure issue by mandating that prenatal drug exposure and/or parental drug use be reported. Many states specifically mention drug exposure in their statutes that define child abuse and neglect. Because these states usually limit drug exposure to mean illegal substances, only a few states require that fetal alcohol syndrome be reported. The condition of the infant that triggers mandatory reporting laws varies from state to state. Some require only a positive toxicology screen. Other states require physical signs of addiction or dependence. The majority of states have no explicit laws requiring the report of prenatal substance exposure (McCurdy & Daro, 1993). In these states the determination of whether professionals should report requires a legal analysis of existing child abuse and neglect reporting laws.

*Reporting parental substance abuse.* In some states, it is not exposure to the fetus but drug use by parents that must be reported. Some statutes characterize parental substance abuse as evidence of child abuse or neglect, thereby requiring that it be reported. A growing number of states will accept reports of parental substance abuse during pregnancy to enable child protective agencies to mobilize. Under existing requirements, prenatal substance exposure must be reported when the parent is severely addicted to a debilitating drug. In such cases, it would be reasonable to expect that the child is harmed or threatened with harm. Severely addicted parents may be impaired significantly in taking care of themselves and their child; intervening to remove may be the only way to ensure the welfare of the child.

### Criminal Prosecution

Prosecuting mothers who use harmful substances during pregnancy is a controversial legal issue. Due to an alarming rise in the number of births of infants exposed prenatally to drugs, specifically attributable to the current popularity of crack cocaine, there has been rising frustration in the legal and health care community about permissible action that can be taken to address the problem of prenatal drug exposure. One result has been an attempt by various public officials, including prosecutors and district attorneys, to criminalize pregnant drug addiction by imposing legal penalties or criminal sanctions. Should pregnancy by a woman addicted to illegal drugs and/or alcohol be a crime?

*Legal viewpoint.* Public officials who attempt prosecution of pregnant drug users have the best interest of the child in mind. In advocating criminalization, they believe that the threat of incarceration will deter pregnant addicts from using drugs and that being incarcerated will motivate addicts to forgo drugs in hopes of getting out of jail and getting their children back. Prosecutors have widespread support for holding women responsible for harm they cause the fetus during pregnancy. Since 1987, as a result of these beliefs and popular support, criminal cases have been brought in several states. Charges range from child abuse and neglect, to delivery of drugs, to manslaughter. Judges are reluctant to make criminal findings unless such criminal behavior is specified explicitly in the statutes (Madden, 1993).

The Supreme Court has protected the woman's right to privacy in the landmark decision of *Roe v. Wade* (1973). Some pregnant addicts would have to compromise their right to privacy by feeling forced to obtain an abortion to avoid criminal conviction. The Supreme Court decided in 1925 and again in 1942 that drug addiction is a health matter, "a sickness," rather than a criminal matter. These decisions argue against criminal intervention.

*Medical and social services viewpoint.* Although some public officials believe criminalization is the answer, most health and social welfare experts strongly disagree, citing many reasons for feeling that criminalization is not the solution. Most feel that addiction during pregnancy is best treated as a health rather than a criminal issue. Although it may not seem unreasonable to assume pregnant addicts should get treatment for their addiction or suffer the legal consequences, effective treatment, unfortunately, is not widely available. In a 1989 survey of the 78 drug treatment facilities in New York City, 54% refused treatment to pregnant addicts, 67% refused treatment to pregnant addicts on medicaid, and 87% did not provide any services for crack-addicted pregnant women (Kirk, 1989). A more recent study showed that substance-abusing women are excluded on the basis of their pregnancy or mental illness or because they had children (Soman et al., 1993). Most centers that accept pregnant addicts do not offer prenatal or child care. Those that do offer services to pregnant women often have long waiting lists and cannot provide the newest treatments because they may harm the fetus.

Criminalization may deter women from seeking prenatal care for fear of being reported and incarcerated. This is especially serious because prenatal care can significantly improve the prognosis for drug-exposed infants even if the mother remains addicted throughout the pregnancy. The doctor/patient relationship and prenatal care can be jeopardized if women fear to disclose their addiction problem to the doctor. Some

experts believe pregnant addicts who are impoverished have been sin-
gled out unfairly for prosecution. One study showed that drug use by
pregnant women crosses racial and socioeconomic lines. Using urine
test results from public and private clinics, the study found 14.8% of
all women tested positive for drugs: 15.4% of White mothers and 14.1%
of Black mothers. Despite the higher percentage of White users, Black
women were found to be almost 10 times as likely to be reported for
substance abuse during pregnancy. The study has been criticized for
including marijuana in the types of drugs used (Chasnoff, Landress, &
Barrett, 1990).

Neither addicted fathers nor drug dealers giving drugs to pregnant
women are being charged with harming the fetus. Cocaine addiction
is prosecuted; however, other potentially harmful behaviors for pregnant women are not criminalized. For example, although cigarette
smoking can cause low birth weight and a higher rate of spontaneous
abortions, it is not prosecuted. Use of alcohol is prosecuted rarely even
though it may lead to fetal alcohol syndrome and its disabling mental
and physical anomalies.

Another argument against incarceration is the poor sanitary environment of many jails and prisons. Most likely a pregnant woman would
have limited access to adequate health care and little opportunity to
exercise in fresh air if she were jailed. Two major recommendations, if
put into practice, would begin to remedy the dilemma associated with
prenatal substance exposure: Offer adequate prenatal care, free from
fears of being reported or incarcerated, to all pregnant women; and
offer effective drug treatment facilities geared specifically toward the
needs of pregnant addicts. California's innovative statute requires an
inhospital assessment of any child born with an indication of prenatal
drug exposure. Even when a toxicology screen is positive, other infant,
family, and social factors must be considered to determine if a report
should be made to child protective services.

## Comprehensive Psychosocial Assessment

The substance-abusing pregnant woman who enters treatment has
a variety of legal, social, and medical problems and a high probability
of dysfunctional family relationships that must be addressed before
effective treatment can be initiated. The assessment should include the
woman's family of origin, adult relationships, parenting experience,

mental health status, living environment, work history, and education. After consent forms are signed by the client, information must be gathered from the agencies that serve her, including mental health, alcohol and drug treatment, Head Start, medical centers, primary physician, department of children's services, public health nursing, and school district or other infant development center. As part of the evaluation, a visit to the woman's home is essential to observe her family relationships and home environment. Coordination of services will increase the likelihood for successful treatment (Edelstein & Kropenske, 1992).

## Social Services

Child protective services intervention can help to stabilize substance-abused infants in their own homes. A study by one state found that unless the baby and the mother were together almost directly from birth, it was unlikely that the child and the parent would be reunited later (California Senate, 1990). The acute shortage of foster homes, especially in large urban areas, is a major consideration when children are threatened with separation from parents who may be fit (Moss, 1990).

The Adoption Assistance and Child Welfare Act of 1980 requires states that receive funds for foster care to make reasonable efforts to prevent unnecessary placement of children and to return them to their homes as early as possible. Agency policies have clarified reasonable efforts to include a caseworker's best efforts to evaluate the individual child and family situation regarding service needs. Prevention is the key element of services to the family, with the caseworker responsible for service coordination to ensure optimum development, safety, and well-being of the child in the parent's home. Reunification services are directed toward helping the parents develop adequate parenting skills.

In states in which a positive toxicology screen at birth is considered indicative of child abuse or neglect, the mandate to make reasonable efforts to prevent placement of the infant at birth could require that the state offer adequate prenatal care, free from fear of being reported or incarcerated, to all pregnant women together with effective drug treatment facilities designed to meet the special needs of pregnant addicts. As previously stated, because treatment programs for pregnant drug addicts are lacking in most communities, effective rehabilitation services usually cannot be offered to the pregnant woman before the child is born.

Reasonable efforts must be made also for mothers who are allowed to take their substance-exposed infants home from the hospital. Even when those addicted parents place their own addiction needs above the needs of their children, the social worker should make reasonable efforts to prevent removal of the children. Such efforts might include training in parenting skills needed for handling the complex medical, emotional, and developmental needs the child may develop; financial assistance while parents are in rehabilitation; respite services for occasional stress relief; and cooperation with public health nurses, physicians, and mental health professionals to provide close in-home supervision and support.

Innovative programs are in scattered use throughout the United States to provide the specialized care the substance-abused infant may need. Reforms suggested to improve services include:

— Increased funding to support the statutory preference for placements in home of parent or relative

— Funding for day care and respite care to enable parents involved in the system to participate in substance abuse rehabilitation treatment programs

— Increased training and payments for foster parents by using funds now allocated for group or institutional care (foster care costs one tenth of the state's cost for group home and institutional care providers)

— Transportation for parents to visit their children who have been removed

— Comprehensive day treatment programs that integrate health care, social services, and substance abuse treatment at one site and link clients to additional services in the community through coordination and case management

— Aggressive community outreach with home visits to enhance aftercare for the newborn

— Residential treatment facilities for pregnant addicts and mothers to facilitate child care training on site, with hands-on and other counseling, vocational, and medical treatment plans integrated into the daily program

— Intensive in-home family preservation services by counselors who work with only two families at a time

— Specialized group homes or foster homes with intensive training and supportive services readily available

## Mental Health and Rehabilitation

Psychiatric disorders or medical problems may undermine or even render ineffective drug and alcohol treatment. Thus a careful assessment must be made as to whether the pregnant addicted woman is suicidal, is depressed, or has a medical problem that lies at the root of the addiction (Edelstein & Kropenske, 1992). Currently, services are funded in an inflexible manner that may not respond to the specific needs of an addicted parent. Under those funding structures, services are made available only to individuals who meet explicit eligibility requirements. Where funding is limited to the provision of a specific service, a woman with both drug and alcohol problems might not be able to receive therapy for both addictions. A pregnancy exacerbates the difficulty in finding a service to meet her complex needs (Wilker, 1990). Ideally, drug and alcohol rehabilitation should be integrated closely with parenting education and medical as well as child development orientation to provide the coordinated intervention demanded by the family that is caught up in substance abuse.

## Costs

Significant financial costs are associated with prenatally exposed infants. The cost rises when premature babies are admitted to neonatal intensive care units. A UCLA study found that 20 prenatally exposed infants spent a total of 570 days in the neonatal intensive care unit. The aggregate cost was more than $1.2 million. At Martin Luther King Drew Medical Center the aggregate annual cost of providing care for approximately 500 withdrawing infants who did not require intensive care was more than $3 million (Wilker, 1990). The number of children born prenatally exposed to drugs in Los Angeles was 210 per month in 1992, but by 1993 the monthly tally reached 300. The cost of hospital care for this increasing number of children is staggering.

The social cost for children suffering the effects of fetal substance abuse is unmeasurable. A child development specialist in the Preschool Educational Development Program at the Salvin Special Education Center in Los Angeles reported that 13 children in the program who had been exposed to drugs in utero had been placed in a total of 35 foster homes before reaching the age of 3 (Cole, 1988). The lifetime dependency needs of the FAS child is a major burden for society. The emotional fragility of some cocaine babies can produce a precarious adulthood, neither stable nor productive. Economic and political strategies must be designed to provide structure and security for these children as they mature into adults.

*Cost comparisons.* In 1990 the average cost for placement in a state developmental center was estimated at $70,000 per year per client. Foster care costs averaged $13,000 per year per child. Expenditures for a community care client served by a mental health center was $5,500 per year. A residential drug program for women, which, if successful, would alleviate the necessity for permanent placement, costs $23,000 per year per client (Wilker, 1990). Clearly, less restrictive care is cost effective.

*Multiagency costs.* An interdisciplinary approach is necessary to deal with children affected by substance abuse. Teachers, administrators, social workers, physicians, public health nurses, physical education teachers, psychologists, speech and language specialists, community resource agencies, and parents or caretakers must team together to develop home/school partnerships whenever possible. Funding for services needed by pregnant substance abusers and their infants comes from multiple federal, state, and county sources as well as private foundation grants. Chapter 13 discusses Public Law 99-457 (Part H Early Intervention Program for Infants and Toddlers, 1990), which provides federally funded services to children age 0 to 3 at high risk for developmental disabilities, and Public Law 94-142 (Individuals With Disabilities Education Act [IDEA] of 1975), which provides special education services for preschoolers and school-age children with disabilities. Funds may be available from state departments of alcohol and drugs for substance abuse treatment programs. The federal government provides medicaid funds to poor children through the Early Periodic Screening, Diagnosis, and Treatment Program (EPSDT), which includes medical and mental health services.

Chapter 8 discusses more fully the department of children's services' use of federal funds for in-home services aimed at keeping children out of foster care. Other programs especially may target health or educational problems of pregnant teenagers or minority families. Eligibility criteria and the process of obtaining eligibility may present insurmountable problems to women and children needing to receive services. The key to serving effectively the broad spectrum of needs of substance-abusing families and to saving tax dollars from multiagency provision of overlapping programs is to provide a seamless system of services that is comprehensive, coordinated, and case managed (Soman et al., 1993).

*Case study.* The mother's 7-month-old baby had been exposed prenatally to various drugs. Her 12-year-old daughter was living with her and the baby; the baby's father was not living in the home. The mother initially had excluded her boyfriend from involvement with the agencies assisting her when she learned she was pregnant. After all, his drug dealing was what supported her and her daughter. She was afraid that if he knew of her involvement with a recovery program and with the department of children's services, he would become violent. She had been consistently free from drug use the entire 6 months she had been receiving treatment and services. She was enrolled in a 6-hour-per-day, 6-day-a-week drug treatment program that provided child care for the baby. The DCS worker is in a dilemma concerning whether or not he should close the case. He is worried that if all services are removed from the woman just when she is doing so well, she may relapse, especially when involved with a boyfriend still in the drug culture. She is in the "honeymoon" period of abstinence, the first year of sobriety when supports are plentiful and abstinence seems easiest. Her baby, although developing normally thus far, remains at risk for later developmental difficulties. Funding by DCS for in-home services is approaching a 1-year limit. Other agencies will need to begin taking over case management and support to improve this mother's chances of success.

## Permanent Placement

In some cases the parents will never be able to give safe care to their children. When a child is removed permanently from the custody of a substance-using parent, the options for permanent placement include legal guardianship, long-term foster care, and adoption. Although the object of permanency planning is to select the option that offers the child the best resources for reaching maximum potential, the substance-exposed infant poses special problems. Studies show that over half of the 3- to 7-year-old children of addicted parents had a poor prognosis for early school success. The children may be irritable and display poor impulse control. They may be attached less securely to caregivers. Immediate placement of babies into boarding institutions interferes with the child's ability to develop normal bonding and decreases the child's development from stimulation (Kirk, 1989).

Fortunately, the future can be hopeful for many of these children. A study in California reported that after 2 years in their adoptive homes, drug-exposed children were found by their adoptive parents to have the behavior patterns, temperament, and educational levels of non-drug-exposed adopted children. Parents of children in both groups reported equal satisfaction with their children (Barth, 1991). The study is controversial in that it lacks in-depth reporting from physicians or pediatric developmental experts who can measure differences more skillfully. It does provide the good news, however, that the adoptive parents are pleased with their children, whether or not those children suffer long-term effects from early drug exposure.

## Conclusion

Although drug exposure does place children at high risk for developing special needs, a child's unique constellation of environmental influences can help modify long-term outcomes to produce consequences ranging from minimal to severe. Chaotic environments alone can lead to poor outcomes for children. When drug exposure, foster care placement, and reunification attempts are added to the equation, children's lives are at increased risk. Providing a stable and nurturing home and school environment for the child maximizes optimal outcomes (Tyler, 1992).

# 6

# Emotional Abuse

*The child's sob in the silence curses deeper*
*Than the strong man in his wrath.*
Elizabeth Barrett Browning,
"The Cry of the Children," 1844

The parents, Robert and Adrian, have significant limitations in their backgrounds and abilities. Robert has been diagnosed as having a borderline personality disorder, and Adrian has cognitive deficiencies that affect her judgment and capacity to care for her children. Their first child, Ennett, was reported as abandoned when less than a year old. The child protective services worker found Adrian in the hospital severely injured from an assault by Robert. When another daughter was born, Adrian asked CPS to remove herself and the children from the home because of her fears for the safety and well-being of the children after Robert had threatened to kill her. She later decided to return home.

By the time Ennett was 4 years old, she showed evidence of physical injury as well as troubling emotional symptoms. Her severe disability soon bordered on a psychotic condition that was attributed to her early exposure to violence in the home. Both children were returned to foster care. Within the next two years, the couple had two boys. When a third son was born and died in suspicious circumstances, the caseworker visited the home. She discovered that the two surviving little boys showed minor signs of physical neglect but major signs of inadequate emotional and developmental growth. She then placed them in foster care. On evaluation, the older boy was found to have significant developmental delays. He was a year behind in ability to form the simplest perceptions of the world about him. The professional who evaluated the younger son believed his protracted lack of nurturing care eventually would doom him. After 10 years of intervention and services, the court overturned a lower court by holding that the trial court incorrectly emphasized the economic and social disadvantages of respondent-parents as factors that excused or outweighed in significance the essentially uncontradicted showing of serious harm suffered by the children as a result of a lack of nurturing care in the home. The court stated, "The mental health of the child and its best interest psychologically must always be considered. . . . The absence of physical abuse or neglect is not conclusive" (*New Jersey Department of Youth and Family Services v. A. W.,* 1986, p. 604).

The facts of this New Jersey case illustrate that in some cases emotional maltreatment that causes developmental delays can be serious enough to justify termination of parental rights. The mental health professionals involved with these children provided evaluations that helped the court determine that the harmful influence of these parents on their children should be terminated. Emotional abuse and neglect can have devastating effects on children, yet it is unlikely the state will intervene to protect the emotionally abused child unless other factors are present, such as a history of violence, physical or sexual abuse, or neglect. A national survey showed that although only 4% of child abuse reports were for emotional maltreatment, 10% of substantiated reports were for emotional maltreatment (McCurdy & Daro, 1993).

## Definition

The National Center on Child Abuse and Neglect (1978) defined emotional abuse as a verbal or emotional assault, close confinement, and threatened harm. Emotional neglect was defined as inadequate nurturance or affection, allowance of maladaptive behavior (delinquency), and any other refusal to provide essential care.

Incorporating emotional abuse and neglect into juvenile codes is especially difficult because the terms that define cause, treatment, and consequences are vague. Goldstein, Freud, and Solnit (1973) urged staying out of the trendy emotional abuse/neglect area. They expressed the belief that the so-called objectively observable symptoms of emotional abuse, such as depression or withdrawal, could arise from many causes. They found symptoms of emotional neglect even more difficult to pinpoint. Other professionals argue that parental behavior can have such devastating effects on the psychologically battered child that a finely drawn definition must be included. Believing that all parent-child interactional breakdowns lead to emotional distress within the family, Helfer suggested eliminating emotional abuse from being classified as a primary entity, using instead the term *verbal abuse*. His broad definition of child abuse and neglect is "any interaction or lack of interaction between family members which results in non-accidental harm to the child's physical and/or developmental state" (Helfer & Kempe, 1987, p. 61).

Psychologist James Garbarino favored a general definition of maltreatment as "acts of omission or commission by a parent or guardian that are judged by a mixture of community values and professional expertise to be inappropriate and damaging." He defined emotional maltreatment as "assault on the psyche," which he divided into five categories: (a) terrorizing, (b) isolating, (c) ignoring, (d) rejecting, and (e) corrupting (Garbarino & Gilliam, 1980, p. 7).

A general definition allows the judge or social worker to use subjective social and cultural standards when applying the definition to the known facts. Interpretations that draw on social and cultural factors are almost impossible to avoid when looking at conduct within the home and family, especially in relation to conduct that can support an allegation of emotional maltreatment. Who is to determine when a parent has crossed over that vague line into the area of publicly condemned emotional abuse or neglect? Physical and even sexual abuse and neglect are usually much easier to evaluate as to cause and effect. Emotional neglect is less visible and the results may not be immediate. It is much more difficult to determine whether an emotionally disturbed child's illness results from the parent's behavior than whether a parent caused a child's broken bones. Parents are overheard frequently in shopping malls voicing such threats to fretful toddlers as "Any more crying and I'm going to walk out and leave you here alone!" How is that type of damage measured, especially when it can be assumed that similarly terrorizing predictions are commonplace in that parent-child relationship?

The Child Abuse Prevention and Treatment Act of 1974 includes a definition for *mental injury* that serves as a general guideline for states to follow if they wish to receive federal funding for child protective services. That general definition includes acts or threatening statements made and/or allowed that result in mental injury or harm to the child and specifies that (a) *mental* refers to emotional, intellectual, or psychological functioning; (b) connection exists between parent's behavior and child's mental problems; (c) parent's behavior must cause or perpetuate mental difficulty of the child; and (d) parent's behavior may be obvious, subtle, explicit, stated, or implied.

In most states the statutory language related to emotional abuse and neglect is vague and general. To be eligible for federal funds for child abuse prevention and treatment, states must require that emotional abuse be reported; all states accept voluntary reports of emotional maltreatment.

## Incidence

No statistics are available on current incidence of emotional abuse and neglect, but the most recent estimate is that of almost 3 million reports, 200,000 were for emotional neglect and 188,000 for emotional abuse (McCurdy & Daro, 1993). Rarely does an incident of sexual or physical abuse or neglect occur without accompanying emotional maltreatment. Conversely, emotional abuse and neglect can occur without accompanying physical or sexual abuse. Charting the rate of incidence is difficult because although emotional maltreatment may be present, it is the physical or sexual abuse or neglect that is reported more often.

Few juvenile court decisions are based solely on emotional neglect. Because this category of neglect is so difficult to prove, such decisions are based often on professional opinions as to the effects of parental conduct on a child's emotional stability. The mental health professional must prove to the court that the expert opinion is not based on conjecture about harm to the child, but must specify how the child is suffering perceptible, severe harm directly attributable to the parent-child relationship.

To increase reliability the mental health professional's testimony should be based on interviews with both the minor and the parents, preferably over time. Testimony based primarily on past history gleaned from social casework and psychiatric records rarely is convincing in juvenile court.

## Case Studies

An expanded construct of Garbarino's psychologically destructive patterns of behavior provides a framework for studying the legal and psychological parameters of emotional maltreatment. The following case studies illustrate a range of emotional maltreatment.

*Terrorizing.* Donnie was 2 years old when he saw his mother strike his sister on the head with a soda bottle and then place her in a hot oven that burned her severely. An expert witness testified that Donnie had been so traumatized that he had to expend excessive emotional and intellectual energy to deal with both the trauma of his sister's abuse and his mother's alcoholism. The court found that the child's environment had injured his emotional, psychological, and developmental welfare. Although there was no question that the sister had been abused, attorneys for the mother argued that Donnie had not suffered any physical abuse and was too young to have suffered emotional harm. The testimony by experts who had kept careful records of their evaluation and treatment of Donnie convinced the judge that the boy, too, had been abused and neglected. The mother's parental rights subsequently were terminated.

*Isolating.* Irena's new husband did not get along with her teenage son, Mark. Forced to live in the garage, Mark was never allowed to have meals with the family or socialize with them. He was given a cardboard box to sleep in. A neighbor befriended Mark, gave him a home, and asked the court to appoint her to be his guardian.

*Ignoring.* Lynne was the gifted 14-year-old daughter of a graduate student. Her mother was rarely at home because of her studies and her boyfriend. Lynne was responsible for buying groceries, fixing her own meals, keeping the apartment clean, and getting herself back and forth to school. Lynne wore baggy clothing to camouflage her body, which was showing signs of anorexia. Her hair began falling out. The school counselor was alerted to her critical condition when Lynne fainted as she stepped off the school bus. When her mother was notified, she blamed Lynne and refused to alter her rigid schedule to spend any time with her daughter. After brief hospitalization, Lynne was placed in foster care with professional parents especially trained to work with

emotionally disturbed teenagers. Lynne remained in therapy for months
with a psychiatrist who appeared at court hearings to make specific
recommendations regarding Lynne and her contacts with her mother.
While in foster care and in therapy, Lynne's fragile health came under
control as her confidence and social skills improved. She began making
friends at school and writing for the school newspaper.

*Rejecting.* Louise lived on a houseboat with her two boys—Tyrone, age
9, and Jason, age 6. Jason was born 4 months after his father deserted
Louise. Although she wanted an abortion, her pregnancy was too advanced. After being reported for neglect, Louise entered therapy on the
advice of her caseworker. Louise explained that she never really wanted
Jason, who reminded her of his father. She couldn't tolerate having
Jason touch her. When she sat the boys down to read them a story, she
would yell at Jason to take his hand off her arm if he happened to touch
her. The two brothers were the best of friends. Tyrone tried to protect
his little brother from his mother's rage. She had no trouble with
Tyrone; it was Jason she never liked. A year after therapy began, Jason
was removed from Louise after she physically beat him. Although
there was a clear legal case for removing Jason from his mother, the
severing of his ties with Tyrone was devastating. To prevent revictimization by a sometimes impersonal system of state intervention, a
sensitive mental health professional would have considered removing
both boys or recommending extended periods of sibling visitation.

*Corrupting.* Jimmy and Johnny lived across the street from the neighborhood school. Their family had much less money than their neighbors, who had moved into a new subdivision surrounding their old
farmhouse. Their father taught them that their wealthier neighbors
took advantage of the poor; he encouraged the boys to get even. Soon
the front yard was filled with bicycles the boys stole from subdivision
homes and then repainted with paint taken from the school. As the
boys reached adolescence, they terrorized their classmates, demanding
lunch money or larger payoffs. They began breaking and entering
homes for stereo and sports equipment. The father saw the bikes and
stolen equipment; he knew the boys had money they had not earned.
He continued to encourage their illegal behavior. Before Jimmy and
Johnny were out of high school, they were in prison for rape and murder.
Early in their career of bicycle theft the boys were brought to the

attention of the authorities who attempted to work with the family to improve the boys' behavior. When the father resisted supervising any positive change, a petition for neglect was brought against the parents. Despite testimony from victimized neighbors and school personnel, the court was reluctant to find that the parents had neglected their sons because the parental behavior did not fit the usual neglect definition of failure to provide food, clothing, or shelter. It wasn't long before the boys were in delinquency court for breaking and entering. Therapy and rehabilitation in training school or detention halls proved futile when Jimmy and Johnny returned home. Their father seemed proud of the record his sons were making for themselves and continued to encourage them.

*Mental illness of the parent.* During Lee's pregnancy the doctor discontinued all her medication for schizophrenia to avoid possibly harming the fetus. Unable to care for herself or the new baby, Lee was forced to place the baby in foster care. Visits with the infant had to be supervised closely because of Lee's tendency to nod off when holding the baby. In contact with Lee's poor personal hygiene and malodorous apartment, the baby cried constantly during permitted home visits. Lee also had a difficult time remembering to take her medication. This lapse was evident when she appeared in court wearing mismatched shoes and could not answer the simplest questions about her life.

The psychiatrist who testified at her termination of parental rights hearing had seen Lee for only a few minutes every few months to regulate her drugs and did not know her lengthy history of mental illness. Thus, as an expert witness, she gave unconvincing testimony about Lee's inability to provide parenting to meet the child's needs. Family members and neighbors were much more convincing as they described her numerous evictions and told how difficult it was for Lee to care for herself, much less her baby.

## Community Services

In-home services can provide guidance and supervision to help the parent learn how to reframe destructive family dynamics. If the mental health professional or public health nurse can make home visits, the parent can be seen interacting with the child in a natural environment.

Parents feel less threatened and are more likely to respond positively if the services they need are provided in the home. Infants and pre-schoolers ignored by their parents benefit from day care, especially care designed for developmentally delayed youngsters. Training in parenting skills stresses the importance of infant stimulation and provides the parent with a range of techniques for improved parenting. Community mental health services are sometimes needed to treat individual and family pathology. The juvenile court may order such services for some parents as a condition of keeping their children or having them returned. See Chapters 8 and 9 for a fuller discussion.

Emotionally fragile children can benefit from in-school services designed to develop the child's self-esteem and autonomy. Those who are seriously emotionally disturbed should be tested by the local school and provided an individualized education program (IEP). Federal funding is available to all school districts to provide services for any child who is seriously emotionally disturbed. Before qualifying, the child must be tested and evaluated. If the school has not first identified the child for testing, a request may be made to the school for tests and evaluations. Chapter 13 discusses educational services for children with disabilities.

When emotional abuse in the home is serious, the mental health professional must evaluate the current harm to the child versus the emotional harm inherent in separating family members. Because foster care placement often means a change in school for the child or adolescent, this factor must be included in the equation before recommending a removal. If the child must be removed, ideally the recommendation would be for placement in the home of relatives or in a foster home in the child's familiar school district.

When foster care is considered, the juvenile court needs to hear evidence from the professionals and other witnesses before deciding whether the parent did emotionally abuse or neglect the child. Only after such a conclusion will the court then determine whether the child should be placed in the custody of the department of children's services for placement in the home of an approved relative or in foster care. In the most serious cases the child may need to be evaluated for special group home living, residential treatment center placement, or institutionalization in a psychiatric hospital. The latter recommendation could require another administrative or court hearing with professional testimony supporting commitment.

## Role of the Mental
## Health Professional in Court

The New Jersey case involving Ennett and her brothers and sister illustrates the importance of the mental health professional in providing evaluations of parents and children and the harmful influence these parents had on their children. The court chided the professionals for using language that had a cultural cast. By emphasizing factual discoveries in their evaluation and by describing age-appropriate skills the children had or did not have, the witnesses could have given an unbiased, clear picture of the dire situation of the children.

The only witness in the New Jersey hearing who advocated return of the children to their parents was a clinical psychologist who had not been given access to the voluminous history of the family. His opinion was based solely on interviews with the parents. The state supreme court specifically instructed the psychologist to review all the social service records before presenting an opinion at the second hearing.

Reports to the court should be detailed, clear, and timely. If the child in therapy is experiencing serious emotional problems because of prolonged or frequent change of placements or because of traumatic visits with the parents, the court should be informed immediately so that court orders and time frames can be reassessed. The mental health professional should try to coordinate efforts with other family-serving agencies as well as the court to make sure that all are working toward the same goal within the same time frame.

The mental health professional provides more than assessment and therapy in today's emotional abuse and neglect cases. Often the primary interviewers and experts for the prosecution are behavioral scientists. In the emotionally charged arena of the courtroom, the professional must take care to stay within the limits of the professional role and expertise. Child welfare, family privacy, and personal liberty must not be compromised by overstepping ethical boundaries. Opinions should be based on scientific research or on specialized knowledge. Parental motivation must be considered as well as a specific cause-and-effect relationship. A child suffering from nightmares or enuresis could have underlying medical or mental health problems that are not related to a parent's emotional abuse or neglect. Other behaviors such as aggression, withdrawal, truancy, low self-esteem, and destructiveness without guilt could have multiple causes. Tying the child's behavior directly to the parent's emotional abuse or neglect requires careful analysis of complex factors. The expert witness must limit court testimony to hard data, not clinical intuition (Melton & Limber, 1989).

## Long-Term Effects
## of Emotional Maltreatment

Emotional maltreatment can result in long-term fear, anxiety and anger, impaired physical development, withdrawal, apathy, and severe damage to cognitive, emotional, social, and moral development (Kincannon, 1989). In a sample of 223 runaways in New York State in 1986-1987, 42% were reported to suffer from emotional abuse defined as extreme verbal abuse, name calling, derogatory remarks, constant yelling, blaming, scapegoating, and rejection. Over one third of the runaway children had been pushed out of their homes by their parents (Powers, Eckenrode, & Jaktitsch, 1990). Adolescents who have a history of emotional neglect may be more difficult to rehabilitate. In a study of delinquents in a juvenile detention home, Polansky (1981) found that the unsocialized aggressive delinquents and unsocialized runaway delinquents had suffered the most parental rejection and were less able to be rehabilitated than the remaining group of socialized cooperative delinquents.

## Emotional Neglect by the State

A succession of placements in foster care or emergency shelters can cause the emotional stability of many children to deteriorate. It is important to evaluate children before they enter out-of-home placement to have an accurate record of problems existing in the home prior to the state's taking custody of the child. Evaluations then should be continued after the children are in custody. The federal Adoption Assistance and Child Welfare Act of 1980 was intended to minimize the length of time children remain in foster care. Because the support services necessary to allow children to remain at home were not funded, the purpose of the legislation was defeated. Ironically, foster care funds continue to be budgeted, although in-home services over a decade later are just beginning to receive serious funding (Omnibus Budget Reconciliation Act of 1993).

Foster care drift, a major problem for children, inflicts serious emotional harm on children through multiple losses, resulting lack of trust, and in the worst cases, the development of psychopathic personality disorders. Children who have been in foster care for over a year or in an emergency shelter for over 3 months should be evaluated by a mental health professional. Los Angeles Dependency Court Judge Paul Boland listed the following conditions as typical of these children:

___ Conduct disorder with aggressive tendencies or antisocial behavior
___ Attention deficit disorder treated by psychotropic drugs
___ Self-destructive or suicidal behavior
___ Use of psychotropic drugs
___ Developmental disability
___ Fire setting
___ Manifestation of psychotic symptoms such as delusion, hallucination, and disconnected or incoherent thinking
___ Somaticizing or psychosomatic problems such as sleeping and eating disorders
___ Chronic depression or social isolation
___ Severe sexual acting-out behavior
___ Substance abuse

Judge Boland (1990) recommended that these children with special needs should have a detailed, individually tailored court order for evaluation, treatment, or placement and possible representation before an administrative agency. Court review every 3 months would keep the judge better informed of the state's action to meet the pressing needs of these special children. The professional who evaluates the child in foster care must be aware of the statutory time frames for children to be allowed to remain in foster care before decisions must be made for a return home or termination of parental rights. Most states have a 12- to 24-month time frame for reunification efforts before filing a petition to terminate parental rights. In cases of severe abuse, most states allow a termination petition to be filed immediately, thus preventing any effort at reunification. The professional treating the foster care child will keep the child's social worker and the court apprised of the child's mental health status so that the state will not become liable for inflicting unnecessary emotional abuse on the child by ignoring or neglecting the child's basic need for permanent attachment to a parent figure. Asking the county to provide in-home services tailored to the needs of the child's family could help avoid foster care placement in the first place if money can be found for these needed services.

Providing therapy for the child and parents during the sometimes lengthy process of reunification will maximize the possibility of an earlier, more stable return home. Infants in foster care should be visited at least three times a week by biological parents in order to foster healthy attachment. An ideal placement would have the infant in a foster home or day care center where the biological parents would go daily to care for the infant under the close supervision of the foster parent or day care specialist. Ideally, teen mothers can be placed with their infants in foster care together with the same high-quality supervised learning and support available.

The mental health professional could provide the evidence the court needs to make firm orders requiring the department of children's services to provide strong reunification services and requiring the parents to respond positively within a given time frame. A 3-month period gives most parents the time pressure needed to motivate responsive action before the next court hearing. Review hearings scheduled at 12- or even 6-month intervals may cause delays by both social services and parents in taking the steps required to meet the child's pressing need for a safe, permanent home.

*Case study.* Anne was given up for adoption at birth by her biological mother. She was placed with foster parents who did not want to adopt her. The policy of the adoption unit of the county department would not allow Anne to be placed in an adoptive home until the biological father's rights had been terminated; his address was unknown. Anne lived with her foster parents for 18 months until the legal work on her father finally was completed. Because she was doing well in foster care, her case was not viewed as an emergency. As soon as Anne was placed in her adoptive home, she developed a state of acute grief that lasted for weeks. Her adoptive parents felt deep anguish because they had been unable to prevent this emotional trauma for Anne by providing a continuity of love and care during her first year and a half of life.

*Case study.* Cary was abandoned by his mother when he was 2 years old and left in the care of his paternal grandparents. When the grandmother died, the grandfather was reported for neglecting to send the boy to school. The department of social services placed the child in his uncle's home and supervised the placement until the marriage of the aunt and uncle became strained by their frequent disputes over how to discipline Cary. He was placed in an emergency shelter for a week until a foster home could be found. Cary was forced to leave the school where he had been receiving special education services and was transferred to a school in the foster parents' district. Cary's severe problems adjusting to the new classroom situation carried over and made him difficult to handle at home. Because the foster parents worried that his behavior would endanger the other three children in their home, they asked that the boy be removed.

Cary was returned to the emergency shelter for a 2-week stay pending the finding of a foster family who could care for a special needs child. He was sent back to the shelter three more times. He was admitted to a residential treatment center that could provide the therapy and special education he needed. Before he was 11 years old, Cary had lived in 12 placements, none of them permanent. A counselor at the residential treatment center took a strong interest in Cary and pushed for consideration of an adoptive placement. Then he helped prepare Cary, emotionally and socially, for an adoptive home. Because of his counselor's advocacy, Cary avoided further placement in long-term foster care or institutional settings, which is all too often the placement for foster children with serious behavior or educational problems.

*Case study.* Jayrene's father moved into his converted bus with Jayrene after her stepmother threatened to punish her with a belt. Her father drove the bus to the shopping plaza parking lot adjacent to the laundromat where he worked. Although the bus had no plumbing or cooking facilities, the father bought hot meals for them at the grocery store and had access to the bathroom at the laundry. After three days of living in the bus, the father was reported for neglect. Late one evening, a social worker making the initial investigation removed Jayrene from her father's custody and placed her in an emergency shelter. As soon as she reached the shelter, Jayrene began vomiting. At the custody hearing in court, the county used her illness as evidence of the unhealthy environment she had been living in for 3 days. Jayrene's symptoms of illness actually resulted from the emotional trauma she experienced when the social worker came in the night and took her away from her father, who had been doing all he could afford to do to keep her safe from harm.

## Conclusion

Most foster children enter foster care with emotional scars from their home environment or develop emotional problems because of the care the state provides. If fragmenting agency services for investigation, foster care, emergency placement, adoption, and court hearings caused the prolonged temporary placements of Anne and Cary, how can agency services be restructured to ensure timely permanent placement? What services could have been offered Jayrene and her father to avoid having her emotionally abused by the state, the agency officially responsible for her protection? These questions will be explored more fully in subsequent chapters.

# 7

# Neglect

*He who saves a child is as if he saved the whole world—he who neglects a child destroys the world.*

Adaptation from the *Talmud*

The extremes of child neglect that bring parents into conflict with the law are scarcely imaginable by those who have had a relatively orderly and well-cared-for childhood. This chapter will discuss the indications and the consequences, both legal and social, of parental neglect that is serious enough to warrant the attention of child protection authorities.

At the edge of a supermarket parking lot, a crowd gathers around an automobile in which a red-faced toddler is screaming. The car doors are locked and the windows closed. These anxious and increasingly angry men and women, standing in 95-degree heat with their shopping carts, await the return of the child's mother and loudly cheer when, on her return, she is apprehended by a security guard.

A neophyte social worker makes a home visit to offer help, if needed, to the wife of a soldier stationed overseas. He has had no mail from home for 3 months and is worried about his wife and young children. Because there is no home telephone and he is unacquainted in her new neighborhood, he has asked a community agency for assistance. A knock on the front door produces no response. On hearing the cry of a baby, the visitor looks through the large front window and sees an infant and two young children on the floor amid pieces of broken glass, piles of trash, dishes of rotting food, scattered diapers, and overturned wooden chairs. When she raps on the window, a somber little girl opens the door. She doesn't know where her mother is, but almost before the child can answer that question, the visitor is overcome by the stench from the house and by the sight of the living conditions of these apparently unsupervised children. While rushing next door to call child protective services, she struggles for self-control, then vomits all over the sidewalk.

In an affluent neighborhood, a mother arrives one morning at an unfamiliar private home to attend a community meeting for which child care has been promised. She delivers her toddler son to the baby-sitter in the backyard, where small children are chasing balls. Half an hour later, she goes out to check and finds that her son and another child have wandered behind the garage where she sees, to her horror, a number of empty metal nursery cans lying on the ground with their roughly cut bottom circles protruding dangerously.

In two of these examples of child neglect, the responsible adults are shocked to learn they have been guilty of seriously endangering the children in their care. In the other, the soldier's wife will insist that she has no support system and insufficient funds to provide better care for her children.

What kinds of parental behavior constitute legally reportable neglect and what are the causes? Is there widespread statutory agreement on definitions of neglect? Who in the community is responsible for protecting children who are the victims? How is the availability of social and legal services for child protection related to decisions by authorities to intervene between parent and child when neglect is discovered?

Parents who are truly incapable of following accepted and reasonable norms of child care unwittingly may produce consequences for their children that are defined legally as neglect. Other parents may be fully aware of their children's basic physical needs and safety requirements but cannot muster the financial resources needed for adequate sustenance and living conditions for their children. Some parents are so challenged by their own addictive behaviors or serious physical, mental, or emotional illness that they lack the capacity to plan ahead and provide for their children's most elementary needs.

A child who is considered neglected may be consistently dirty, hungry, inappropriately dressed, and tired or lethargic. The child often may be left without supervision for long periods of time. The child may be exploited, overworked, or kept from attending school. In some cases the child has been abandoned. The child might beg or steal food or be engaged in vandalism, prostitution, or substance abuse. The parent's behavior may indicate evidence of severe mental illness or retardation, substance abuse, or chronic illness.

Children of the rich and famous can be neglected, too. One mother who was reported for neglect had decorated her living room in wall-to-wall white carpeting and limited her children to only two rooms in the large house. She could not tolerate the sight of soil or any untidiness in the bedrooms or kitchen. A parent who is so compulsive about neatness that the child is placed under unduly severe restrictions is not providing proper care for the child. In an upper-middle-class neighborhood, the parents of two girls departed for a 2-week vacation out of the United States with no plan for adult supervision in the home for their young daughters. This real "Home Alone" episode of child abandonment was discovered only when the older girl ran to a neighbor for help after a smoke alarm went off.

Brief parental absence in an emergency or a poorly kept house are not adequate standards of neglect. But neglect can be found where the home environment of the child poses immediate and continuing danger because of parental absence, structural problems, safety hazards, nonworking utilities, or poor sanitation. If the home is extremely filthy and rodent infested and without appliances or utilities in working order, the child probably would be removed unless the parents could respond in a timely fashion to services offered that would make the home safe for the children (see Magura & Moses, 1984).

Parents who are confronted officially when their behavior appears to represent neglect often feel that they are the target of unwarranted intrusion into their rights of family privacy and constitutionally protected authority over their children. Authorized state intervention must be based clearly on a substantial need to protect the child from specific harm by the parent. There is great variability, however, in state and federal statutes that define neglect.

Some statutory definitions give wide discretion and little guidance to the child protective service workers who, in most communities, are the persons officially responsible for intervening to arrange for protection. Often the decision to intervene is based not on whether the act meets the legal definition of neglect but on whether the presenting case looks more serious than others or on whether a service is available to meet the particular needs of that child. Identification of neglect based on service availability rather than individual need tends to work against neglected children who usually have a complex pattern of needs.

Vague standards increase the likelihood of inappropriate intervention that may be more harmful to family dynamics and to the child's security than nonintervention. Legal scholar Michael Wald (1975) almost 20 years ago made a stand for a narrow, precisely drawn definition of neglect. The narrow definition would avoid discretionary intervention by judges or social workers that often reflects personal values not supported by scientific evidence. He believed such overstepping intervention may do more harm than good.

*Neglect* is defined generally as abandonment; willful or negligent failure to provide adequate food, clothing, shelter, support, or medical treatment; inability to provide regular care for a minor due to the parent's mental illness, developmental disability, or substance abuse; failure to intervene to protect a child; or failure to enroll a child in school. The neglect definition may specifically rule out minors whose only needs result from poverty or homelessness (see California Welfare and Institutions Code sec. 300(b) and New York Family Court Act sec. 1012(f)(i) (A), 1988). Before looking in more detail at the areas of neglect included in the foregoing definition, this chapter examines two social factors that on the surface may seem like neglect—poverty and homelessness.

## Poverty

Economic stress is often a precursor to all types of abuse and neglect. A recent study found that in over 85% of all cases reported, annual incomes were less than $21,000 (Tjaden & Thoennes, 1992). Another survey found that the factor most frequently cited by state officials for the rise in child abuse reports was economic stress due to poverty, unemployment, and related work concerns (McCurdy & Daro, 1993). It is important for the professional to separate the poverty issue from the pattern of parent-child dynamics to discover whether neglect does indeed exist. The growth of poverty, especially that affecting children, makes this distinction more difficult. Over 30 million Americans live in poverty. Two of five of these are children. Moreover, children are the fastest growing number found to be in poverty (Baker, 1991).

## Homeless Families

Families with young children are the fastest growing segment of the homeless population, constituting one third of the homeless population. In addition to those living in shelters or on the street, a large number of children are doubled up temporarily in the often already overcrowded dwellings of friends or family. The high cost of housing, an unexpected medical expense, or a missed child support check can force a family into the ranks of the homeless. Life on the streets or in shelters is dangerous, for both young families and runaway youth. The lack of family housing stability, which often includes randomly available access to school, is emotionally damaging. A frequent response of the child welfare system is to put the children in foster care, thereby adding to the children's trauma by removing them from their families (Bussiere, 1989).

Homelessness can have serious, permanent effects on children by significantly exacerbating such incipient problems as academic failure, clinical depression, and developmental lags, as well as malnutrition, pneumonia, and other illnesses. Dr. David Wood's (1990) study of homeless children in Los Angeles found that 24% failed the Denver Developmental Test, 30% of the children repeated grades, and 28% were in special classes in school. A survey in New York found that 72% scored below grade level. The Child Welfare League of America (1991) concluded in its report on homelessness that homeless children and youth are at increased risk for physical and mental health problems, dental problems, nutritional deficiencies, developmental delays, acting-out behaviors, truancy, exposure to substance abuse, unplanned pregnancies, and early delinquencies.

Homelessness is particularly damaging for preschool children. In her study of homeless children living in shelters compared with housed children living in a poor area of Philadelphia, Leslie Rescorla found that the homeless preschoolers were not attending day care, although many of the housed children were attending. The homeless youngsters were significantly more delayed in receptive vocabulary and visual motor development, had much higher rates of behavioral and emotional symptoms, and were more likely to be delayed on the Denver Developmental Screening Test. The children who were in school did not show these differences (Rescorla, Parker, & Stolley, 1991). The California Department of Education estimated that there are 25,000 school-age children in the state who are homeless. Of these, 11,000 attend school, but 14,000 do not attend on a regular basis (Lazarus, 1989).

Advocates for children have attempted to address problems for homeless families on an individual basis. Federal legislation created the Family Unification Program, which is designed to provide rental assistance to families who are at risk of separation primarily because of a lack of affordable housing. The McKinney Homeless Assistance Act of

1987 provides federal funds for educational needs of the homeless. Some states have statutes that specify that poverty or homelessness alone should not be sufficient reason to remove children from their family. Individual families may be reluctant to seek assistance from the system for fear the children will be removed. Other families on the brink of homelessness reluctantly may place their children with other relatives or with the department of social services hoping that they will be well cared for until affordable housing can be found. The child welfare system thus becomes the agency for addressing societal neglect of these children by inadequate economic, employment, housing, and income maintenance systems (Child Welfare League of America, 1991).

Outside the framework of societal neglect that includes poverty and homelessness there are specific types of individual parental neglect that generally are included in statutory definitions.

## Statutory Neglect

### Incidence

Neglect is much more common than all other forms of abuse and has been found to cause more fatalities (McCurdy & Daro, 1993). A study of children in foster care found that 67% of all children were removed from their homes for neglect, abandonment, and caretaker incapacity; 17% for physical abuse; and 11% for sexual abuse. The long-term effects of neglect on the child can be much more debilitating than abuse (Watahara & Lobdell, 1990). The short- and long-term effects, which often depend on the particular type of neglect, will be discussed following the description of specific categories of neglect.

### Abandonment

Courts generally define *abandonment* as intentional conduct by a parent showing an intent to forgo all parental duties. Such conduct includes withholding presence, love, care, support, and maintenance for a certain period of time (*In re Cardo*, 1979). In one case, a neglect petition against the mother based on abandonment of three small children was dismissed when the court found that the report of neglect had been made by the father after the mother had left him and their children 3 days earlier. After a marital quarrel, she had left home for a visit out of town and had not told him when she would return. The court could not find that the mother either showed any intent to forgo parental duties or had left the children for a significant period of time. A more common type of abandonment takes place when the drug-addicted parent leaves the child with a neighbor or relative and fails to return for days or even months. Cases involving abandonment are likely to result in an initial dependency filing to allow the child to be placed in foster care immediately so that some type of care and supervision can be provided.

## Negligent Failure
## to Provide Adequate Food

The parents of five children lived on the outskirts of town. The two older children came to school very tired and ravenous on Mondays. The teachers soon realized that the children's only meals were the weekday breakfasts and lunches provided by the school meal program. The children were dressed in filthy clothes, the baby sometimes only in a wet diaper. The home was dirty and without food or heat, but the parents had a large TV, a VCR, and cases of beer. The parents had obtained food stamps but sold them for alcohol and drugs. The youngest child was malnourished when the public health nurse visited the home.

The earliest manifestation of this form of neglect can be seen in some infants with a medical diagnosis of failure to thrive. This term usually describes children who were healthy at birth but have failed to mature at a normal rate of development. Inadequate growth of children can stem from organic or nonorganic causes. In some children both nonorganic and organic causes contribute to the growth failure. Characteristically, the caloric intake has been insufficient for several possible reasons: Food is not being offered, the child is resisting nourishment because of loss of appetite, the child is using calories at an increased rate, or the calories are not being absorbed properly. Medical and psychological evaluations are necessary to clarify the pattern for each child (Smith et al., 1988).

Infants who fail to thrive because of severe feeding problems, a condition often found in premature babies, may further overburden an already overstressed family. Caring for other small children, unemployment, poverty, poor housing or homelessness, and substance abuse are stressors that compete with the exceptionally needy infant for energy and attention. These factors make caring for and bonding with the infant difficult tasks (Drotar, Malone, & Negray, 1980).

Cuddling, vocalization, and other positive forms of interaction help to foster mutual attachment between parent and child. Isolation and poor development of reciprocal bonding can contribute to diminished appetite in the infant. For some parents, especially those who are inexperienced, unrecognized or weak evidence of infant responsiveness can lessen parental motivation to provide adequate nourishment. Factors involved in nonorganic failure to thrive include social isolation, poor parenting skills, poor parental relationship, nonhelpful or critical family members or friends, negative infant behavior characteristics, feeding errors, and intentional caloric deprivation (Broughton, 1989).

The consequences of failure to thrive can be severe when the child's body breaks down muscle and fat to maintain growth of the brain. Nonorganic failure to thrive frequently is accompanied by severe cognitive and emotional deficits (Hathaway, 1989). Many of these children develop subdued and inhibited personalities. Long-term consequences can include mental retardation, learning difficulties, and delay in language skills (Smith et al., 1988).

Older emotionally neglected children who have a separation disorder know that they can gain attention from their parents by not eating. They may fear separating psychologically from their overattentive parents. Children with this disorder develop a pattern of food refusal as a means of attaining autonomy (Chatoor, Schaeffer, Dickson, & Egar, 1984).

*Case study.* Matthew was just over a year old but could not sit up without support. When Matthew was born, his mother had stopped working to devote herself to him full time. She had breast-fed Matthew since birth but did not feed him any other foods. His weight was just below normal; his motor development was extremely delayed. Matthew had never been taken out of the house. During the father's graduate studies, he first became aware of the severity of his son's delayed development. His wife refused to acknowledge any problem and would not consent to have Matthew seen by a pediatrician for evaluation. When a report was made to the child protective services, Matthew was removed from the mother's care and hospitalized so a thorough evaluation could be made of his failure to thrive.

*Case study.* Neglect also can be a crime. A friend of a mother who was caring for the mother's child was found guilty of aggravated child abuse because of willful acts of omission and neglect that caused unnecessary pain and suffering leading to the death of the child. The 4-year-old was forced to run, denied food, and made to drink bath water and urine to be freed from "evil spirits." During a 4-month period of systematic torture and deprivation of food the child became thinner and weaker until she eventually died (*Nicholson v. State*, 1992).

## Negligent Failure
## to Provide Shelter

If the only danger to a child is lack of housing, the state should make reasonable efforts to provide housing for the family. In Pennsylvania a teenage single parent placed her child voluntarily in foster care when she became homeless. The county agency refused to return the child to her care when she returned a month later. The superior court decided that where there was no evidence of abuse or neglect or reason to support a dependency finding, the child could not be removed from the mother for the sole reason that they were homeless. The judge stated also that the agency responsible for removing a child must make all reasonable efforts to prevent removal including provision of housing for the parent and child. The judge in this case recognized the importance of children being raised by their parents and of child welfare agencies making reasonable efforts to keep families together (*In the Interest of S.A.D.*, 1989).

A study of homeless mothers in Massachusetts reported that 22% of those mothers were being investigated actively for child abuse and neglect (Bassuk & Gallagher, 1990). Congressional studies report that many homeless families needing shelter never request it out of fear that their children will be taken away by the very agencies that are supposed to be helping them (Waxman & Reyes, 1987). Chapter 8 will focus on the responsibility of the department of social services to provide shelter and other services to keep families together.

Many single custodial parents must depend on public funds to pay for shelter for the family. When the base AFDC rate for a family of three falls below the fair market rent of a two-bedroom dwelling, the government's double standard puts children at risk of systemic neglect. As a result, a child may be placed in costly foster care because the minimum support provided by the government cannot cover the basic cost of shelter, much less food, clothing, and health care (McKeever, 1989). Another study found that one half of the families reported for child abuse and neglect were headed by a single female head of household (Tjaden & Thoennes, 1992).

### Failure to Provide Support

Parents are required by law to support their children when they are financially able (see D.C. Code sec. 16-2301(9)(b), 1981). In most states the obligation rests with both parents. The obligation continues until a child reaches the age of legal majority, usually age 18. Child support includes the provision of food, clothing, shelter, medical expenses, and education. Only a small percentage of children in broken homes actually receive support from fathers after divorce or separation. In 1989, of women with children under 21 with no father in the household, 25.5% received the full court-ordered award; 11.8% received part of the court-ordered award; 12.3% received nothing of the court-ordered award; and 42% were not awarded support (U.S. Bureau of the Census, 1989). According to a recent study by Children Now, absent fathers enjoy a 41% rise in income after divorce while children and their mothers experience a 31% drop in their income. In many cases, these children are pushed below the poverty line. In 1990 the study concluded that only 39% of child support orders tracked by district attorneys in California resulted in any payment (Roark, 1992). Impoverished women and children who have the greatest need have the fewest resources to obtain court orders and have them enforced. Noncustodial parents are sent notice of court hearings against the custodial parent for neglect, but are themselves rarely charged with neglect for failure to support until it is time to terminate parental rights. Yet this failure to support may be the crucial causative factor in the custodial parent's neglect.

### Failure to Provide Medical Care

Medical neglect includes the failure to provide, consent to, or follow through with preventive, diagnostic, remedial, or prosthetic care. It is reported most often by medical personnel at the hospital or by schools when parents fail to obtain required immunizations (Besharov, 1990b).

*Case study.* A mother failed to provide her child with medical and remedial care that was offered through the department of social services as a free service. In this case, the child suffered from a speech defect and a hearing impairment that would have responded to treatment and prosthetic care. Her poor speech and hearing impeded her learning and socialization. The court concluded that the mother had neglected the child by depriving her of the opportunity for normal growth and development (*In re Huber,* 1982).

*Case study.* A professional who had immigrated to this country was charged with medical neglect for failure to obtain dental treatment for his 4-year-old son whose teeth were decaying because of a steady diet of candy and prolonged use of a bottle, especially at bedtime. Only after a petition was filed did the parents take steps to obtain dental treatment and change their son's feeding habits.

## Inability to Provide Care
## Due to Parent's Mental Illness

A mother believed she was still pregnant although she had not been pregnant for several years. Her five children slept on a mattress on the floor in a filthy home. Both parents were unable to provide adequately for their children's physical and economic needs by reason of mental illness and could not correct the inadequate conditions in their home within a reasonable time. Eventually, their parental rights were terminated. The seriousness of such chronic neglect may be overlooked by a caseworker who views parents who neglect as mentally or emotionally incompetent rather than malevolent. Thus cases involving neglect have been found to be significantly less likely to involve criminal prosecution (Tjaden & Thoennes, 1992).

## Inability to Provide Care
## Due to Parent's Developmental Disability

A young woman with mild mental retardation and a seizure disorder and her husband, who had moderately severe cerebral palsy, had a baby against the advice and wishes of both sets of grandparents. Although very resistant to outside help, they were unable to manage the infant's physical care without assistance from others. They quickly would dismiss anyone the grandparents joined together to hire for child care. As a result, this infant had very inconsistent feeding, bathing, and general supervision. Ultimately, when threatened with removal of the infant whom they both loved, the parents agreed to have a child care worker in the home for enough hours per week to ensure that the child's basic needs were met. The infant care routine of the in-home helper also served as a training model to strengthen their awareness and child care skills.

## Inability to Provide Care
## Due to Parent's Substance Abuse

Children are not removed from parents solely on the basis of parental abuse of alcohol or drugs without proof of adverse impact or high risk for the child. Often the use of drugs or alcohol is the main causal factor in the resulting neglect of the child. Parents use money needed for rent or food for the child to pay for drugs or alcohol. Parents under the influence fail to respond to the cries of the hungry infant or leave the child uncared for as they go in search of another fix. The major deleterious effects of parental substance abuse are discussed in detail in Chapter 5.

## Failure to Intervene to Protect a Child

Parents cannot sit by idly and watch their children be abused with impunity. A mother was found guilty of neglecting her 8- and 9-year-old sons after they told her their father was sexually abusing them and she did nothing to protect them. Although he abused the older son in the presence of the mother and the mother knew the father had been charged in the past with child sexual abuse, she told the boys not to discuss the father's conduct (*In re Scott*, 1992).

## Failure to Enroll Child in School

Parents are responsible for enrolling their children in a public, private, or in-home school and for making sure that they attend. The school the parent chooses must provide the education the child needs. A state court of appeals rejected a father's claim of a fundamental right to educate his mildly mentally retarded son at home in his "School of Universal Studys [*sic*] and Understanding," which met all statutory criteria for nonpublic schools. The court determined that the father was not capable of providing his son the special care and training offered by the public school's special education classes (*In re Devone*, 1987).

## Neglect as a Lesser
## Court Finding Than Abuse

Sometimes parents who are charged with abuse will admit that they neglected the child in order to avoid having the court make a finding of abuse. A finding of abuse carries more stigma than a finding of neglect. Although the practice of plea bargaining in juvenile court saves the county time in proving abuse allegations and gives the court jurisdiction so that services can be provided sooner, the historical court record of neglect may mask the seriousness of the abuse offense if subsequent abuse incidents occur. If the parents become unwilling to cooperate with the services ordered, the county will have to file a petition to terminate parental rights without the strong factual basis of abuse incidents in the court record.

# Intervention

If the investigation following a report of neglect results in substantiation of the neglect, the child protective service will try to develop a treatment plan that allows the child to remain in the home if the parents voluntarily agree to the settlement proposed. Removal of the child in cases of neglect is not an appropriate solution in most situations, especially if the neglect is neither severe nor chronic. Chapter 8 will include a more detailed discussion of the requirement to provide in-home services to prevent the need for removal in most cases of abuse and neglect. Consider the neglect allegation in the following case.

*Case study.* A 16-month-old baby lives with her 18-year-old mother who is 8 months pregnant. The baby is well nourished, developmentally normal, and emotionally secure with her mother. The young mother is responsible for caring for her mother-in-law, an 80-year-old diabetic amputee on oxygen. Weighing 400 pounds, she must be turned four times a day and lifted to use a bedpan. They all live in the house the mother-in-law owns. The father of the baby beats his wife. He is away from the house most of the time while working at odd jobs. The mother-in-law is brought lunch by Meals on Wheels. A home health nurse who visits the home twice a month reported the mother for neglect. The kitchen table, counterspace, stove, and much of the floor are covered with dirty dishes, pans, and empty food containers. The bedroom reeks of urine. Piles of used disposable diapers and adult pads are on the floor. Firewood, old tires, garbage, and several large pails nearly block the entrance to the house.

How best should this and similar home situations be handled? When intervention appears indicated, several options must be considered: Is neglect of the child severe or chronic enough to warrant state intervention? Would it be sufficient to have the court order the family to clean up the house? Is that likely to be effective given the physical limitations of the mother and mother-in-law? What factors should be considered in designing an effective program of intervention for this young child and her family? Would voluntary placement of the child and mother in a battered women's shelter and placement of the mother-in-law in a nursing facility be more appropriate than removal of the child to foster care? What would be the least detrimental alternative available? Consider the case of another child whose home environment went beyond any dirty house standard.

*Case study.* Andrew was born prematurely. After 2 months in intensive care, he was able to be discharged to live with his parents. Twice during his infancy his parents took him to a hospital emergency room. Although the doctor recorded in the hospital chart his concern about Andrew's lack of development as well as his general welfare, especially when the mother commented that Andrew was no better than a dog, the doctor did not make a report for neglect. In the years to come neighbors often heard Andrew crying and were concerned about the unsanitary condition of his home. These parents kept 26 dogs in their home. Following a neighbor's referral, DSS workers went out and found the floor soaked with animal urine but could not find Andrew. Returning with the sheriff, they found the boy, now 4 years old, locked in a closet with several of the dogs. Andrew did not communicate verbally and was not toilet trained. The parents said he was so retarded they kept him in the closet.

After being removed from the family home, Andrew began learning to talk. As he gained weight, he insisted on carrying around a bag filled with bits of food. He learned to use the bathroom. Following his visits with his parents, he would have nightmares and would regress to wetting and soiling himself. The therapist evaluating Andrew recognized the severity of his condition and the importance of keeping Andrew from ever returning to the cruel neglect of his parents. After seeing both Andrew and his parents, she wrote a thorough, descriptive evaluation for her court report and was available to testify at the hearing. To protect Andrew from further suffering, she kept the social worker informed of her conclusions regarding a ban on visitation with the parents and concluded that any effort to reunite Andrew with his parents would not be reasonable.

In this case the parents were convicted of criminal child abuse. Not only did Andrew's home situation fit the legal definition of neglect for juvenile court intervention, but the jury in criminal court found the parents guilty of criminal neglect and abuse. The neglect was so severe that no changes the parents could make in the home environment, even with the support of community agencies, would justify returning Andrew.

## Conclusion

One child who is neglected by parents can suffer physical or emotional scars that will not go away. Another child may respond well to support systems offered to the parents and regain physical or developmental losses without serious permanent damage. Some neglected children will be successful survivors even though neglect continues throughout childhood. When intervention is warranted, it must be fine-tuned to meet the complex physical, emotional, financial, social, and educational needs of the whole child and the family. Coordinating intervention services to enable the family unit to survive intact and to develop healthy dynamics is a formidable challenge for any social service agency.

**III**

# What Are the Options
# for Remediation?

# 8

## Family Support to Prevent Placement

*What we have found . . . is a national disgrace—a pattern of institutional abuse and neglect of our most vulnerable children that cannot wait one more day for correction. The daily plight of these children, often left family-less, makes a mockery of our professed belief in family, our concern for our young, and for the cost-effective use of taxpayers' money.*

Marian Wright Edelman,
*Children Without Homes*, 1978

Sharlene was reported for neglecting her 7-year-old son, Mick, who was found wandering on his home street after school. Sharlene had started working part-time and could not be home after school every day. On close investigation, the social worker found Sharlene extremely depressed and exhausted. Her husband left her after he lost his job because of his drug addiction. Sharlene's pay covered the rent and utility bills. She was able to eat at the restaurant where she worked but did not have money to provide food at home. Mick had breakfast and lunch at school.

The social worker arranged to meet Sharlene before she left for work the morning after Mick was reported. They discussed her financial and child care problems. The social worker took Sharlene to three offices and helped her fill out the forms to apply for AFDC, medicaid, food stamps, and child support. The social worker then called the school to see if Sharlene could place Mick in the after-school program. Finally, Sharlene was put on the waiting list at the local mental health clinic. Although the reported neglect of Mick was entirely appropriate, his mother had the capability and motivation to utilize the community services offered to her so that Mick could remain safely in the home. One can speculate about other useful follow-up efforts that might be made when the immediate crisis is over. This example of appropriate intervention in a neglect case illustrates what a difference timely and well-planned intervention makes, even for children who have been placed in danger.

## Omnibus Budget
## Reconciliation Act of 1993 (Public Law 103-66)

In 1993 Congress enacted a new federal program for family preservation and family support services, PL 103-66. With an estimated federal cost of $1 billion over 5 years, PL 103-66 provides states with funds for services to avoid foster care and to preserve and strengthen families. The family preservation services aimed to reduce foster care placement include follow-up services to families after a child has been returned from foster care, respite care to provide temporary relief for parents and other caregivers, and services to improve parenting skills. The federal act also funds family support services for families not yet in crisis. These community-based activities should help strengthen and stabilize biological, adoptive, foster, and extended families. Designed to increase parental confidence and competence, they should provide children with a supportive, stable family environment that will enhance child development. These funds can fill a major void in confirmed cases of child maltreatment for which one national survey found no access to therapeutic or supportive services (McCurdy & Daro, 1993).

## Foster Care Drift

Prior to 1980 children were slipped into the foster care system almost casually with little or no consideration given to ways to maintain them in their own homes. Once the child was in foster care, visitation between children and parents rarely was encouraged, case planning for the child's future living arrangements was atypical, and services to help biological parents overcome problems that led to placement were offered infrequently. As a result, countless children were never reunited with their biological parents and instead "drifted" from one foster home to another. Foster care drift results partly from a child welfare system that has not appreciated fully the importance of the family and partly from a federal funding system that provided states with substantial federal reimbursement for the costs of foster care for poor children and comparatively minimal funding for child welfare services. This imbalance has given states much stronger incentive to place children than to provide preventive services.

*Medical-legal versus ecological model.* The agencies established 30 years ago to respond to the problems of abuse and neglect were based on a medical-legal model that identified individual psychopathology in the parent. The more recently evolved ecological model of maltreatment nests cultural, political, community, family, and individual factors that interact dynamically and continually, adjusting to shifting internal and external forces. The ecological model recognizes the complexity of change and demands that agencies intervene in families by providing a more complex array of services with delivery gauged to maximize positive change and minimize stress by building on family strengths and matching services to specific needs of individual families (Crittenden, 1992).

*Investigative or treatment role of child welfare worker.* Traditionally, child welfare workers found themselves in conflicting and often antagonistic relationships with the families they were supposed to help. The worker's role was conceptualized as mostly investigative. The interventive role with families was limited to assessing the extent of abuse or neglect of children and recommending placement or treatment. A pattern developed in which families were referred routinely to community mental health or private counseling agencies for psychotherapy. Families referred to these services often felt coerced into treatment plans that seemed to have little relevance to their lives. Because working through a problem in a therapeutic relationship was so different from their usual patterns of coping, many families had increased feelings of powerlessness in a world of daily struggle just to survive. When parents failed to complete these treatment plans, cases were closed and the client was dubbed unmotivated or uncooperative. Placement of children was then recommended or reunification was postponed because clients had not followed through with the alien treatment plan (Laird & Hartman, 1985).

    In the mid-1970s the child welfare profession began to change its views about the importance of family relationships to the welfare of children. Some professionals began to emphasize the need to support and enhance families rather than undervalue their potential strengths. The goal gradually became one of protecting familial bonds and maintaining children with their biological families whenever possible. In contrast, cultural insensitivity by CPS workers may have led to the current overrepresentation of minority children in the foster care system. For instance, in Los Angeles, although African Americans represent only 11% of the county's population, they represent 44% of the children in foster care (Commission for Children's Services, 1992).

## Adoption Assistance and
## Child Welfare Act of 1980

In 1980, alarmed by the large and rapidly increasing number of children placed in foster care who never returned home, the federal government passed the Adoption Assistance and Child Welfare Act, known as PL 96-272. The act requires states to submit a plan for federal approval that designates the preventive and reunification services the state will make available to families in need. To qualify for this federal funding, the state may not place children covered by the act's Title IV E (those receiving AFDC) in foster care unless reasonable efforts are made prior to placement to prevent or eliminate the need for removal of the children from their home and, if they must be placed, to provide reunification services to make it possible for them to return home (Adoption Assistance and Child Welfare Act of 1980, 42 U.S.C.A. sec. 671[a][15]). Further, on the basis of a recent Washington, D.C., circuit court opinion, a foster child may sue the state for failure of the state agency to make "reasonable efforts" as required by D.C. statutes, which are similar to statutes in many states (*LaShawn A. v. Kelly*, 1993). In an earlier Illinois case, the U.S. Supreme Court decided that the Adoption Assistance and Child Welfare Act does not give foster children the right to sue the state for failure to make reasonable efforts to prevent the removal of children from their home and to facilitate reunification of families (*Suter v. Artist M.*, 1992).

### The Indian Child Welfare Act

The Indian Child Welfare Act of 1978 (Public Law 95-608) gives Indian tribes jurisdiction over Indian child custody procedures and authority to provide services that address the needs of Native American children. The act was designed to halt practices that threatened families and Native American cultures. This act requires that *active efforts* be made to provide remedial services and rehabilitative programs and that these be proven unsuccessful before a child may be removed from the home (see also Northwest Resource Associates, 1986). These distinctions between the two federal acts must be remembered when working with Native American families in the context of abuse and neglect and legal requirements for in-home services and removal of the child.

## Reasonable Efforts

Although the federal government left to the states the task of defining reasonable efforts, it did provide a list of suggested services in the Code of Federal Regulations. These services include 24-hour emergency caretaker and homemaker services, day care, crisis counseling, individual and family counseling, emergency shelter, procedures and arrangements for access to available emergency financial assistance, and arrangements for the provision of temporary child care to provide respite to the family for a brief period as part of a plan for preventing removal from home (Adoption Assistance and Child Welfare Act of 1980, 45 C.F.R. sec. 1357.15(e)(2), 1991).

The regulations also give examples of other services the state may identify as necessary and appropriate, such as home-based family services, self-help groups, services to unmarried parents, provision or arrangements for mental health, drug and alcohol abuse counseling, vocational counseling or vocational rehabilitation, and postadoption services (Adoption Assistance and Child Welfare Act of 1980, 45 C.F.R. sec. 1357.15 (e)(2), 1991). Concerned with the urgent problem of drug-exposed infants and children, the National Council of Juvenile and Family Court Judges (1992) recommended additional services that should be considered in determining if reasonable efforts have been made: family-centered drug treatment, inter- and intra-agency coordination of timely delivery of concrete services, and contacts with all relatives, including paternal family, as sources of child care.

*Reunification efforts requirement.* Under the 1980 legislation, the removal of a child must be based on the need for protection from specified substantial danger. Except for emergencies, the child protective service must show that in-home alternative services have been tried without success and that efforts have been made to place the child with relatives. After removal, the social worker must make reunification efforts and service plans for both the child and family. Visitation is mandated except in the most threatening situations. Case plans submitted to the court for timely review must include the projected date of the child's return. Tight time frames facilitate adoption planning if the reunification efforts are not successful (see Chapter 12).

### Putting Reasonable Efforts Into Practice

*Voluntary supervision.* After investigating a report and determining that a child has been abused or neglected, the social worker can undertake a program of supervision that allows the child to remain in the home. This program of supervision can forestall filing a petition with the court that alleges abuse or neglect. Such voluntary supervision can be done only with the parent's consent. During the period of supervision, the social worker must provide appropriate child welfare services to the family in an attempt to ameliorate the problems that created the abuse or neglect. Funding for these services has been limited. Federal fiscal incentives provided open-ended foster care funds of $1.2 billion in 1990 but made available only $270 million in capped funds for child welfare services designed to prevent out-of-home placement (Commission for Children's Services, 1992). As a result, finding funds for mandated in-home services and finding the array of services needed to meet individual family needs has, until recently, been a futile exercise. Additional federal funding for in-home and reunification services was made available in 1993 (Omnibus Budget Reconciliation Act of 1993).

> *Case study.* A Florida study found that the state allocated 80% of its child protective budget for investigation, prosecution, and out-of-home placement—but only 15% for supervision and treatment. The study found that most family treatment plans offered the same basic services regardless of the individual needs of the families. The plans offered protective services, foster care for injured children, day care for young children in the home, counseling, parent education, and an assortment of family-targeted fiscal and medical services. The families were divided into categories based on severity of family dysfunction. Of the services offered in Florida, 51% were found appropriate for only 20% of the maltreating families who were in the more

functional "vulnerable to crisis" category. Only 28% of available services were appropriate for the less functional "restorable" group that comprised 40% of the maltreating families. The 30% of families in the low-functioning group in need of supportive services until the children were grown had only 16% of services appropriate for their individual needs. Thus the state's financial resources were being wasted because the range of services needed did not match available services. Moreover, the study showed that in many cases families did not receive the prescribed services in their treatment plans and court orders. In one third of the cases, the agency failed to make necessary referrals for the family. In over one third of the cases, the treating agency put the family on a waiting list. In less than a third of the cases, the family contributed to the problem because it lacked transportation or caretakers for children. The heavy load and intricate scheduling of parenting classes, group sessions, house hunting, social worker visits, and daily child care was too overwhelming for the parents to manage and sometimes caused further disintegration of family dynamics (Crittenden, 1992).

*Parenting education.* One of the most frequently used services is parenting education. Most parenting education programs train abusive parents in child management, child rearing, and self-control skills, and programs for neglectful parents focus on nutrition, homemaking, and child care. Few definitive studies demonstrate the efficacy of parent training in curtailing reabuse (National Research Council, 1993). Parents who neglect or abuse their children need opportunities to learn how they can meet their children's basic needs without becoming intolerably overwhelmed or resorting to violence. Some parents can learn parenting skills through adult education services in the community. Classes that enable parents to be part of a group focused on child development and child-caring skills offer the additional benefit of group involvement. Working together on common goals may help to alleviate the social isolation some participants otherwise may feel. Especially for young and inexperienced parents, the relief of finding their anxieties and frustrations shared by others as they become more knowledgeable about normal behaviors during a child's development may help to prevent some of the emotional crises that contribute to instances of abuse and neglect.

Some parents who are required to take classes may not respond positively because they feel targeted as guilty patients seeking treatment. Many are hampered by a history of failure in school settings or difficulty with abstract concepts. Unable to sufficiently understand classroom discussions, they are not able to bring new insights, attitudes, or techniques to their ongoing family experiences. Complex family stressors can interfere further with their ability to follow through on the parenting skills taught. Their parental authority questioned, parents may suffer a crisis of identity, confidence, and security. Those feelings of emotional distress can lead to parental malaise that needs to be counteracted if the parent is to feel motivated strongly enough to work on learning to provide good parenting.

*Individual services.* When some parents find the responsibilities that come with parenthood too overwhelming, they may look to the social worker as an authority figure who will allow them to become dependent. Treated as an individual who is capable of working with another in the learning process, the parent is more likely to increase self-awareness and achieve positive results. Home-based intervention by social workers and mental health professionals realistically can introduce and reinforce parenting skills. Individualized training in the home can give even a resistant parent everyday experience in improving parenting skills by testing new attitudes and expectations about children and by using supported opportunities to take additional responsibility for the physical, medical, and emotional needs of the family. Individual behavior therapy, group therapy for both parent and child, and therapeutic day care, coupled with concrete support services such as homemakers, health care, and emergency shelter, have been found to be beneficial especially when it can continue at least 6 to 18 months (Howing, Wodarski, Gaudin, & Kurtz, 1989).

## Family-Centered Placement Preventive Services

Family preservation programs have common elements. They accept only families on the verge of having a child placed. They are crisis oriented, seeing each family as soon as possible after referral is made. Their staff responds to families day and night, maintaining flexible hours 7 days a week. The intake and assessment process carefully ensures that no child is left in danger. They deal with each family as a unit, rather than focusing on either the parents or the children as the individuals with problems. Workers see families in their own homes, making frequent visits convenient to each family's schedule. Their approach combines teaching skills to family members, helping the family obtain necessary resources and services, and counseling based on an understanding of how each family functions as a system. Services are delivered on the basis of individual need rather than according to routinely designated case categories. Each worker carries a small caseload at any given time. Staff members may work in teams of two to a family, providing each other with support and easing the demands of their irregular schedules. Length of involvement with each family is limited to a short period, typically between 2 and 5 months. The staff receives ongoing in-service training. Staff members often are required to have a degree in social work and thorough knowledge of the community. They follow up on families to assess their progress and evaluate the program's success (Edna McConnell Clark Foundation, 1985). In 1988 the projected savings in foster care and administrative costs for a child receiving family-based services was estimated to be $27,000 (Daro, 1988). Family preservation programs, with potential cost-effective and placement prevention characteristics, are currently operating in about two thirds of the states (Spar, 1992). Three types of in-home intensive family preservation programs have developed.

*Homebuilders.* The first model of crisis intervention, called Home-builders, was developed in Tacoma, Washington. The goal is to provide an alternative to foster care, group care, psychiatric hospitalizations, and corrections institutions. Based on a social learning theory, this tertiary prevention model provides in-home multidimensional services including family therapy, advocacy, home management, life skills training, and concrete services, with each component tailored to meet the specific needs of the family. Intervention lasts for 30 to 45 days during the period of crisis, when families usually are most open to change. At a 12-month follow-up, 86% of the families had avoided out-of-home placement. The Homebuilders model was found to be most successful with children who had been abused physically and least successful with neglected children (Bath & Haapala, 1993).

*Families.* The second type of home-based intervention is the Families model developed at the University of Iowa. A therapist uses the family system theory for assessment and intervention for an average period of just over 4 months with the objectives of improving linkages, perceptions, and relationships between the family and its environment. Concrete and coordinated supportive services are provided as well. At follow-up 70% of the families have continued to be intact (Nelson, Landsman, & Deutelbaum, 1990).

*Family treatment model.* The family treatment model provides more therapeutic intervention and less concrete and supportive services than the other programs. Services are provided in the office or the home for an average of 90 days. Twelve months later 66% of the families were found to be intact. Possibly because of less emphasis on concrete services, this intervention model is least successful with neglectful families. Longer intervention with more concrete services might foster more success for neglectful parents (Bath & Haapala, 1993; Daro, 1988).

These three models have generated a mix of in-home service delivery practices throughout the United States. The Child Welfare League of America (1989) uses the term *intensive family-centered crisis services* to describe these services that are targeted for families in serious crisis, including those at imminent risk of losing their children to foster care. Family preservation programs have a common focus, first on the strengths and needs of the family as a unit and, second, on the family in the context of the community and cultural milieu in which it lives.

Not surprisingly, the most challenging families to work with are those with the most severe problems. Homelessness, severe poverty, significantly limited family and community support, high degrees of personal instability in the caregiver often caused by mental illness or addiction, and weaknesses in child-rearing skills pose severe potential risk to the child. An increasing number of families are homeless or are affected by parental substance abuse, parental crime, poverty, or inadequate health care. The child-serving professional may encounter unpredictable interaction patterns in these families. The child may be unable or unwilling to accept the caregiver as an authority figure. In some situations, the child may exhibit unusually passive or deviant behavior. Some children will withhold affection or attention from the caregiver or be mistrustful. At the same time, the parent may be one who rarely demonstrates feelings of affection or positive emotional ties with the child and may argue or threaten as the usual mode of communication, engage in frequent episodes of aggressive physical contact, intimidate or verbally abuse the other caregiver, view the child as the source of all problems, regard the child's presence as a threat, or acknowledge inability to control the child's behavior. The treatment that works for physical abuse may have no effect on the sexually abusive parent.

Child abuse policy expert Giovannoni (1985) challenged researchers and practitioners not to treat child maltreatment as a unitary phenomenon. She recommended more research to show which type of intervention works best for physical abuse, which for sexual abuse, and which for neglect. Assessment and treatment of families must be individualized to account for multiple and interactional causes of problems that are child and family specific (DePanfilis & Salus, 1992). Under the Omnibus Budget Reconciliation Act of 1993, the secretary of Health and Human Services is required to conduct evaluations of family preservation services.

## Court-Ordered Services

When a maltreating parent resists in-home intervention, the child protective service department may file a petition against the parent and ask the court to order the in-home delivery of service. The National Council of Juvenile and Family Court Judges recommends as a primary consideration allowing the child to remain at home under protective orders of the court, which can include removal of an alleged abuser and must include the delivery of in-home supportive services (Note, 1986). In some cases, court-ordered treatment evokes a more responsible parental response than voluntary intervention (Irueste-Montes & Montes, 1988). A recent study found little difference between the services provided through voluntary and court-ordered services. Both included counseling, parenting classes, and drug and alcohol testing and treatment. Less commonly offered services are parent aides, homemaker assistance, and help with housing, day care, or financial problems. In this recent study of 833 substantiated cases of abuse or neglect in Los Angeles, Denver, and Newcastle (Delaware), use of family preservation services was not evident. Child protective services intervened in 75% of the cases by developing a treatment plan. Rather than providing in-home services, the intervention resulted in out-of-home placement in half of the opened cases (Tjaden & Thoennes, 1992).

If the family fails to cooperate or the problems are not satisfactorily resolved during the period of supervision, the social worker may then file a petition in juvenile court (see next chapter). Families who refuse to accept such services and whose children remain at risk and families in which the parents are not capable of utilizing preservation services would not be appropriate choices for in-home intervention. Other inappropriate situations for family preservation efforts include sexual abuse cases in which the alleged perpetrator cannot be removed from access to the child victim; families in which the parent is severely developmentally or psychiatrically disabled and there is a weak or nonexistent support system; cases involving a child under the age of 2 in which a strong likelihood exists for further risk despite the provision of service; and cases involving significant violence such as the use of a deadly weapon or serious physical abuse resulting in broken bones or other severe injury.

## When to Remove
## the Child From the Parents

In an emergency, a doctor, child protective services worker, or other professional authorized by state law may take temporary custody of an abused or neglected child. The child may have inadequate parental supervision, be left with no provision for support and with immediate need for medical care, be in immediate danger of physical or sexual abuse, or be in a physical environment that poses an immediate threat to the child's health or safety. Before taking a child into custody, however, the CPS worker must consider whether reasonable services can be provided to the family that may eliminate the need to remove the child from the home. In some states the CPS worker must have the approval of the juvenile court judge before taking the child into emergency custody.

Before a child is removed from the biological parent's home, the following questions must be answered: Has the child been harmed seriously or threatened with serious harm or is the child ill? To what extent is the parent responsible? What harm might the child suffer if removed? Does the parent have the ability and motivation to make rapid changes necessary to make the home safe for the child, or has the parent failed to respond to intensive in-home services? Did the agency provide services needed to meet the family's individual needs and keep the family together? If the services did not remedy the identified problems, were other services tried? Is this an emergency situation in which the child cannot be protected without removal from the home prior to providing services? (see Hardin, 1983).

The social worker must assess the danger to the child and collect information from doctors, teachers, neighbors, mental health professionals, police, and others to support the decision to remove the child. *Real evidence* from photographs, X rays, mental health evaluations, and school records are critical for court. *Direct evidence* from firsthand knowledge of events can be elicited from neighbors or family members who saw the child being beaten or wandering on the street at night and who can testify in court. *Circumstantial evidence* could identify the boyfriend as the child's caretaker when the injury occurred (Stein & Rzepnicki, 1983).

The social worker must be aware of the long-term implications and consequences as to permanent placement of the child whenever there is failure to obtain substantial evidence at the outset. If the child remains in foster care and the parental response to reunification efforts is unsatisfactory, the evidence used for the court-approved removal of the child will be presented again when the case is made for termination of parental rights. When the decision is made initially to remove the child, the social worker must be planning for reunification and at the same time consciously preparing to meet the higher burden of proof required for termination if reunification efforts fail. If adequate evidence is not available for the termination of parental rights hearing, the child is likely to remain in long-term foster care rather than being freed for adoptive placement. Long-term foster care continues to be a major problem. In Los Angeles, 57% of the 33,000 children in out-of-home care are in long-term foster care (Commission for Children's Services, 1992). This startling statistic illustrates how important multidisciplinary observations, evaluations, and recommendations are at every stage of the decision-making process.

### Psychological Considerations

*Evaluating the child.* In preparing an evaluation for court determination as to whether the child has been abused or neglected and whether the child can remain in the home safely or should be removed, the psychologist looks at the child in relation to certain general characteristics. Is the child excessively shy and inhibited, fearful and anxious, or aggressive and provocative? Is the child unusually serious, or does the child have difficulty forming normal relationships with peers and adults? If these characteristics are absent, the psychologist will question whether the child has been mistreated. Many abused children have problems of physical aggression and anger (Egeland & Sroufe, 1981), as well as conduct disorder characterized by repetitive and persistent conduct that violates the rights of others or is extremely inappropriate for the child's age (Rogeness, Amrung, Macedo, Harris, & Fisher, 1986). Certain types of severe neglect may lead to developmental delays, attention deficits, poor social skills, and less emotional stability (National Research Council, 1993). One recent study found that children with developmental disabilities are more likely to be neglected than abused (Bath & Haapala, 1993), but with intensive support these children can be kept at home.

> *Case study.* The local pediatric hospital referred the family to the Specialized Family Program in New York, which provides in-home services to parents with mental retardation and/or psychiatric disabilities. The father, diagnosed as paranoid schizophrenic, had spent 12 years in a state psychiatric hospital. He met the mother at a community group home after she was discharged from a 10-year-stay in a state developmental center. Their baby was born with hydrocephalus, which required surgery after birth to insert a shunt, followed by continuous watchful and hygienic care. In the first week of intervention, the worker came to the home at 7:00 each morning to help the parents develop a morning routine of arising when the baby cried, preparing her breakfast, bathing her, and dressing her in clean clothes. The parents followed a simple checklist of morning activities. The second week the worker came twice and called three times. By the third week the parents, devoted to their baby, were independently completing their tasks and feeling successful. Over 20 agencies provided services to this fragile family to help keep the triad intact. Through case management, the services were coordinated and consolidated so the parents could learn management of the baby without being unduly overwhelmed (Pomerantz, Pomerantz, & Colca, 1990).

*Evaluating the parent.* Not all communities have that quality of intensive services available for similarly at-risk families. The mental health professional must ascertain to what extent the parent is responsible for mistreatment of the child. A comprehensive evaluation of behavior and conditions in the family unit should identify parental strengths and weaknesses. Child abuse specialist David Wolfe (1987) has suggested that many parents who neglect or abuse their children show a severe lack of self-esteem and a poorly integrated sense of identity. The parents may be somewhat socially isolated with a history of emotional deprivation, physical abuse, and chaotic family experiences in their early years. The parent may have a general character defect that allows impulsive aggression. Many parents in this category have distorted notions of child rearing. Psychosis in the parent is characterized by a major abnormality in the areas of thinking, emotionality, or perception. Delusions and hallucinations are typical. Parenting ability is quite limited. Wolfe believes that the sociopathic parent is a real danger to the child emotionally, because the parent cannot give or receive love, warmth, and affection. Moderate to severe mental retardation of parents, with an IQ below 50, indicates a poor prognosis for the ability to parent. Parenting with this level of ability will be particularly difficult when the child reaches puberty and enters adolescence. It is difficult also if the child requires special care because of physical or mental disabilities.

Parental addiction to drugs and alcohol is present for an increasingly large majority of children at risk of foster care placement. Parents not amenable to treatment who chronically abuse alcohol or drugs may need continued supportive services to meet the basic physical, intellectual, emotional, and economic needs of their children (Crittenden, 1992).

*Parent-child interaction.* After evaluating the overall parental behavior and level of functioning, the psychologist observes parent-child interactions and looks for evidence as to how the parent copes with stress, for parental awareness of both normal behavior and age-related needs, and for general parental understanding of the child together with signs of warmth and caring. To measure potential of trauma that would result from separation, the psychologist evaluates evidence of attachment. The initiation of foster care always presents the eventual possibility of multiple placements that can destroy the child's ability to form trusting relationships. When removal is the only recourse to protect the child, meaningful parental contact should be maintained, especially for the already bonded young child. Separating the child from siblings, the extended family, friends, and school presents significant risk for the child's basic attachments and therefore should be considered cautiously.

The evaluator must look for clues as to whether the parent rapidly can modify the kinds of behavior that are harmful to the child. Are parental acts of mistreatment linked inextricably with an underlying condition that has a poor prognosis for rapid change? Is the parent motivated to work intensively to improve the quality of care in order that the child will be safe at home? If the child is to be removed, the psychologist should evaluate the potential for visitation between the child, parent, and siblings. The court will need to know the basis for any recommendation that visitation should be restricted, supervised, or denied. Visitation normally occurs at least once a week with both parents and siblings. Unless the court is presented with evidence of danger to the child, the recommended visitation site would be the home of the parents or the foster family, rather than a less comfortable office of the social worker. Visitation with infants and toddlers can be recommended on a daily schedule if appropriate.

The National Council of Juvenile and Family Court Judges (1992) recommends that the drug treatment services provider evaluate whether family functioning is impaired by substance abuse and, if so, create a comprehensive interdisciplinary plan for alcohol or drug treatment for all affected family members. If adequate treatment cannot be provided in the community while the child lives with the parent, the child may need to be placed with relatives or in foster care so that inpatient treatment can proceed quickly and effectively.

Even when all known positive steps have been taken following a report of abuse or neglect and the provision of intensive in-home services, there always will be some children who must face the future separated from their biological families. Studies of families brought before the Boston Juvenile Court indicated that parenting classes and referrals for other services would not have a positive effect on children who are severely neglected because of the multifaceted problems of their families. Two thirds were desperately poor, most were headed by a single mother, and more than half included a parent with a serious psychiatric disorder. Parental substance abuse or alcoholism was a major factor in cases reported in Florida, Massachusetts, and Washington, DC (Jellinek et al., 1990; Select Committee on Children, Youth, and Families, 1990). In 1990 the Los Angeles Department of Children's Services estimated that 80% of the 108,000 referrals for abuse or neglect involved parental substance abuse, including an average of 200 drug-exposed babies reported each month (Commission for Children's Services, 1992).

Critically needed substance abuse rehabilitation programs that integrate training in parenting skills rarely have been offered by social services. The Training in Education and Management Skills (TEAMS) approach pioneered at UCLA is a model multidisciplinary program serving families with prenatally drug-exposed infants. Children's services workers and public health nurses work together to assist these high-risk infants and their caregivers through intensive services in their homes and through support groups (Howard & Kropenske, 1990). A pilot project in Connecticut includes links to child- and family-focused mental health services; substance abuse treatment; legal advocacy; linkages to concrete services such as housing, energy, and financial assistance; employment counseling and training; adult education; and respite child care (Blau, Whewell, Gullotta, & Bloom, 1994). Intervention coupled with a continuum of services can make court proceedings unnecessary for some substance-exposed infants as well as other maltreated children.

> *Case study.* An 18-year-old unwed, unemployed mother asked the local agency for assistance in caring for her 14-month-old until she found housing and employment and was able to enroll in a drug treatment program. The agency indicated voluntary placement in foster care was the only recourse for the mother. The agency then provided the mother with a bus pass and referred her to several public and private human services agencies and drug rehabilitation programs. On finding a part-time job, drug treatment, and a place to stay with a friend, the mother returned for her child. The agency refused her request and filed a dependency petition. Did CPS make reasonable efforts to prevent placement? What services might have prevented foster care placement of this child? Did this mother neglect her child? What plan would be in the best interest of this child?

Making reasonable efforts requires more than referral to other agencies for assistance. Many parents neglect their children only because they cannot cover basic family expenses or cannot piece together the services that might be available to meet their children's minimum needs. Should a child be left in a home in which he is not fed properly or in which there is no heat or where, as in a crime-ridden housing project, the neighborhood conditions place him in serious danger? Should a child remain in the home in which he has been battered or sexually abused and the parents have been unwilling to participate in therapy or in-home services? Two important distinctions always must be made: (a) Is the neglect or abuse caused by poverty, cultural practices, substance abuse, stress, isolation, or insufficient education or resources, all causes of maltreatment that might be remedied better by support services for the family than by removal of the child? and (b) What will be the effect on the child of removal or of remaining?

## Effects of Removal or Remaining

Although fiscal concerns are significant, the major consideration is the anticipated impact on the child as a result of removal or remaining. The removal of a child from the home solves an immediate problem: The child is protected from the harmful situation that necessitated the intervention, but the separation could create trauma, especially for the child who blames him- or herself for the separation (Stein & Rzepnicki, 1983). Removal is only the beginning of a much more serious challenge, that of establishing a suitable permanent home for the child. Continuity in relationships is a critical need of all children. To develop self-esteem and security, every child needs to be the apple of someone's eye, ideally a parent. In treatment, the family needs to be seen as a unit; dysfunctional family dynamics rarely can be improved significantly when only one family member has therapeutic counseling or when family members are living apart in different family constellations. Family-based therapy can help the at-risk child maintain crucial relationships while total family resources are supported and strengthened.

Sometimes, there is no clear-cut preferred choice. A study of children in foster care in a California county found that of neglected children remaining in the home approximately one half continued to have significant emotional problems. Relations with their parents remained poor (Wald, Carlsmith, & Leiderman, 1988). Some children do not survive chronic neglect in the home. Endeavoring to distinguish between the most vulnerable children and those who can be left safely with their parents can be extremely difficult.

No matter how much some parents love their children, their own incapacity to provide even minimally acceptable care finds them threatened with removal. Although it is heart-wrenching to remove these children, the courts approve removal when parents who have neglected or abused their children do not respond to a high level of supportive services.

## Case Plans

Under the Adoption Assistance and Child Welfare Act of 1980, an individual case plan for a child must be developed within 30 days after the initial removal of the child or after an emergency in-person response when the child is not removed from the home. The case plan must include an assessment of the circumstances that required child welfare services to intervene; specific goals and the planned services to meet these goals; identification of the original abuse or neglect allegations or the basis for declaring the child a dependent; a schedule of social worker contacts with the child and family; the frequency of contact between the parent and the child if the child is in an out-of-home placement; and to the extent available, the child's health and education records, including any individual education programs. The individual case plan for each child must be designed to "achieve placement in the least restrictive (most family-like) setting available and in close proximity to the parent's home, consistent with the best interest and special needs of a child" (Adoption Assistance and Child Welfare Act of 1980, 42 U.S.C.A. 675[5][a]). Parents are entitled to review and receive a copy of the case plan. Chapter 9 discusses court review of case plans.

## Reunification

Planning for reunification begins with out-of-home placement. When possible, parents should be involved in the placement process to ensure a transition that will be least damaging to the child and to the integrity of the family system. Parents can provide information to help in the selection of a foster home, communicate information to the foster parents, and prepare the child for foster care placement.

Parental accessibility to the foster home is critical to eventual reunification. The foster home should be close to the biological parents' home and transportation must be provided, if necessary, in order to maintain ties to the child through visitation. Once placement has occurred, the next responsibility of the caseworker is to make a postplacement assessment of the family that includes an identification of supports and stressors in the family's environment and a clarification of the family's needs, strengths, and competencies. The worker should encourage parental involvement in the assessment and try to help the parents understand the relationship of environmental stressors to their current situation and the importance of using social supports. Within this larger perspective, it is necessary also to focus on specific topics of immediate relevance to family reunification and the establishment of specific goals that will assist in the return of the child.

After an assessment is made, the caseworker and parents should discuss and agree on a reunification plan. This process begins with a consideration of the facts the court found to be true that caused the child to be placed out of the home. The parties then should define clearly the objectives, time frames, and outcomes that can be evaluated. The parents' objectives may include intent to work toward reunification; maintain regular contact with the child through visitation; utilize specified services such as parenting education, substance abuse treatment, and sexual abuse therapy; and provide financial support of the child if required. There also should be an indication that the parents understand that failure to meet these objectives may result in termination of parental rights. The caseworker may agree to keep the parents informed of the child's progress, ensure regular visits, provide direct services or link the family with other helping agencies, and meet regularly with the parents to help in the family's rehabilitative efforts.

*Case study.* Derek Burns is a homeless child whose 17-year-old mother, Judy, was also a homeless child who had grown up in foster care in the state of Delaware. When Derek was 3 months old, Judy asked CPS, which had custody of her, to provide a home for both mother and child until Judy could find housing. Judy signed a voluntary placement agreement and a consent giving custody to CPS. The sole reason for the agreement and custody consent was Judy's lack of a place for them to stay. The social worker explained to Judy that unless she signed both documents, she and Derek would be in the streets and the department would have to take Derek from her.

When Judy and Derek were placed together in a foster home, Judy began job training and narrowly missed passing her GED (high school equivalency diploma) test. Trained in the clerical field, Judy was offered only a part-time job at a fast-food restaurant, which she accepted. When Judy turned 18, she notified CPS she was leaving to live with her father and was taking Derek with her. The foster mother called the police who forcibly took Derek from Judy. From that time on, CPS did nothing to provide Judy and Derek with housing to allow them to continue living together. A new social worker tried to put Judy in parenting classes and counseling. When CPS refused to return Derek to Judy, Judy submitted to a psychiatric evaluation, which recommended reunification. Derek remained in foster care.

Over the next year Judy moved from place to place in search of stable employment and housing. In January 1985 Judy moved to the Philadelphia area, where she supported herself by working at odd jobs and living with various friends. In March 1985 CPS sought to terminate Judy's parental rights, completing that action in the family court. The Delaware Supreme Court reversed the termination and held that the CPS had an obligation to make all reasonable efforts to prevent the removal of the child and to reunify the family after separation. Because the only reason for placement was the lack of suitable housing and because the agency had failed both to continue joint foster care placement for the mother and child and to assist the mother to obtain alternative subsidized housing, CPS could not terminate parental rights (*In the Matter of Derek W. Burns*, 1986).

This case illustrates how the misapplication of a neglect standard can disrupt the life of a mother and child, jeopardize their relationship, and threaten permanent separation with no prospect for future reunification. Appropriate application of the concepts of reasonable efforts and family preservation as set out in the Adoption Assistance and Child Welfare Act of 1980 may well have prevented 2 years of unnecessary emotional turmoil and floundering in the young mother's quest for a home that would satisfy the authorities who had control over her son.

## Conclusion

As increasing numbers of children find themselves homeless, poverty stricken, or at risk with their families, it is ever more critical that the goals and procedures of the Adoption Assistance and Child Welfare Act of 1980 be put into practice responsibly throughout the nation. Funding available through the Omnibus Budget Reconciliation Act of 1993 must be adequate to provide needed concrete services. In-home supportive and therapeutic services must be tailored to meet individual family needs to prevent avoidable foster care placements. The Adoption Assistance and Child Welfare Act was passed to curtail unnecessary or prolonged placement in foster care. Yet children whose families could be preserved still are being placed in foster care prior to the provision of effective individualized in-home services and are remaining in foster care when with proper supervision and support, it would be safe for them to return home.

# 9

# The Child in Court

*The lack of appropriate services and facilities for . . . neglected children has contributed more than any other single factor to negating the purpose of the court.*

Judge Justine Wise Polier,
*A View From the Bench,* 1964

This statement, made more than three decades ago, still rings true for many children involved in court proceedings. What services are being provided? How are courts accommodating procedures to serve their youngest citizens?

A 2½-year-old girl is abused sexually by her drunken father and is found wandering in the apartment parking lot at 2 a.m. She is placed in a county emergency shelter, a petition is filed, and she is scheduled for a dependency court hearing. The criminal trial cannot be scheduled for at least a year. The only evidence the investigator has to identify the father is the child's statement to the person who found her in the parking lot, "Frank did it with his dick." What questions could the investigator ask the child to help her identify the perpetrator? What cognitive and memory problems will the criminal court encounter a year later in finding the child qualified to testify? Should efforts be made to reunify this child with her family?

## Juvenile or Criminal Court Intervention

The child victim of abuse or neglect may be caught up in two philosophically different types of courts. The purpose of criminal court proceedings is to determine guilt in order that the guilty may be punished.

The purpose of juvenile court is to protect the child if it is determined that the child is abused or neglected. The burden of proof in criminal cases is beyond a reasonable doubt. In juvenile court the burden, with a less stringent standard, is by a preponderance of the evidence. Court action may be pending simultaneously in both criminal and juvenile courts. If there is substantial evidence that a child has been abused seriously, the department of social services has several options to ensure protection for the child.

The first option is to remove the perpetrator from the home. If a criminal warrant is issued for an arrest, the perpetrator may be safely behind bars, but this occurs only in the most egregious case. The court can set bail for the indicted perpetrator and order the defendant to stay away from the child as a condition of bail. If the perpetrator is a parent, another condition can be the provision of support for the family to sustain them economically. The nonabusive parent may seek a temporary restraining order against the perpetrator that may help keep the accused away from the child and the home.

If the nonoffending parent does not believe that the child was abused, it is often emotionally difficult for the child to remain in the home. When a parent or stepparent perpetrator is sent to prison, the family's economic security will be jeopardized, and the label of criminal abuse may stigmatize the family. The child may be blamed for the negative consequences of the imprisonment. For any of those reasons, the child who remains in the home may incur more harm than benefit. The department of social services will want to protect the child from further emotional trauma. The least restrictive method is to require the child and parents to be in therapy before, during, and after any court hearing. If the defendant is released on probation, therapy can be a condition of the probation. Sometimes the child needs an alternate placement, especially if the alleged perpetrator continues to live in the home. If another family member can offer a home, the child will have the continuity of family relationships to provide security and personal support. When kinship care is not available, placement in a foster home may be necessary even though removal tends to make the child feel at fault. The loss of security in being uprooted from home may strike another blow against the child's ability to trust others.

In communities that provide a multidisciplinary approach for assessing and treating victims of abuse, trauma to the child can be minimized. Stuart House, in Los Angeles, is a model sexual abuse treatment program. The facility's professional team includes a deputy district attorney, a law enforcement investigator, a department of children's services worker, and a child advocate. The team follows procedures designed to eliminate repetitive interviews and ensure proper evidence collection. Stuart House therapists are clinical social workers and psychologists with knowledge, skill, and experience in helping sexually abused children and their families. Services offered include individual, family, and group therapy; crisis intervention; court accompaniment; consultation to the child's school; and assistance in obtaining victim compensation. The child is supported through any criminal court prosecution as well as in juvenile court.

## Criminal Court Involvement

The process in criminal court that centers on establishing the guilt of the parent has punishment as its aim, not rehabilitation for the offending parent. For this reason, most court-referred cases are brought to juvenile court, where the judge may order rehabilitative services that will protect the child and may keep the family together. Usually only the most extreme cases of harm to the child go to criminal court.

In a recent study an allegation of sexual abuse was the primary predictor of whether a substantiated child abuse or neglect report went to either dependency or criminal court. Criminal filings were significantly more likely to occur in cases of sexual abuse. Nonparent perpetrators and juvenile perpetrators were much more likely to face criminal charges than biological parents. The study found that if the victims were very young children, they were seen as noncredible witnesses. If they had reached adolescence, they were viewed as promiscuous or angry, which would cast doubt on their testimony. Criminal prosecution was more likely with a female victim age 7 to 12 years (Tjaden & Thoennes, 1992).

### Child as a Witness

A child called to testify in criminal court can be frightened by the formality of legal proceedings. Perry and Wrightsman (1991) have offered a number of ways the child can be prepared. Explaining the court procedures, giving a personal walk-through of the courtroom, introducing court personnel, and providing personal support during the time the child has to appear in court should help allay the child's fears.

Prior to giving testimony, the child must be qualified. As a matter of law, there is no age below which one is incompetent to testify. If a child can show a capacity to recall a past event and relate that memory to the court and the child demonstrates understanding of the concept of truth, the child can be found competent to testify (Green, 1986).

*Memory.* To testify in court, the child must be able to recall the event. Children, like adults, present both strengths and weaknesses in their memory. Their reports may be accurate but less complete than adult reports. Errors of omission are common especially when the child is giving an account of a highly personal and emotionally charged event, such as sexual abuse (Yates, 1987). When asked more specific questions, the child can fill in details if the questions are concrete, understandable, and objective (Goodman & Reed, 1986). Cognitive interview techniques help the child recall details regarding the abuse without the use of leading questions. These memory enhancement techniques help the child to reconstruct mentally the circumstances by using all four senses as well as emotions, feelings, and reactions. The child is encouraged to be complete by reporting things that may seem unimportant. Reverse recall provides extra incidental details. By prompting the child with "What happened *just* before that?" the interviewer will avoid the child's tendency to make great leaps backward in time. A child over age 7 can be asked to change perspective to another person or thing at the scene in order to obtain more details (Saywitz et al., 1992).

Prior to testifying, the child should be informed of the court process and what information the court needs to hear from the child. Although it is not a good idea to tell the child how to answer specific questions, the professional can refresh the child's memory by reviewing a tape of the child's previous statements or pictures the child drew of the events or just review what happened with the child to jog the child's memory prior to testifying (Feller, Davidson, Hardin, & Horowitz, 1992).

*Ability to communicate.* Child victims of abuse might be too traumatized to be able to talk when having to face the defendant in a courtroom setting. Iowa tried to protect all child abuse victims by mandating that defendants be placed behind a screen so that the child could not see the defendant while testifying. The Supreme Court declared this practice unconstitutional because it was highly prejudicial to the defendant and did not give the defendant the opportunity to see the accuser face-to-face (*Coy v. Iowa*, 1988). A more recent Supreme Court decision (*White v. Illinois*, 1992) allows certain hearsay statements of the child into court without giving the defendant the opportunity to see the child face-to-face and without having to prove the child is unavailable to testify.

A procedure in Maryland allowed the court to use one-way closed-circuit television. Before using the procedure, the court heard expert testimony and found that testimony by the child in the courtroom would "result in the child suffering serious emotional distress such that the child cannot reasonably communicate" (*Maryland v. Craig*, 1990, pp. 841, 3161). The trial judge permitted four child witnesses, aged 4 to 7, to give closed-circuit televised testimony after the state presented expert testimony that if the victims had to testify in the presence of the defendant, they would suffer such serious distress that they would not be able to communicate effectively or would not talk at all. The judge, jury, and defendant remained in the courtroom where the testimony was displayed. The Supreme Court concluded that the state's interest in protecting the physical and psychological well-being of child victims may be sufficient to outweigh the defendant's right to face-to-face confrontation. The Court emphasized that the state must make a showing of necessity justifying the use of a special procedure and that the court's finding of necessity must be specific to the particular facts of the case.

*Case study.* In a case in which such a procedure was not available, the judge refused to allow the child witness to be subjected further to courtroom trauma. The trial judge stated: "This child is utterly terrified . . . I've seen her hands tremble and her throat quiver; I've seen the look of fear cover her eyes. . . . She's looked at the defendant and dropped her head and lowered her eyes and I've observed her little legs up here shaking. Whatever information she may possess just is frozen by fear and will not come out, and I don't know of any point in traumatizing her further" (*State v. Chandler*, 1989, p. 734).

Experts disagree as to whether the courtroom experience is consistently traumatizing or cathartic for child witnesses. A study of a limited number of sexually abused children who provided testimony in court found that children aged 6 to 17 who testified in juvenile court resolved their anxiety more rapidly than peers who did not testify in juvenile court (Runyan, Everson, Edelsohn, Hunter, & Coulter, 1988). Other studies have found that testifying in court can be very traumatic for the child witness and that not testifying may be even better for the recovery of the child (see Naylor, 1989; Nuce, 1990; Perry & Wrightsman, 1991).

> *Case study.* A 9-year-old boy had been abused sexually by his baby-sitter. At the first trial, which ended in a hung jury, he left twice during testimony to go to the bathroom and after his testimony reportedly threw up. During the second trial, when the defendant was brought into the courtroom, the boy covered his eyes and put down his head. The boy cried and begged that he not be asked any questions. The judge described the boy as "totally distraught" and allowed him to leave. The videotape of his interview with police was allowed into evidence because most of the questions were nonleading, and the child's spontaneous statement to a psychologist he had been seeing was admitted also because, again, there was a lack of leading questions and the child's demeanor indicated reliability (*State v. Lonergan*, 1993, p. 353).

*Telling the truth.* In addition to the ability to recall and communicate the event, the child must be able to understand the difference between truth and falsehood. Children below the age of 3 may be able to communicate the event but may not be able to testify because they lack understanding of the concepts of telling a truth or lie. Burton and Strichartz (1991) found that younger children may make better witnesses than do adults when the question of potential for honesty is considered. They examined available evidence on the development of the concept of lies and truth and concluded that young children will be as motivated, if not more motivated, than adults to tell the truth on the witness stand. Kaplan (1990) suggested that the desire that children have to please others such as parents, therapists, and lawyers may be one reason why children often do not tell the truth when they are called as witnesses in court.

People are sometimes afraid that children mix fantasy with reality. In her survey of experimental and clinical considerations, Saywitz (1990) concluded that children 10 to 11 years of age are no more suggestible than adults; findings regarding the suggestibility of children 5 to 9 years of age were inconsistent. She concluded further that some suggestibility effect is due to demand characteristics whereby children go along with what they perceive to be the adult questioner's expectations. By the age of 2 most children know the difference between truth and falsehood but may not be able to identify an act as a lie or a mistake. Differentiating fact from fantasy is no more difficult for a child than for an adult. Certain children under the stress of courtroom testimony may not be able to resist suggestion or retrieve detailed memories. But in other cases, the seriousness of the courtroom may promote enhanced performance by some children. In contrast, Ornstein, Gordon, and Larus (1992) have found that 3-year-olds are more prone than 6- year-olds to make false claims in response to suggestive questions.

In *White v. Illinois* (1992) the Supreme Court held that a 4-year-old girl's spontaneous statements made to her mother, her baby-sitter, a police officer, an emergency room nurse, and a doctor could be admitted as hearsay testimony without requiring the child to testify or to be declared unavailable as a witness. The defendant charged with sexual assault on the 4-year-old girl did not have the right to confront the child, whose out-of-court statements were admissible when the state accepted spontaneous utterance or medical examination hearsay exceptions. This decision is especially important for the professional who wants to spare the child the experience of testifying in court; it also should encourage prosecutors to proceed against the perpetrator even when the child would not be a strong witness in court or might be incompetent to testify.

## Reducing Stress for the Child Witness

There are major factors in the court process that increase the stress of the child. Long delays between the incident and the trial are particularly stressful because the child must relive the abuse over and over again every time the details of the story have to be repeated. Children's mental health can be affected adversely by long delays in the criminal process (Runyan et al., 1988). Rescheduling the trial exacerbates the situation because the child witness must prepare psychologically for trial once again. When the trial has begun, the child may feel uneasy waiting in the courthouse. The longer the child has to wait in the courthouse, the harder it may be for the child to testify.

A lack of personal support is also a significant factor that causes stress for the child witness. If the abuser is a family member, the rest of the family may be supportive of the abuser rather than the child. In such a case, the child may fear the family's rejection. The closer the relationship of the abuser to the child, the more distress the child may feel in testifying. In cases in which the abuser has threatened the child, the child fears rejection from the family and, perhaps, bodily harm from the abuser. In addition, the child may feel guilty for breaking apart the family and bringing them under the scrutiny of the public. Where there is available a staff of professionals who are sensitive to the anxieties of the child witness and are working to alleviate this stress, the child may be better prepared psychologically to cope with testifying in court. The federal Victims of Child Abuse Act of 1994 provides child victims in federal courts rights and protection such as testimony by two-way closed-circuit television, videotaped depositions, appointment of a guardian ad litem, adult support persons for child witnesses, and restrictions on delays in court.

## Expert Testimony of Professionals

In child sexual abuse cases, expert testimony from a professional should be admissible when relevant and helpful in the determination of factual issues. These issues fall into three groups: (a) those relating to the child victim's competence and general credibility; (b) those that corroborate or dispute that a child was abused sexually; and (c) those given during rebuttal to rehabilitate the child's credibility about the allegations of sexual abuse after the child's testimony has been attacked (Lloyd, 1990).

Expert testimony has further limitations. To qualify as an expert witness, the professional must demonstrate specialized knowledge that will aid the fact finder in reaching a determination of the case. The expert's credibility could be demonstrated by evidence of skill, experience, training, or education. The expert witness may give an opinion, including a diagnosis, based either on personal knowledge or observation or on information supplied by others, including the patient. Such information must be inherently reliable even though not independently admissible into evidence. In most states the expert witness may not give an opinion on what the verdict should be, although some courts allow testimony as to whether the expert believes the child was abused (see Myers, 1992). The jury or the judge is the decision maker and cannot substitute the expert's opinion for that ultimate decision. The expert may state that the child has a diagnosis of sexual abuse. The expert may testify about the propensity or lack thereof of children in general to fantasize about sexual assaults. The expert may testify also in general about behavioral and psychological indicators of abuse. This type of testimony may be used to rebut testimony that the child witness is not credible. The expert may not testify that a particular child's testimony at trial was truthful or that the child was not fantasizing about the specific incident for which the defendant is being tried. Expert testimony may be given in either criminal or juvenile court.

## Juvenile Court Involvement

### The Petition

When the child protective services worker reaches the decision that the child cannot be protected safely in the home despite the reasonable efforts made, a petition will be filed by the department of social services requesting immediate custody of the child. Some states also allow private citizens or specified public officials such as physicians or police to file. The petition states how the facts of the particular case fit all elements of the state definition of abuse or neglect. Each parent must be served with a copy of the petition and notice of subsequent court hearings. Except in an emergency, a child should not be removed from home without a court hearing. In most cases the child is removed from the parents and placed with relatives or in foster care pending a preliminary hearing on the need to take immediate custody, usually scheduled the next day.

### Emergency Shelter Care Hearing

Both parents and the department of social services are represented by an attorney. A guardian ad litem or attorney is appointed to advocate for the child. In some states a trained volunteer court-appointed special advocate serves with the attorney or guardian ad litem who represents the child. Because the attorneys often are appointed at or just before the hearing, they are not able to advocate fully for their clients at that first hearing. The hearing may last only long enough for the judge to hear sufficient evidence that the allegations in the petition have adequate weight to warrant keeping the child out of the home until the adjudication hearing. In order to receive federal foster care funds, the department of social services must prove at the hearing that reasonable efforts were made to prevent the placement of the child outside of the home.

## Pretrial Settlement

The parties can use pretrial negotiation to reach a mutual agreement to settle all or part of a case before the actual hearing on the issues. The parents may be willing to agree to charges of neglect rather than face a hearing for what they perceive as the more serious charge of abuse. This pretrial negotiation may prevent unnecessary judicial intervention into a parent-child relationship. The use of pretrial conferences, mediation, and consent orders can simplify and provide for early dismissal of a case when appropriate. Parents may become emotionally upset and confused at the court hearings, and such additional emotional stress may hinder the parents' ability and willingness to adhere to a treatment plan and work toward becoming responsible parents. If the parents voluntarily will accept services and training to improve the home situation relative to family dynamics and, if pertinent, substance abuse problems, there may be no need for a judicial decree ordering these same services. Most pretrial settlements allow for subsequent court adjudication if the parents do not follow the terms of the agreement.

## Adjudication

For the cases that do not settle, the full hearing, called an *adjudication*, usually is scheduled within a few weeks of the child's removal from the home. Evidence is heard as to whether the allegations in the petition are true and as to whether the child should be placed in the custody of the state because of parental abuse or neglect. The parents and child may present evidence and cross-examine witnesses. These witnesses may include the doctor or mental health professional seeing the parents or children concerned, the schoolteacher, the day care center worker, the neighbor, the relative, the public health nurse, and the social worker who investigated the home or provided services to the family. Testimony at the adjudication will support or refute the allegations in the abuse or neglect petition. The CPS worker will present evidence to support the abuse or neglect allegation, reasons why the child was removed, and the need, if any, for continued out-of-home placement. Unless the petitioner can show the court that the child comes within the statutory definition of abuse or neglect and that there is a danger to the child if returned home, the court will return the child to the family. Following the adjudication the court may return the child to the parents or place the child in the home of a suitable relative, in an emergency shelter, or in a licensed foster home.

## Dispositional Hearing

After a finding that a child has been abused or neglected, the court must hear evidence concerning the proper disposition of the child. The primary purpose of the dispositional hearing is to determine what will be in the best interest of the child. The CPS worker's social study of the child will be presented. This information includes documentation of the efforts made to protect the child within the home and services offered or provided to parents. A case plan for reunification of the child and parents must be presented also.

At the hearing in juvenile court, the judge is extremely cautious about making a decision that removes a child from parental custody or allows the child to remain in state custody. As previously discussed, separation from the parent is often traumatic for the child and, for an infant, can critically impede the bonding process with the parent. The court will take into account several factors when considering the foster care placement of the children. These factors include:

___ Extended family support
___ Willingness of parent to receive in-home services
___ Willingness of parent to participate in court-ordered services including alcohol and drug rehabilitation programs and testing, if indicated
___ Safety of home environment
___ Age of child
___ Medical and psychological records
___ Substance abuse history
___ Prior court referrals

Extended family support can be the key to maintaining the family unit and successfully rehabilitating the parent. The court report should contain an evaluation of resources available to the family, concrete services the family needs, the ability of extended family members to provide care for the children if out-of-home care is required, and the feasibility of permitting a child to remain at home if needed services are provided. In the case of an infant whose mother is abusing drugs, consideration should be given to the availability of a mother/child residential program or the possibility that the mother and baby can reside with an extended family member to facilitate bonding while providing supervision.

Parental participation in court-ordered services including drug rehabilitation and testing programs may be an indicator of the parent's commitment to deal with the abuse or neglect and resume active care for the child. The parent's physical and emotional abilities; parental awareness of the impact of physical, sexual, and substance abuse and neglect on the child; level of parental concern; and parental acknowledgment of the problem are major considerations for the court. Lack of accessible testing and rehabilitation services, specialized day and after-school care, and housing may cripple the efforts of social service agencies, courts, and parents to keep the family together.

Safety of the home environment should be considered if the parent resides in a house or neighborhood in which violence or drugs are prevalent or in a home in which sexual abuse is condoned. The younger the child, the greater the potential danger if the parent abuses substances, is violent, or neglects the child's needs for food, medical care, and emotional security. In most cases, infants and preschoolers rely completely on their parents to meet all their basic needs and to protect them from harm. Although there are no monitors in the general community to check on parents who have not been reported to make sure they are providing for the infant, toddlers in day care and school-age children will be observed by caregivers or teachers who can report any sign of abuse or neglect.

Medical and psychological records containing specific history of the child's needs provide guidance for the court in determining how sophisticated the caregiver must be to meet the specific needs of an abused child. The court may order release of the parent's records to determine whether the parent can safely resume visitation or care of the child. A recent study found that parents diagnosed as psychotic or character disordered were significantly more likely to reabuse their children and return to court (Murphy, Bishop, Jellinek, Quinn, & Poitrast, 1992). The history of the parent's abuse or neglect, including substance abuse, should be documented carefully in the court record. The more pervasive a parent's past abuse or neglect, the greater the danger a child faces.

Prior court referrals should alert the judge to the risk of returning the child. A study in the Boston Juvenile Court found that a prior juvenile petition serves as a very serious warning sign of likely future return to court (Murphy et al., 1992).

## Review Hearings

Federal funding statute PL 96-272 (Adoption Assistance and Child Welfare Act of 1980) requires review hearings following the disposition in order to ensure that a permanent placement is found for the child without unnecessary delay. Case plans developed when the child is removed from the home may be clarified or revised, actions by parents or agencies will be reviewed, and a court record will be made of time frames for action. The reviews remind the parents and agency personnel that parental rights may be terminated if progress is not made. Phased-in visitations may be required along with other treatments or evaluations. The record made at the court reviews may influence later litigation. Reviews are held 6 months after the disposition and at least once more prior to the 18-month permanency planning hearing.

## Placement Alternatives

Placing the child in kinship or foster care should be considered only when informal supervision cannot provide protection for a child. Alternatives that a court will consider include:

___ Release to a parent

___ Release to a parent on condition that the parent receive appropriate in-home services and needed treatment

___ Order for community-based services for the family such as parental attendance at Alcoholics Anonymous or Narcotics Anonymous and parent education, mental health services, or vocational rehabilitation

___ Placement in kinship care with visitation allowed provided that a stable family member is present

___ Placement in foster care in close proximity to the parent in order to prevent change of school or day care for children, to facilitate the visitation plan, and to minimize transportation obstacles

___ Placement in foster care with limited supervised visitation only or no visitation allowed

___ Separate placement of siblings because of lack of foster homes to accommodate all the children together or because of particular emotional or physical disabilities of one or more of the children

___ Placement in specialized foster care for the child whose physical or mental health requires specially trained foster parents with parental visitation if appropriate

___ Placement in group home with visitation only as appropriate

___ Placement in a residential treatment center usually for an extended duration to work on major behavior or psychiatric problems

___ Placement in a hospital for medical or mental health needs of the child

## Visitation

Recommendation for visitation should be specific as to duration, frequency, and monitoring. These issues should be addressed in the court report with facts to support each recommendation. Visitations should be frequent and unmonitored unless the court is made aware of dangerous circumstances or a clear detriment to the child. The visitation order of the juvenile court is crucial in supporting the need of the parent and infant to develop a natural bond. Older children need to spend time with parents to participate in work on family issues that will make reunification efforts successful.

In making recommendations for visitation orders, the social worker, mental health professional, and the court will consider such factors as parental motivation to regain custody; parental participation in drug and alcohol treatment, counseling, and testing programs; circumstances of the protective services referral; child abuse or neglect history; caregiver's acknowledgment of parental abuse and/or neglect; location, frequency, flexibility, and need for supervision of visitation; need for provision of transportation to facilitate visitation; time frame for reunification; and the next court review date.

Visitation between parent and child is essential to reunification. Besides allowing and arranging visits, the caseworker should aggressively promote regular contact. Parental visitation is often an indication of the progress the parent is making in other areas. A missed visit should act as a signal to all concerned to explore the parent's situation and provide additional needed services. If visitation does not occur, the parental rights are likely to be terminated within a year and the child ultimately placed in an adoptive home.

Infants in foster care should be visited at least three times a week by biological parents to help with formation of a healthy attachment. An ideal placement would leave the infant in a kinship or foster home or day care center where the biological parent could attend daily to care for the infant under close supervision of the foster parent or day care specialist. Teen mothers and their infants can be placed in foster care together. The professional treating the foster care child will keep the child's social worker and the court apprised of the child's emotional health to prevent possible state liability for further emotional abuse by ignoring or neglecting the child's basic need for permanent attachment to a parent figure.

### Realistic Time Frames

Goldstein et al. (1978) stressed the importance of adopting a child's sense of time when striving to achieve what is in the best interest of the child. A child's sense of time is much shorter than an adult's. Therefore, adults who work on the child's behalf must move quickly and effectively to provide a safe, permanent home for the child. Courts recognize the importance of balancing the time required to reunite the families of abused or neglected children against the need to place a child in a stable, long-term living situation as soon as possible. Thus, reunification efforts with parents should not continue indefinitely.

### Permanency Planning Hearing

The professional who evaluates the child in out-of-home care must be aware of statutory time limits for children to remain in foster care before either they are allowed to return home or the parents will lose their rights. Most states have an 18-month time frame for reunification efforts before a petition is filed to terminate parental rights. Agency personnel may be required to prove that they have made reasonable efforts to reunify the family before this ground for termination is allowed to be used.

The medical, mental health, and educational professional can supply evidence that the court needs to firmly order the department of children's services to provide strong reunification services and to require the parents to respond positively within a given time frame. A span of 3 months gives most parents motivating time pressure to respond before the next

court hearing. When review hearings are scheduled at 12- or even 6-month intervals, social service agencies and parents are less likely to give prompt attention to the child's pressing need for a safe, permanent home.

When there has been severe abuse, most states allow a termination petition to be filed immediately, thus forgoing any effort at reunification. Strict time frames can pose special problems for addicted parents who are unable to get off waiting lists and into effective rehabilitation programs. A high recidivism rate for even the best treatment programs does not provide much hope for the addicted parent who is not committed seriously to change. Parents with multifaceted problems will have an even more difficult time turning their lives around within the time frame of the child.

## Conclusion

Court can be the setting for parental affirmation when the children return home because the parents have worked with the agencies in resolving major problems. If the parent fails to follow through on reunification efforts despite court orders, the petition should be filed for termination of parental rights. Once the court has determined that the parents are unfit, parental rights can be terminated and the court can focus on a disposition that will be in the best interest of the child (*Santosky v. Kramer*, 1982). Termination will be discussed in Chapter 11.

# 10

# Foster Care and Guardianship

*No one would seriously dispute that a deeply loving and interdependent relationship between an adult and a child in his or her care may exist even in the absence of a blood relationship.*

U.S. Supreme Court,
*Smith v. Organization of Foster Families for Equality and Reform*, 1977

Candy, one of six children, was 10 when placed in her third foster home and only 11 when she became the oldest child in a group home. Moved out just 2 weeks short of graduation from the sixth grade, she could not return for that milestone event. Candy had been abused in her third foster home and had to be removed to an emergency shelter, which became her favorite place because there was so much recreation: field trips, toys, videos, and wide-screen televisions. She sat in the middle of the floor and cried when her social worker came to take her to her fourth foster home placement. An older sister and brother had been luckier. Mrs. Griffin had been their foster mother for over 5 years. They felt like part of a real family. Candy often wished she could live there with Christi and Kevin, but her social worker didn't think that would work. He let the children visit each other only once a year at Christmas time. Lynette and Jeanette, her 14-year-old twin sisters, had been placed in a group home away from Candy. Lynette liked living there, but Jeanette recently had run away for the third time. This time, no one even was looking for her. Older brother Dan was now at a training school for delinquents.

All six children were placed in care when their mother was killed 6 years earlier. At first an aunt tried to take care of them, but her own family was so big that the extra six boys and girls had to be placed in foster care a year later. The children had the same social worker, the same attorney, the same CASA, and the same judge, but different parent figures, neighborhoods, friends, and family. They had attended only one court hearing and only then because the CASA volunteer picked up each of them and brought them to the hearing. Their father had sexually abused all the children; when he was released from prison, he was forbidden to see any of them. Because his parental rights never had been terminated, none of the children had been considered for adoption. By now, that family of children represents a typical picture of what happens to children placed in the custody of the county. Two of the six remain in a wholesome long-term foster home placement. One is in a group home for six teenagers that has a rotating staff 24 hours a day. One has been in five different foster homes, was abused in one of them, and is now living in a group home for six young girls. One is a runaway living on the streets as a prostitute. The oldest is in a training school for delinquents.

Foster care is a complex program of providing substitute care. It works well for many children whose own homes are more destructive than supportive. Foster home care generally is preferable to institutional care because the home atmosphere that all children need usually is provided. But foster home placement has a sorry history of use as a first rather than as a last resort for children from poor or troubled families.

## History of Foster Care

The power of the government to remove children from the home and place them in some form of foster care is grounded deeply in American history. Seventeenth-century laws in Connecticut, Virginia, and Massachusetts authorized magistrates to "bind out" or indenture children of the poor over parental objections. In 1909 the first White House Conference on the Care of Dependent Children resolved that a carefully selected foster home was the best substitute for families who did not want their children or could not provide adequately for them even with outside help. By 1933 half of the neglected children in the United States were in large institutions and a large proportion were supervised by a religion-connected and -sponsored voluntary agency. Two years later, the Social Security Act of 1935 created a program of federal tax-supported foster care as a temporary last step to protect children at risk of imminent and grave harm at home.

### Reasons for Placement in Foster Care

Historically, foster care has been a child welfare system based on a set of deep-rooted values and beliefs:

— Removing a child is the best means of protection.
— Troubled families do not want their children.
— Troubled families are incorrigible.
— Children and families can be considered separately from each other.
— Parents do not deserve government help and support.
— Individual pathologies should be treated.
— Racial and cultural prejudice bring children of color into foster care more often and longer.

By the 1960s children were being placed in foster care for a variety of reasons, including physical illness or incapacity of the parent, mental illness of the parent, the child's personality or emotional problems, severe neglect or abuse, an unwillingness or inability to continue child care on the part of an adult other than a parent, children left or deserted, and parental arrests or incompetence. Many parents made the placements voluntarily without any court review.

The California State Department of Social Services gave the following breakdown in reasons for removal from home for over 46,000 dependent foster children in 1987: severe general neglect (41.5%); caretaker absent or incapacitated (25.4%); physical abuse (16.7%); sexual abuse (10.9%); child disabled, emotional abuse, exploitation, relinquishment (5.5%). A national survey on the reasons children entered substitute care in 1988 is less specific as to abuse or neglect allegations but paints a more accurate picture of reasons for foster care: protective services (46.9%); parent condition or absence (22.3%); delinquency or status offense (10.9%); handicap of child (3%); relinquishment of parental rights (1.7%); other (parent-child interaction problem, adoption, deinstitutionalization, training/education, and unwed motherhood) (11.8%) (Spar, 1992).

## Foster Care Population

By 1978 the number of children in out-of-home placement reached 503,000. Federal funding laws discussed in Chapter 8 required the state to reduce unnecessary placements and shorten the length of time spent in out-of-home care. Accordingly, by 1982 the average length of placement decreased from 47 months to 35 months (U.S. Department of Health and Human Services, 1984). This remarkable decrease occurred when states were forced to take a census of the children currently in foster care and make major efforts to reunite them with their parents or risk losing federal foster care funds. An increase in the mid-1980s could reflect the high number of substance-abused infants born and the failure of the government to provide a safety net for families plagued by poverty.

## Foster Home Characteristics

A foster home is defined as a residential facility providing 24-hour care for six or fewer children and serving as the foster parent's residence. Foster homes must be licensed by the state. The child's health and education records must be provided to the foster parents and kept updated. The entry point for referral into foster care can come from schools, law enforcement agencies, health care facilities, and social service agencies (Schor, 1987). If the child must be placed outside the home, preference is given to placement in kinship care, a practice that has become increasingly common. The Supreme Court ruled that a relative who is providing foster care is entitled to the same federal foster care payments as other foster parents (*Miller v. Youakim*, 1979).

If the child cannot be placed with family, proximity to the home of the natural parents is preferred to promote increased visitation and to give the child continuity with school, peers, and neighborhood. Most states list an order of preference for placement to be first with a relative, then in a foster home with the same racial or ethnic identity as the child, and next in a foster family of a different racial or ethnic identification if there is evidence of sensitivity to the child's race and culture. Consideration is given to the child's religious background. A child's extraordinary physical or emotional needs are considered also when specialized care is needed.

## Foster Parent Characteristics

Foster parents, typically older than the average parent, have a family income slightly below average. They own their own home and move less often than the average family. With a generally stable marriage, they have raised two or more of their own children and have a strong sense of family and kinship. Foster parents are usually sensitive to children's traumatic history and maintain firm but fair discipline. The average foster parent has a strong sense of personal and social tradition (Simms, 1991).

# Foster Care Problems

*Case study.* A child who had been left with a baby-sitter was brought to the emergency room when he developed serious breathing problems. After treatment in the hospital, the boy was released to the custody of the foster care social worker with medication to control his asthma. When the social worker placed the child in a foster home, she transferred the medication to the foster mother. Neither the social worker nor the foster parent requested any information about the child's continuing need for treatment. On the second day in foster care placement, after the boy finished the medication, he told the foster mother he was having trouble breathing. She told him to lie down in his bed. When she checked on him later, he was in grave condition and died when he reached the hospital. In a suit brought by the boy's family, the court would not allow the state to use government immunity to hide behind their legal duty to provide care and protection to a child in custody. Their deliberate indifference to the serious medical needs of the child left them open to the liability suit brought by the family (*Norfleet v. Arkansas,* 1992).

## Neglect and Abuse by the County

Some foster children face neglect and abuse once they enter the system. The multiple moves and extended stays characteristic of foster care threaten the stable permanent family ties a child needs. This is particularly hard on the very young. In many states the Adoption Assistance and Child Welfare Act of 1980 has not stopped foster care drift. The Utah Department of Human Services reported in 1992 that over 30% of the state's foster children had been in four or more placements. Michigan reported that 73% of infants entering foster care had multiple placements within 4 years (Abbey & Schwartz, 1992). An increasing number of very young children are now in foster care. In 1985, 37% of children entering foster care were under 6 years of age. By 1988 that increased to 42% (Select Committee on Children, Youth, and Families, 1989).

Although the majority of children in foster care are White, the minority percentage has increased to just under 50%. The drastic increase in the number of children born drug exposed in the past decade is reflected also in their increased numbers in foster care. As a result, there are not enough foster homes for children. Of the children living in foster care in the United States, one in five lives in California. The number of foster care homes in California increased 11% from 1986 to 1988, although the number of children needing foster care increased 28%. There is a very high turnover rate among child welfare workers who are underpaid, poorly trained, overworked, and demoralized by massive problems. Some foster parents are not adequately selected, licensed, trained, supervised, or matched with foster children. The average monthly cost of foster care is $801 per child in Los Angeles, where the department of children's services has not been able to provide adequate psychological, medical, and educational services for foster children. Although in-home services cost less than foster care, 97% of the children petitioned to dependency court in Los Angeles are removed from their homes (Watahara & Lobdell, 1990). Chronic substance abuse is a major problem in those families, yet most child protective services do not provide substance abuse programs for the parents. Rehabilitation programs offered outside the agency have waiting lists and rarely address the particular problems faced by the addicted parent.

Many children who come into foster care bring serious emotional problems from their earlier lives with their biological families. Once in foster care, children may develop greater emotional problems from drifting through multiple or prolonged placements. The most frequently identified disorder of children in foster care is emotional illness. At the same time, services for emotional problems are the least available (Halfon & Klee, 1986). A major problem for resolving treatment needs of foster children is the absence of a mechanism to guarantee that children in the custody of the state receive needed services from other public agencies and private providers. Needed are practices that will fuse the multiple efforts of agencies into a cooperative continuum of cost-effective services for all foster children who need them (Halfon & Klee, 1991). The lack of permanent adoptive homes for older, disabled, and even some healthy minority children holds children in the foster home system instead of in permanent adoptive homes. A paucity of effective support services for adoptive families leads to disruptions and feeds children back into foster care with the added emotional burden of adoption failure.

> *Case study.* Maria was brought to the emergency room by her parents when she was less than a year old. She had broken bones, a fractured skull, and signs of long-term physical abuse. The court removed Maria from her parents and placed her in foster care where she thrived. Because of the severity of her injuries, Maria did not have to be reunified with her parents. When she was 3 years old, the county attempted to begin visitation with her grandmother who had come from Mexico in hopes of seeing the little girl. The grandmother did not believe the parents had abused the child. She hoped to gain custody of the child and return to Mexico where the parents lived. The foster parents adored Maria. She and their biological daughter were inseparable. Except for an eye injury requiring future surgery, Maria had recovered. At the court hearing to review the permanent plan for Maria, the county made it clear to the foster parents, who were not Latino, that the grandmother would have increased visitations and that eventually Maria would be placed with her. The CASA volunteer strongly opposed this plan, as did the foster parents, but the court refused to consider any evidence of bonding between the foster parents and Maria and eventually approved placement of the child with her grandmother.

## Continuum of Foster Placements

Since the Adoption Assistance and Child Welfare Act of 1980, foster care has changed its orientation from child welfare to family treatment (see Chapter 8). Instead of a system that is largely custodial, a treatment perspective for entry into foster care is beginning to provide a continuum of services for children and families. Entry to foster care ideally accompanies a diagnostic component on family strengths, family system dysfunction, placement requirements for the child, and recommendations for treatment of family members. Follow-up continuum services include day care, day treatment, facilities for the perpetrator, core shelter facilities, regular foster homes (allowing for high-risk adoption placements), therapeutic foster homes tiered in levels of need, couple group homes (four to six residents), rotating shift group homes (four to six residents), residential treatment facilities (10 to 15 residents), and finally, hospitalization (Woolf, 1990).

Children who need to be in therapeutic foster homes may have to be hospitalized because only a hospital bed is available at the time placement is needed. A child who is ready for discharge from successful hospitalization may have to remain in the facility for days or even weeks until a place opens in a less restrictive home facility. When all these services can be operated by one entity, there is a fiscal incentive to move the child to the least restrictive placement that meets the child's needs. Most types of care in the foregoing list are not grouped under the same organization. Thus a child can experience major disruptions when the child's needs are in transition. If he lives in a residential treatment facility but has progressed enough to move into a group home, he will face three problems: finding a place in a group home that might not want to risk taking a child from a treatment facility or does not have a bed available; losing the relationship he has built with those who operate the treatment facility; and having no guarantee that if his condition worsens, he will be able to return to the treatment facility or if he improves he will be able to advance to less restrictive settings.

*Shelter care.* Shelter care is designed for very short-term needs but, in fact, may last many months. Children in shelter care may not have an advocate to help protect their rights. Health and school records, often slow to be processed, may arrive weeks after the child has been at the facility. A model shelter care facility would provide living quarters for children to ensure individual privacy. Placements of infants would be discouraged. Court review every 15 days for any child remaining in an emergency shelter longer than 1 month would guarantee advocacy for protection of the child's right to parental reunification, if deemed possible, or permanent placement.

Problems with institutional placement of children are well documented. Overcrowding, poor staff training, and lax supervision can lead to a daily occurrence of behaviors such as verbal abuse, hair pulling, slaps, shoves, pinches, sadistic behavior, sexual exploitation, kicking, or other assaultive behavior against the institutionalized child (Rindfleisch & Hicho, 1987; Rindfleisch & Rabb, 1985). Appointment of a legal advocate for the child on entry into out-of-home care can help prevent such abuse and exploitation. Children's developmental and psychological needs cannot be met well in institutional settings. Federal funding for temporary emergency shelter is provided through the Social

Services Block Grant, Title XX of the Social Security Act. Funding limits encourage placement in kinship or foster care. Institution use should not be caused by poor planning and management that, instead, fails to utilize foster care placement. Children learn best how to interact with others in a homelike setting. Until a permanent home can be found for the child, the foster home is the preferred option for out-of-home care (Simms, 1991).

*Core shelter facility.*   In the continuum of out-of-home care, a core shelter facility should be available in large urban areas. This important link in the continuum permits an agency to have a significant, positive impact on hundreds of children each year. The core shelter facility serves as a primary placement resource for police and social workers; a resource for parents seeking assistance during crisis; and a safe, caring temporary environment in which to prepare the child for the next placement—either return home, entry into foster care for first time, move to another foster home, or entry into a residential treatment program.

The core shelter facility is characterized by a short length of stay, usually 7 to 10 days. In a city of 1 million people, the core shelter will have 40 to 50 beds. Such a facility is open to receive children 24 hours a day. It accommodates large sibling groups and offers a setting for daily visitation to support the parental role. The social worker can benefit from child observation to better recommend an appropriate placement for the child. The facility personnel evaluate and record each child's condition at admission and arrange for health services. Staff can make referrals to many community resources to address other specific needs of the children. The core shelter facility provides an alternative for families in crisis that avoids social service or legal involvement. An on-campus school ensures continuous education that is sensitive to each child's needs. A high level of recreation, field trips, and structured activity is provided for the children. The per diem cost is three to four times foster care cost (Fox, Graves, & Sanders, 1986).

*Kinship care.*   Placement of children with relatives is increasing as the mandate to preserve families is taken more seriously by child protection agencies. What happens to the children placed in kinship foster care? A recent study by Dubowitz, Feigelman, and Zuravin (1993) at the University of Maryland found that the reasons given for placing children in kinship care are generally the same as for other foster care placements except for sexual abuse, which accounted for only 7% of kinship placements.

One of the most interesting findings in the study was that only 39% of the caregivers thought there was a long-term plan for the child to remain in their care as compared to 58% of the social workers. Thirty-five percent of the caregivers were unsure of the permanent plan for the child. Dubowitz et al. (1993) suggested that uncertainty about the permanent plan for the child might diminish the caregiver's investment and involvement in the child and aggravate the child's feeling of insecurity. The majority of children in the study did find a relatively stable home with a single caregiver. A major difference found between kinship and other foster care was the infrequent contact caseworkers had with children. One fourth of the caseworkers had seen the child fewer than four times in the previous year despite court orders for bimonthly visits. Twelve percent of these Maryland children were reported for maltreatment while in kinship care.

A national survey found 7% of children in foster care being reported for maltreatment compared with only 2% of all children in the country being reported (Bolton, Lane, & Kane, 1980). The American Academy of Pediatrics criticized social workers for providing less supervision of relatives and limiting family support services to relatives providing kinship care. The academy recommends that a kinship care plan should be based on a careful assessment of the child's needs and of the ability of the relatives to meet those needs (Committee on Early Childhood, 1993).

## Effect of Foster Care on Children

Wald et al. (1988) reported on their study of the foster care system in their book *Protecting Abused and Neglected Children*. Wald and his colleagues compared families in a county with intensive in-home services for families in crisis at risk of having their children removed with families in a neighboring county whose children already were placed in foster care. The study found that foster care was not detrimental to most children. There was little major change among children in either group. Foster care was somewhat more beneficial to the children most at risk, at least with regard to improving physical health, school attendance, and academic performance and preventing deterioration in social behavior at school. Both foster care and in-home placement involved emotional stress for children. Stress caused by conflict and chaos in the home environment may have had a more negative impact on the home children than the stress that separation, movement, and adjustment to new parents had on the foster care children.

All children do not thrive in foster care. A national study of runaway youths found that more than a third had been in foster care the year before they ran away. In California the percentage reached 45%. Ninety-six percent of these youths in California ran away because of physical and sexual abuse. The problems found by this study led the survey director to conclude that "our foster care facilities are failing. They are not addressing the long-term problems of these kids" (Toth, 1992, p. A5).

## Legal Limits on Foster Care Services

Legal scholar Robert Mnookin (1973) proposed specific standards for removal in his seminal article "Foster Care—In Whose Best Interests?" Removal should occur only when the child cannot be protected within the home. The decision for removal should be based on legal standards applied in a consistent and even-handed way. The state should make every effort to provide children who must be removed with as much continuity and stability as possible. Mnookin believed the judge's decision is based often on the best interests of the child standard, which fails to consider the parent's rights and responsibilities. It looks instead at the child's happiness, parent's spiritual goodness, economic productivity, stability and security, and intellectual stimulation in the home. Mnookin believed that the best interests standard should not be used until the jurisdiction of the court has been adjudicated by a finding that the child is abused or neglected. At the dispositional phase of the dependency court hearing, the best interests standard can be used to determine which placement is the most appropriate or is the least detrimental alternative. Many of Mnookin's principles have been adopted in state and federal laws.

### Court Action Involving Foster Care

An action was brought against the director of a state division of family services challenging the provision of foster care to children in a metropolitan area. Highlighting some of the problems of foster care nationwide, the issues brought before the court included licensing of foster homes, mandatory training of foster parents, proper matching of foster children with foster parents, investigation of and response to suspected incidents of abuse and neglect or unsuitable care, preplacement process, prohibition of the use of improper (corporal) punishment, elimination of overcrowding, and the rate of reimbursement (*G. L. v. Zumwalt*, 1983). The consent decree entered into in *Zumwalt* affirmed the constitutional rights of foster children to care that is adequate. Among the more noteworthy aspects of the decree is the absolute prohibition against the use of corporal punishment of children in foster care and insistence on mandatory training for foster parents and social service staff members in the prevention of abuse and neglect in foster care. A limitation on the maximum size of caseloads carried by child welfare social service workers was fixed at 25. Similarly, the consent decree specified a maximum ratio of one supervisor to seven social service workers. The decree also mandates extensive preservice and inservice training for all social service workers and the supervisory staff.

Social service workers were required to visit each child in the foster home at least once every 2 weeks; a telephone contact was not an acceptable substitute for a home visit. During the home visit the caseworker was to speak with the child in private as well as in the presence of the foster family. Weekly visits between the child and the biological family were required except where specific factors made such visits inadvisable or physically impossible, and this is noted and incorporated in an approved case plan.

Each child was to be enrolled in a health maintenance organization or prepaid medical plan. Each child was required to receive a physical examination within 24 hours after coming into care and an eye, hearing, and dental examination within 30 days. A treatment plan was required for the correction of any identified problems. Foster parents are to be assisted in meeting a child's medical needs, including the provision of baby-sitting services and transportation expenses when necessary. When no other arrangements are possible, the agency bears the final responsibility for ensuring that the child is taken for the required examinations and treatment.

In addition to the treatment of medical problems, the decree requires the agency to assess the psychological, emotional, and intellectual needs of each foster child within 30 days of the child's coming into care. If a problem is identified, the agency must ensure that the child receives adequate professional services. A uniform case record system is to be developed to capture essential information about foster children, their biological parents, and the foster parents in a concise and reliable way. A preliminary case plan must be developed for each child within 30 days. Long-term foster care is an inappropriate plan for any child under the age of 15, absent special circumstances. Similarly, without special reasons, the agency may not continue to plan to return a child home when there has been no contact between the parent and child for 6 months. The decree mandates supervised preplacement visits in the foster home and an overnight preplacement visit whenever possible. Careful matching of the foster child with the foster family is required, and in no case may the placement of a foster child violate the licensing restriction or stated preferences of the foster parents (Mushlin, Levitt, & Anderson, 1986).

The county department of family services (DFS) in *G. L. v. Zumwalt* (1983) failed to submit a proposal on how to provide medical care until 5 years after the consent decree was issued. After numerous other delays, the DFS proposed in 1990 to use a system of case management to organize and coordinate health services. Ongoing monitoring shows that DFS has met some of the requirements, such as providing a medical exam within 24 hours, but has failed to comply with others (Halfon & Klee, 1991).

## Attachment

Children who are being abused physically can find a safe, secure environment in a foster home, but the child's break with the abusive parent can lead to serious emotional harm. For decades the common practice for foster care agencies was to discourage foster parents from becoming attached to the children in their care. Before children were placed, contracts were signed to confirm that foster parents understood they had no long-term hold on the child. Often children were moved out of a foster home when the social worker felt that the foster parent was becoming too emotionally attached to the foster child or vice versa. Such a lack of attachment leads foster children to experience identity problems, conflicts of loyalty, and anxiety regarding the future. Wald et al. (1988) ask the poignant question: Is it worse to be beaten or to lack an attachment figure?

Despite this paradox in foster care, there is convincing evidence that most foster children show wide-ranging improvement in cognitive and social development during placement (Simms, 1991). Some foster parents who become emotionally attached to children in their care make attempts to replace the temporary relationship with a permanent, legally protected bond through adoption. A U.S. Supreme Court decision supports the viewpoint that foster parents indeed should be considered for permanent adoptive placement. The *Smith v. Organization of Foster Families for Equality and Reform* (1977) decision helped pave the way for more serious consideration of the child and foster parent's emotional bond and the need for the child and the foster parent to form a permanent legally binding parental relationship. Foster parents now are considered first for adoptive placement when parental rights have been terminated and no family members are able to adopt the children.

## Legal Alternatives for Foster Parents

Foster parents may be the first choice for permanent placement when reunification efforts fail, when the child has been abandoned, or when the abuse was so severe that no reunification efforts will be made. Some foster parents may not want to take steps to build a stronger legal attachment to the child. They may prefer to have the child remain with them in long-term foster care. Other foster parents may want to solidify their legal relationship with the child by becoming guardians.

### Long-Term Foster Care

The Adoption Assistance and Child Welfare Act of 1980 was designed to "lessen the emphasis on foster care placement and to encourage greater efforts to find permanent homes for children either by making it possible for them to return to their families or by placing them in adoptive homes" (U.S. Code Cong. & Admin. News, 1980, p. 1450). Despite this strong emphasis on adoption, long-term foster care remains the permanent placement of choice for most children who are not reunited with their parents. In Los Angeles 57% of all children in foster care have long-term foster care as their permanent plan (Commission for Children's Services, 1992). In the case study that opened this chapter, Christi and Kevin were in long-term foster care with Mrs. Griffin, with whom they had lived for 6 years. The other sisters were also in long-term foster care but with placements in various group homes. The instability and lack of parental figure had caused Jeanette and Dan to run away from foster care altogether, preferring for themselves life on the streets.

*Long-term foster care when adoption is forestalled.* Long-term foster care placement may be used as a matter of convenience for the agency having custody of the child because adoptive homes may be more difficult to find than foster homes. Involved legal procedures needed for adoptive placements may discourage adoption as a preferred placement. In California the number of preschool children in long-term foster care without an adoption goal increased from 1,860 in 1987 to 4,889 in 1990 (Barth, Berrick, Courtney, & Pizzini, 1990). Long-term foster care is an option that keeps the child in the custody of the county. Another problem with long-term foster care is the absence of a guarantee to provide stability of placement. A history of multiple foster care moves makes an eventual adoptive placement more difficult to accomplish. However, long-term foster care can give the child continuity with the natural parent if that is what the child desires and it is safe to continue the relationship.

To prevent prolonged foster care placement after parental rights are terminated, the Adoption Assistance and Child Welfare Act of 1980 requires that a judicial review of the child's placement occur 6 months after the termination proceeding and at regular intervals thereafter. This time frame should allow the agency to find an appropriate home for the child so that court review will be unnecessary. The guardian ad litem or CASA gives the child a voice in court after parental rights are terminated if the adoption process is too slow or placement does not meet the child's needs.

> *Case study.* A guardian ad litem represented five children whose parents' rights had been terminated. When the children were first placed in foster care, DSS could not find a home that would take all five children. They became separated by being placed in three different homes. One foster parent was interested in adopting two of the children, but not all five. The guardian ad litem was able to locate a relative with a big home and a big heart. When the adoption worker continued to move forward on a plan that would keep the children permanently separated, the guardian ad litem motioned the court for a review and succeeded in having all the children placed with their relative.

*Cost.* To the high cost of foster care must be added the administrative cost of required social worker visits and court reviews. Despite being the least desirable for the child needing permanence and the most expensive of the options available, long-term foster care is still, by far, the most widely used type of permanent placement.

# Guardianship

Guardianship is a legal action that gives someone other than the parent the care, custody, and control of the child. Guardianship can be initiated completely separately from the juvenile court or can become the permanent plan for a child who is in foster care. A family member or adult friend of the child may seek guardianship when the parents are unwilling or unable to care for the child. A parent's will may appoint someone to become the child's guardian in case of the death of both parents. A parent who must be hospitalized or be absent for an extended period may leave the child with a person appointed as guardian to allow the child to enroll in school and receive medical care.

## Guardianship of the Person

An appointment as guardian of the child's person does not give the guardian control over the child's estate. The adult needing to control the child's finances also must be appointed guardian of the child's estate. A caregiver related to the child may apply for AFDC without being appointed guardian of either the person or the estate (Social Security Act of 1935, 42 U.S.C. sec. 606, 607). If a guardian is not related to the minor, neither the guardian nor the youth is eligible for federal AFDC (*Curry v. Dempsey*, 1983).

*Standards for appointment.* In deciding whether to grant guardianship, the judge will be guided by the best interests of the child standard and will grant guardianship to promote the child's health, safety, and welfare. The court will consider the wishes of the parent but will not necessarily require parental consent before granting guardianship.

*Differences from intervention for abuse or neglect.* Although juvenile court intervention requires proof of parental neglect, abuse, or abandonment, guardianship is not necessarily the product of juvenile court interven-tion. The petitioner seeking guardianship is not the county, but a person who wants to or is providing personal care for the child. Although intervention by the department of social services almost always re-quires efforts to reunify the child with the parents, guardianship obtained outside of dependency court does not have that same requirement. The guardian, not the parent, will have the right to determine whether and when the parent can visit the child, unless the court order states other-wise. A judge granting guardianship does not have a staff of social workers to keep in regular contact with the child and to provide needed services to support the child's special needs. These responsibilities fall on the shoulders of the guardian. Just as in abuse and neglect cases, the court will maintain jurisdiction over a child involved in a guardi-anship until the child reaches 18.

> *Case study.* Mary Lynn and Sarah were orphaned when their parents were killed in an automobile accident. The parents had not left a will. Immedi-ately after their death, the girls went to live with friends of the parents. Too elderly to provide a home for the girls, their grandfather was glad that they could live with family friends. The friends asked the court to appoint them as guardians of the person and of the estate so that the children could live in their custody and the insurance proceeds from the parents' estate could be used to meet the girls' financial needs.

*Parental rights.* Parents do not lose permanently their rights to the child during a guardianship. Rather, the parental rights are held in abeyance. When able to resume parental responsibility, the parent must petition the court to have the guardianship terminated and custody of the child returned to the parent. Depending on state laws, the guardianship may be temporary or come into effect only on the occurrence of a certain act. This type of guardianship is helpful particularly for parents with AIDS who want to ensure that their children are cared for during any time that they are incapacitated.

> *Case study.* Laura was HIV positive. She had three very active young children. Her best friend provided respite care to allow Laura to get away from the stress of child care and tend to her own medical needs. Laura knew that her health was unpredictable and didn't want to worry that her children would be placed in foster care if she had to be hospitalized. Her friend was willing to become guardian for the children through a court order that went into effect only when Laura became incapacitated.

*Guardianship after foster care.* If the department of social services places a child in a caregiver's custody, the caregiver should be offered foster care benefits. Instead, the DSS may advise a caregiver to obtain guardianship status. In some states foster care benefits are not allowed if the caregiver is a relative of the child (*Lipscomb v. Simmons*, 1990). A relative who is licensed or approved as a foster parent is entitled to foster care payments (*Miller v. Youakim*, 1979). A caretaker receiving foster care benefits who is related to the child may become ineligible for those benefits on becoming the child's guardian. Eligibility for federal foster care benefits may be preserved if the judge includes in the guardianship order the following language: "The placement and care of the child is the responsibility of the Department of Social Services or an agency contracting with the Department" (Adoption Assistance and Child Welfare Act of 1980, 42 U.S.C. sec. 670 et seq.).

*Case study.* James had lived with his grandmother almost since birth. She received AFDC payments for him and qualified for low-cost government housing. Paul Andrews, a railroad pensioner, lived with James and his grandmother but had never married the grandmother. When she died Andrews was not able to obtain AFDC to continue caring for James because he was not a relative. They received an eviction notice because Andrews's name was not on the lease. A children's lawyer called by the school social worker was able to help Andrews obtain guardianship so he could receive AFDC-FC, a special state program available for nonrelated guardians. With the guardianship established, Andrews also could qualify for the low-cost government housing.

*Case study.* Patricia had cared for her two grandchildren since the youngest was born addicted to cocaine. She received foster care benefits from the time the children were placed with her by the department of social services. When the parents failed to get off drugs and follow through on reunification efforts, DSS decided that the permanent plan for the children should be long-term placement. The grandmother told the court she would continue caring for her grandchildren but wanted a more stable plan. She did not want to have to terminate parental rights for the children's parents because of the emotional turmoil such an action would cause her family. She did want to become guardian of the children, but without the foster care funding and medicaid that came with it, she could not afford specialized services they needed. To maintain the family unit and provide structure, continuity, and services for the children, the judge awarded Patricia guardianship, but ordered that placement and care of the children remain the responsibility of DSS.

## Conclusion

Foster care and guardianship provide homes for children when their parents are unable or unwilling to be responsible parents. Entry into foster care can be limited to children who cannot live safely with their own parents despite an array of in-home support services. The observance of statutory time frames for reunification or termination of parental rights can best ensure that children are placed in a safe, permanent home as soon as possible. Supportive and visitation services to foster parents, foster children, and their parents during the foster care stay will help to keep children more emotionally stable and strengthen families. Guardianship rather than long-term foster care can provide the stability children need when they cannot return to their parents or be adopted.

# 11

# Termination of Parental Rights

*Sometimes I feel like a motherless child,*
*A long ways from home.*

Traditional

John Santosky II and Annie Santosky are the natural parents of Tina, John III, and Jed. After incidents reflecting parental neglect, the Ulster County Department of Social Services initiated a neglect proceeding and removed Tina, age 2, from her natural home. Removal proceedings were commenced in response to complaints by neighbors and reports from a local hospital that Tina had suffered injuries at her home including a fractured left femur, treated with a homemade splint; bruises on the upper arms, forehead, flank, and spine; and abrasions of the upper leg. About 10 months later John Santosky III, the second oldest child, was also removed from the parents' custody. John, who was less than 1 year old at the time, was admitted to the hospital suffering malnutrition, bruises on the eye and forehead, cuts on the foot, blisters on the hand, and multiple pen pricks on the back. On the day John was removed, Annie Santosky gave birth to a third child, Jed. When Jed was only 3 days old, social services transferred him to a foster home on the ground that immediate removal was necessary to avoid imminent danger to his life or health.

The family court concluded that the parents were unable to resume their parental responsibilities due to personality disorders. Under a court-approved plan, the Santoskys received training by a mother's aide, a nutritional aide, and a public health nurse, and counseling at a family planning clinic. In addition, the plan provided psychiatric treatment and vocational training for the father and counseling at a family service center for the mother. The parents rejected social services they found offensive or superfluous.

After the department of social services took custody of the three oldest children, the Santoskys had two other children, James and Jeremy. The state made no effort to remove these children. At the next hearing, the family court found that petitioners had "failed in any meaningful way to take advantage of the many social and rehabilitative services that have not only been made available to them but have been diligently urged upon them." In addition the court found that the "infrequent" visits "between the parents and their children were at best superficial and devoid of any real emotional content." The family court then terminated parental rights (*Santosky v. Kramer*, 1982, p. 782).

## Parental Responsibilities

Parenthood, whether biological or established through adoption, carries responsibilities for the child that at a minimum include the duties to provide food, clothing, medical care, and shelter. These general parental obligations are avenues for a parent to give emotional support and to express personal concern and love for a child. In cases in which parental rights are being questioned, there must be proof of fulfillment of parental responsibilities. Proceedings for termination of parental rights should begin only when it can be established that the parents have failed to function adequately as caregivers for the child, despite the efforts of the child protective services and other community agencies to strengthen the parent-child relationship. Some parents may realize that it is futile to contest the termination and voluntarily relinquish parental rights. This chapter focuses on those parents who contest the termination.

Terminating parental rights is the most critical decision a judge must make in any juvenile proceeding. The result is complete and permanent severance of all ties between the biological parents and their child. Not only do they lose custody forever, but they permanently forfeit the right to correspond, visit, or have any communication with the child. In some cases, the termination of parental rights resolves prolonged and highly disturbed family situations in which the prognosis is very negative for reunification of the children with their natural parents. Only after termination proceedings can these children be free for adoptive placement.

Permanency planning is a watchword of the social worker involved in providing protective services for children. Seeking termination of parental rights is the natural and legal outcome of parental failure to respond to the reunification and rehabilitative services the social worker offers. In most courts, termination of parental rights is a relatively rare occurrence (Bross, 1990).

Interest in permanency arises only when it is clear that the biological parent cannot or will not provide a minimally adequate family home for the child. In some instances this decision can be made immediately after an incident of abuse or neglect, as when a drug-using mother's parental rights were terminated 5 weeks after giving birth to the child (*In re Gentry*, 1985). Often the decision to terminate is not made until after months or even years of attempts to keep the family together. When children are moved in and out of foster care or from one foster home to another or separated not only from their parents but from brothers and sisters, a timely order for termination will allow a permanent home to be established for the children. Placement of children in adoptive homes soon after termination will reduce fiscal and administrative costs of foster care and the high costs of making reasonable efforts to reunite the family as a federal requirement for reimbursement of foster care expenditures.

## Legal Framework

Statutes for terminating parental rights are extremely detailed and demanding. Because parental rights have constitutional protection (see Chapter 1), the termination of these rights requires strict adherence to state laws and constitutional requirements.

### Jurisdiction

First, a petition is filed to initiate termination proceedings. Personal jurisdiction is established by the child's presence within the county in which the petition is filed. A summons with a copy of the petition is then served on the parents and, in some states, on a child of a specified minimum age.

### Grounds for Termination

A number of factors generally considered sufficient to terminate parental rights are abandonment, willful nonsupport, severe or chronic abuse or neglect, parental incapacity to care for the child, willfully leaving the child in foster care for an extended period of time without responding to the DCS reasonable efforts for reunification, and severe alcohol or drug dependency that endangers the child's welfare.

*Abandonment.* Abandonment is intentional conduct by a parent showing an intent to forgo all parental duties. Although failure of a parent to contribute to the support and maintenance of a minor child in another person's custody does not necessarily constitute abandonment, it can offer some evidence that the parent has relinquished a claim to the child.

> *Case study.* A mother had not communicated with her children for over a year when the termination petition was filed alleging abandonment. She indicated that she had wanted to contact the children, but her current husband had threatened her life if she tried. Because her lack of communication was not willful, her parental rights were not terminated.

*Willful nonsupport.* Neither the single factor of incarceration nor the inability to support one's children during incarceration will constitute abandonment. If the incarcerated parent has the ability to take gainful employment while imprisoned and fails to accept the opportunity to earn money that can be sent for child support, such failure can be used as evidence of a willful abandonment of parental responsibilities (see *In the Interest of Baby Girl W.,* 1987).

A finding that the parent has the ability to meet the financial needs of the child is essential before parental rights can be terminated on this ground. Ignorance of the legal obligation to support is not a sufficient excuse to obviate termination under this section. The parent's adherence to a court order to pay even a minimal amount of support while the child is in foster care will help the parent maintain parental rights.

*Severe or chronic physical abuse or neglect.* Termination of parental rights may occur without any efforts at reconciliation in the rare cases in which the abuse or neglect has been so severe that a return to the parent's care would put the child's life in jeopardy.

> *Case study.* The little boy was admitted to the hospital with severe bruises and abrasions on his neck and head after his father attempted to strangle him. The father was charged with criminal child abuse and was sent to prison. His parental rights were terminated with no efforts made for reunification.

*Parental mental or physical incapacity to care for the child.* Before the parental rights of a parent with developmental disabilities can be terminated legally, the record must show clear and convincing evidence that services designed to meet the needs of the developmentally disabled parent have been explored. The court must look at alternatives to terminating parental rights such as the services available through mental health clinics and specialized service centers for developmentally disabled persons (*In re Victoria M.*, 1989).

The incapacity of the parent is usually required to be of a long-standing nature. Factors such as emotional instability, mental illness, retardation, and physical disability are relevant only as they might limit the parent's ability to provide essential care for the child. Because the parent may not mean to harm the child, intent is not an element that must be proved. Inability to understand the special needs of the child and failure to meet those needs is sufficient grounds for terminating parental rights in those cases.

*Willfully leaving the child in foster care.* This ground for termination carries with it the mandate for child protective services to make reasonable efforts to provide supportive, reunification services to the family to prevent the necessity of parental rights termination. The agency must show that the required reasonable efforts have been made, or termination of parental rights on the grounds of leaving the children in foster care may be challenged. It may be the parents who fail to complete court-mandated treatment or to follow other orders of the court and thus prevent reunification with the result that their children are left in foster care.

> *Case study.* The children were removed from the parents because of the filthy, unsafe condition of the home. When the parents were offered extensive services by the CPS, they failed to follow through on almost all their opportunities. The court found that by failing to pursue those avenues, the parents were not making diligent efforts to strengthen the parental relationship in an effort to regain custody of the children. The fact that the parents moved to a neat, clean apartment just prior to the termination proceeding was not sufficient to establish that substantial progress had been made in light of the extreme filth and unsafe disorder in which the parents had lived for the previous 6 years (*In re Wilkerson*, 1982).

*Case study.* In an Iowa case, parents failed to complete a sexual abuse treatment program and refused, at first, to admit to charges of sexual abuse. Termination of parental rights was based partly on parental refusal to participate or admit (*Interest of H.R.K.,* 1988).

*Severe alcohol or drug dependency.* In most states the child must be endangered as a result of the drug or alcohol dependency before this ground can be used for terminating parental rights. Despite a high correlation found between substance abuse and child abuse or neglect, substance abuse should be seen as associated causally with but not as a single factor basis of child abuse. Findings that a parent abuses alcohol, without proof of adverse impact on the child, have been held an insufficient basis for termination of parental rights (*In re Adcock,* 1984). In New York, the Family Court Act allows for prima facie evidence of neglect in cases of extensive parental addiction to the extent that the parent who repeatedly uses a drug is in a state of "stupor, unconsciousness, intoxication, hallucination, disorientation, or incompetency or a substantial impairment of judgment, or a substantial manifestation of irrationality" (New York Family Court Act 1046(a)(iii) McKinney, 1983).

*Case study.* Katie was referred to the child protective services on numerous occasions due to her mother's substance abuse and inability to provide proper care for the child. The mother experienced a serious relapse from years of sobriety when her husband was killed in an accident during Katie's infancy. The mother entered a drug rehabilitation program and provided care for her daughter when she could. When after 3 years of attempting rehabilitation the mother was not yet able to provide care for the child, her parental rights were terminated.

## Representation at Court Adjudication

*The parent.* The parent has the right to receive notice of the hearing and to contest the petition by filing an answer or appearing in court. The parent has neither the right to trial by jury nor the constitutional right to be represented by a court-appointed attorney (*Lassiter v. Department of Social Services,* 1981). Most states provide court-appointed attorneys for indigent parents even though it is not required constitutionally. To give continuity to the parent's legal representation, the attorney representing the parent in the abuse and neglect hearing also should represent the parent at the hearing to terminate parental rights. Some states do not make this provision.

*Department of social services.* Some counties use attorneys with specialized experience to represent the department of social services at termination hearings. Attorneys may be on contract with the county only to do termination hearings because they have much experience in appellate court and are aware of the need for a strong record that can withstand an appeal. When a different attorney is used for the termination, precious time is lost in becoming familiar with the record and with the pressing needs of the child. When attorneys represent the county at the initial abuse and neglect hearings as well as at the termination hearings, they are better able to make a strong record at the beginning of the court process instead of having to wait for the termination hearing to patch things together.

*The child.* Some states only recently have enacted legislation that guarantees the child the right to representation at the termination hearing (Massachusetts General Laws c. 210, sec. 3; see also Colorado Revised Statutes 19-1-106). Other states have guaranteed the child continuity of representation by the same attorney from the time of the initial emergency shelter hearing through termination of parental rights and adoption (North Carolina General Statutes 7A-659-660). In states where the right to representation is not statutory, the argument has been made that the court has the inherent authority to appoint an attorney for the purpose of fulfilling the court's obligation to protect the child's best interests (Monopoli, 1990). Ideally, the child should be represented by the original attorney, guardian ad litem, and/or CASA appointed at the emergency shelter hearing. Some states have followed the suggestion of the American Bar Association's Juvenile Justice Standards Committee that an attorney who represents a child capable of considered judgment on his or her own behalf must advocate what the child wishes, which may not be what is in the child's best interests (*ABA Standards,* 1979). Other states require the attorney as guardian ad litem to present to the court what is in the best interests of the child (see North Carolina General Statutes 7A-586).

Keeping the same attorney for each of the parties has the advantage of helping the court process move more quickly and efficiently. The child's attorney who begins representing the child when the initial abuse or neglect petition is filed can apply permanency planning principles from the beginning of the representation and promptly move for termination of parental rights when the parents refuse services or demonstrate within a reasonable time that services provided will not benefit them sufficiently to allow return of the children.

> *Case study.* The 16-year-old biological father had a history of delinquency, drug use, and emotional problems. He had never supported the toddler or provided care for him. The mother of the toddler voluntarily had relinquished parental rights when he was born in hopes that the baby would be adopted. After the baby had lived for 18 months in the same foster home, the department of social services filed a termination of parental rights petition against the teenage father and then, in a reversal, decided to consider placing the child with his teenage father while attempting to dismiss the termination petition. The district court judge exercised his inherent power to appoint a guardian ad litem who was able to proceed with the petition to terminate. The father was found to be an unfit parent, DSS was relieved of any further responsibility for the child, and the court placed custody with the foster parents (*In re Scearce*, 1986).

*The judge.* Many courts are trying to keep the same judge on the child's case from the abuse or neglect adjudication through the termination of parental rights to save court time and help children achieve permanency within a more reasonable time frame. Florida Appellate Judge Hugh Glickstein (1990), a strong advocate for children, encouraged other appellate judges to write opinions in support of the concept that the same trial judge hear all phases of the case from the determination of abuse or neglect to the termination.

### Standard of Proof at Adjudication

Absent a finding of parental unfitness, the child and parent "share a vital interest in preventing erroneous termination of their natural relationship." Because the private interest affected is commanding and risk of error substantial, the parent has the right to a clear and convincing burden of proof on the petitioners (*Santosky v. Kramer*, 1982, p. 790). In most states the burden of proof is higher than the standard used to remove the children for abuse or neglect, but it is not as high as the criminal standard of beyond a reasonable doubt. *Cynthia D. v. San Diego* (1993) is a California Supreme Court case that allows termination of parental rights despite requiring only a preponderance of the evidence standard of proof. The court said that it is only because of the precise and demanding substantive and procedural requirements that the petitioning agency must satisfy before it can propose termination that the lesser standard of preponderance of proof is adequate. Other states follow the *Santosky* standard. The facts in the Santosky case that introduced this chapter are compelling, but because the family court failed to state that its decision was based on clear and convincing evidence, the U.S. Supreme Court would not allow to stand the lower court decision to terminate parental rights (*Santosky v. Kramer*, 1982).

## Disposition

In the hearing on the merits of the termination case, the judge must hear evidence, find facts, and adjudicate the existence or nonexistence of any of the grounds for terminating parental rights that have been alleged in the petition. Once such a determination is made, the court can find that it is or is not in the best interests of the child to terminate parental rights.

The dispositional phase of the hearing can be based solely on the best interests of the child. After the adjudication is made, the interests of the parent and the child diverge. At that point the judge considers only what is in the best interests of the child. In some states a termination petition cannot be considered until an adoptive placement has been found for the child. In other states only after the termination is approved is there a search for an appropriate adoptive placement.

## Appeal

Any party to a termination proceeding can appeal a termination decision. Pending the appeal the child may remain in foster care. In some jurisdictions the child is placed in an "at-risk" adoptive placement to avoid attachment and bonding problems inherent in temporary foster placements. Appeals can be dragged out for years until a final appellate court decision is made. The practice of leaving the child in foster care with the knowledge that an adoptive placement will be necessary if the parents' appeal is unsuccessful, as is common, may protect the emotions of the prospective adoptive parents but seriously can endanger the child's emotional well-being. In many cases the foster parent who has been caring for the child seeks adoption, a less emotionally complex solution.

> *Case study.* A father appeals termination of his parental rights to a child who has been in foster care since birth. By the time the case reaches the state supreme court, the child is 7 years old and still lives with the foster parents who want to adopt him. Evidence shows that the agency did not attempt to place the baby in the care of the father at any time. The court decides the termination decision was not supported by evidence of parental fault. The child, of course, is dependent psychologically on the foster parents. Should the termination be upheld? If the legal criteria for removing a child from the parent were increased to the level required for terminating parental rights, perhaps children would not be kept floundering in foster care for a prolonged period while waiting for sufficient grounds to be established for termination.

### Review

Some children remain in foster care even after parental rights have been terminated. In 1980, according to New York State Child Welfare, 75% of foster children free for adoption in New York City had remained in foster care for over 1 year. To encourage a change in this policy, the Adoption Assistance and Child Welfare Act of 1980 requires annual review hearings of children who remain in foster care. Despite this federal requirement, only 33% of children in Michigan eligible for adoption in 1992 were adopted within 3 years after termination of parental rights (Binsfield Commission on Adoption, 1992). Some states require hearings every 6 months after parental rights are terminated in an effort to keep pressure on the DSS to find an adoptive home for the child.

## Role of the Mental Health Professional

The child involved in termination hearings will need strong advocacy and support from the mental health professional. Evaluations of the child, the parents, the foster parents, and interaction between the child and the biological and foster parents should give the professional significant information the court needs to hear. Advocacy means action. The professional who is working with the child should understand the importance of court testimony, especially in termination hearings. If the child would be shattered emotionally by the loss of the biological parent, the court needs to know. If the child's fragile emotional health was caused by abusive or neglectful acts of the parent, the court needs to hear that testimony to make a finding of unfitness. The child may have emotional needs that require a specific permanent plan for placement that the court should be informed about at the dispositional hearing. If the child has been so severely harmed by parent abuse or neglect that he or she is determined to sever the parental relationship and find a permanent place in another family, the court needs to be aware of the child's state of mind.

*Case study.* In 1992 a boy in Florida brought a termination of parental rights case against his mother in a highly publicized case of the boy who "divorced" his parents. The mother had neglected the boy for years, leaving him to drift in and out of foster care. When the boy finally found a family who wanted him, the boy located an attorney to file a petition against his mother so he could be freed from her permanently and be adopted into a family who had demonstrated that they really cared for him (*Kingsley v. Kingsley*, 1993).

*Case study.* A termination of parental rights was overturned by the appellate court in Michigan because the evidence against the parents was too weak to withstand the burden of clear and convincing evidence. The mother had failed to keep the child on an apnea monitor for the full time advised by the doctor and failed to give the child the proper doses of medicine. There was nothing in the record against the father for neglect or abuse. One psychologist gave the mother only two tests: the Rorschach and the Early Memory Test. On the basis of the results of these tests, he diagnosed the mother as having borderline personality disorder, concluding, "There is a real possibility of neglect of physical and emotional needs in this case." The lower court decision that was overturned had been based on the speculative opinions of three mental health professionals who testified that the parents' personality disorders could lead to child neglect (*In re Hulbert*, 1990, pp. 602, 37).

*Case study.* The testimony of two psychiatrists was pivotal in providing clear and convincing evidence that the mother's parental rights should be terminated on the basis of mental health evaluations of the children and the mother. The mother complied with the agency requests to enroll in parenting classes and counseling, to participate in supervised visitation, to enroll in college, and to secure a job. The mother had beaten one child with a belt and verbally abused the three oldest children, all of whom showed signs of severe emotional abuse. The youngest child was so traumatized by upcoming visits with his mother that he spread his feces on himself and his room. Both psychiatrists testified that the mental condition of the mother was unlikely to improve. The mother's parental rights were terminated.

## Conclusion

Parental rights are terminated when the parent has demonstrated little or no parental responsibility toward the child. When time frames are followed and careful records kept by all professionals serving the child and biological parents, the court can free a child for adoption without unnecessary delay. Termination gives the child the opportunity to become part of a permanent adoptive family, often with familiar foster parents or with relatives. Unaided DSS workers cannot carry the burden of testifying in court regarding termination. CASAs, guardians ad litem, psychologists, physicians, and other child-serving professionals share the responsibility for that crucial decision. In addition, the child depends on the teacher, doctor, social worker, counselor, coach, relative, and neighbor to inform the court about knowledge they have that may influence the decision. Unless this responsibility is taken seriously, adults who professionally serve these families will be doing a disservice to vulnerable children. In the absence of termination and a permanent adoptive family, the best alternative that can be hoped for is a stable foster care placement or guardianship.

# 12

# Adoption

*The king's daughter, who adopted him as her own son, said, "I pulled him out of the water, and so I name him Moses."*

Exodus 2:10

The recorded history of adoption dates to Moses in biblical times. Because the English gave so much importance to property inheritance through bloodlines, adoption did not become a part of English common law. In the United States, the adoption statute of Massachusetts, enacted in 1851, became a model for the other states (Kawashima, 1982). The Massachusetts law affirmed that the state has an obligation to protect biological parents from an uninformed and coerced decision to relinquish and also the duty to protect adoptive parents from the consequences of an uninformed and hasty decision to take a child (Cole, 1983). W.E.B. DuBois described the early history of the adoption of African American children as a natural response to charitable appeals. African Americans had few orphan asylums, and a large number of children were adopted by families who could ill afford it (DuBois, 1898).

Following World War II, the management of adoptions by physicians and attorneys shifted to the official jurisdiction of social welfare agencies. More recently, infant adoptions once again began to originate more frequently with members of the legal and medical professions. Many states enacted statutes limiting or forbidding adoption activity by persons other than licensed adoption agencies, thus hoping to control the black market in babies whereby biological parents or brokers sold them for profit.

Psychological theories influenced adoption practices into the 1960s by encouraging parents to adopt infants at as young an age as possible, when, presumably, they would be easy to mold. Starting in the late 1960s, with increasing social acceptance of single and unwed parenthood and the increase in abortions, fewer and fewer infants became available for adoption. As a result of the ensuing intense competition among applicants for infants and years-long waiting periods, older children began to attract more serious consideration as candidates for adoption by both adoption agencies and adoptive parents. The emphasis in matching children to their adoptive parents changed dramatically. Instead of focusing on finding a perfect blue-eyed blond child for the blue-eyed blond parents, adoption workers were encouraged to seek the best possible home for the child.

Of the children living in foster care, less than 8% are adopted each year. The National Commission on Children (1991) encouraged child welfare agencies to terminate parental rights more quickly to facilitate adoption of infants abandoned at birth and other young children who cannot be returned safely to their biological parents. The commission encouraged agencies to be sensitive to the emotional needs of children, biological parents, and adoptive parents. The commission recommended that counseling before and after birth for the biological parents and before and after adoption for the adopting parent should be supplemented with health and social services especially for the medically fragile infant.

Stressing the need to fund in-home services to prevent the necessity of out-of-home placement and adoption, child welfare authorities Billingsley and Giovannoni (1972) emphasized the need to change the primary aim of adoption from providing a baby for a couple wanting to adopt to providing homes and services to children. In this way the natural parents become a valuable resource, and the multidisciplinary in-home services become vital for natural parents and their children.

The Child Welfare League of America supports this emphasis on providing services to the natural parents but establishes principles for adoption when it is necessary:

___ All children, regardless of age, sex, race, or physical, intellectual, or emotional status, are entitled to a continuous, caring environment.
___ For most children, the biological family in its broadest definition provides the best environment.
___ When a child's birth family is not willing or able to nurture him or her, the child is entitled to timely placement with a family.

___ For most children, adoption provides a new family better than any other type of substitute parenting.

___ Adoption is and will continue to be the most cost-effective method of substitute parenting that can be made available as a child welfare service.

___ Adoption is a means of finding homes for children and not finding children for families. The emphasis is on the child's needs. (Cole, 1983, p. 454)

The department of social services controls the process of adoption for children in their custody after a termination of parental rights. In many communities the service of adoption is under contract with private agencies. Some states regulate private placement adoptions, requiring all direct placements by the biological parent into a private home to be approved by the public adoption agency. However, in the case of stepparent adoptions, many persons who decide to adopt their stepchildren are subject to little if any investigation or postplacement monitoring by the local child services agency. In some states family members of the children, especially if they have been providing care all along, are the first to be considered as the adoptive parents. Transracial adoptions, especially those involving children from Third World countries, add cross-cultural factors to consider in determining whether the adoption is in the best interests of the child.

## The Legal Framework

Adoption is the legal procedure that establishes a new parent-child relationship. Adoptive parents assume all the rights and responsibilities of natural parents. The child's interests are advanced by relieving the child of the often prolonged uncertainty as to where and with whom the child permanently belongs. Stepparent adoptions and private placement adoption, including transnational adoptions, will not be discussed further. The primary focus of this chapter is adoption of the child whose parental rights have been terminated because of abuse, neglect, or abandonment.

In looking at the future for many children in the custody of the state whose parents have had their parental rights terminated, one court stated:

It is an unfortunate truth that not all children who are "freed" from their legal relationship with their parents, find the stable and permanent situation that is desired even though this is the implicit promise made by the state when it seeks to terminate the parent-child relationship. Multiple placements and impermanent situations sometimes mark the state's guardianship of a child. This unstable situation is frequently detrimental to a child. Indeed, the detriment may be greater than keeping the parent-child relationship intact since the child's psychological and emotional bond to the parent may have been broken with nothing substituted in its place. (*In re Angelia P.*, 1981, [dissent] pp. 929, 210)

The legal process ensures that the social process for adoption protects the child from assignment to inappropriate adoptive parents. Legally, the child must be free of biological ties; the adoption is difficult to rescind once it is decreed. Most states require legal due process, comprehensive family studies, and usually the safeguard of a 6- to 12-month period of supervision between the filing of the petition and the court order that makes the adoption final. This gives the court time to receive progress reports on the newly constituted family as well as the opportunity to intervene, if necessary, while the child is in a transitional stage with the new family.

## Consents Required

Infant placement involves the mother's consent and either the father's consent or termination of his parental rights. In many states, older children must give their own consent to adoption.

*Father.* Most states require the father's consent if he was married to the mother at the time of conception or at any time after, if the minor was his child by adoption, or if he otherwise legitimized the child under state law. A state statute that eliminated the need of consent by the natural father if notice of paternity was not filed within 5 days of the birth of the child was found to be constitutional (*Shoecraft v. Catholic Social Services Bureau, Inc.*, 1986).

*Mother.* Problems arise when the mother alleges fraud by the adoption agency or alleges personal incompetence to consent. The mental health professional may be asked to provide expert testimony for the court.

> *Case study.* The biological mother was mentally retarded. Adoption proceedings were brought alleging that the consent of the mother was not necessary

because she was incompetent to give her consent. The court ruled that the mental retardation did not of itself render her unfit and thereby allow the child to be adopted without her consent but that retardation could be considered along with other evidence on her fitness (*Helvey v. Rednour*, 1980).

*Case study.* In the case of another mother, expert testimony regarding her psychological disorders was admissible even though the opinions were based on documents not admitted into evidence. The court decided that psychologists are allowed to present opinions based on hearsay if members of the profession generally and reasonably rely on such facts in reaching their professional conclusions (*Scott v. Prince George's County Department of Social Services*, 1988).

*Child.* Most states have a requirement for the adoptive child to consent to the adoption if the child has reached a certain age, usually 10 to 14 years. Although younger children may express their preference to the court, the court is not required to follow it.

## Factors to Consider for Placement

*Foster parent preference.* Foster parents are ideal adoptive parents in many cases and are given preference by law in some states. Before foster children can be removed from foster care for placement elsewhere, a hearing for foster parents who contest such placement is indicated (see *Smith v. Organization of Foster Families for Equality and Reform*, 1977). Foster parents who sign agency agreements that bar them from adopting the child have received mixed support in the courts when they later attempt to adopt the child against agency policy (*Knight v. Deavers*, 1976; *Re Adoption of S.C.P.*, 1987).

*Race.* The Supreme Court has ruled that the effects of racial prejudice cannot justify placement of a child (*Palmore v. Sidoti*, 1984). The difficulties inherent in interracial adoption justify consideration of race as a relevant factor but only as one factor among many and not as the sole factor to reject adoption (*Drummond v. Fulton County Department of Family and Children's Services*, 1977). Some professionals believe that African American children need to be raised in African American homes to develop the identity and values of their ethnic/racial culture (Bowen, 1988). Of the 1,500 children in the National Adoption Center register,

67% are Black or Black/White, although the majority of parents wanting to adopt are White ("Barriers to Same Race Placement," 1991). One legal scholar (McCormick, 1990) who questioned the constitutionality of allowing race to be used as a factor suggested that a new standard be used to determine whether to allow a transracial adoption. She asked whether the outcome would differ if race were not a factor. She suggested that if the court does recognize race as a key determining factor, the court should have specific proof based on circumstances in the family life or community that the adoption by a racially different parent will have a negative effect on this specific child. McCormick suggested that if, at the outset, the court determines that the child will suffer a negative impact from the racial difference, the adoptive family must then have the opportunity to show the court that they are ready and willing to support the child's heritage.

*Religion.*  Religion may be a factor to consider in placement especially when the birth parent requests that the child be brought up in a specific type of religious home (*Wilder v. Bernstein,* 1988).

*Parental choice.*  Choice of the natural parent is another factor that may be considered. One state encourages the biological parent to choose the adoptive parent from three selected sets of parents. This enlightened process gives the biological mother a sense of power and control over her own and the baby's life. It reassures her of the important role she is playing in the child's future. The adoptive parents feel comforted and special because the mother chose them. The adopted child benefits by knowing that the biological mother did not reject him or her but participated in a life plan for the child (Fish & Speirs, 1990). In a recent development, parental choice is being used by mothers who know they face death from an active case of AIDS.

> *Case study.*  Tanya was one of hundreds of mothers in that terminal situation. Worried that her two little girls would be placed in foster care and perhaps separated, Tanya was determined to find parents to adopt them before she died. Tanya, like many mothers with AIDS, lacked family support, partly because of the stigma attached to the disease. Before she died Tanya was able to find an adoptive family she could trust to give her children a better life. Her choice helped the children make the transition from their mother to their new parents.

Because the legal process might take several months, most infants relinquished at birth for adoption are placed in "legal-risk" adoptive homes, often licensed as foster care homes. An infant with no disability usually can be placed immediately. Although adoptive placements are not as readily available for infants who are victims of substance abuse, nearly 25% of children adopted in California in 1988-1989 were drug-exposed children (Barth, 1991). Placement with relatives is ideal for these infants if the home provides a healthy environment and is free of substance abuse. Whether the adoptive parents are related or unknown to the infant, special parent training and support services will be needed by the new parents to help them cope effectively with the physical and emotional difficulties these children may develop. Long-term foster care is another alternative that is preferable to making the babies grow up as "boarder babies" in institutional care (National Commission on Children, 1991).

## Adoption Assistance
## and Child Welfare Act of 1980

Some prospective adoptive parents, whether relatives, foster parents, or strangers to the child, may need a special subsidy to enable them to provide an adequate home, especially for a child with special needs. Foster parents who want to adopt may experience economic hardship if they have to lose both the foster care funds and the federal health insurance they were receiving. To encourage adoption by foster parents or others, the state and federal governments provide monthly supplements and medicaid coverage for children with special needs. Although the supplement may be less than the former foster care payment, the health coverage is helpful especially for children with preexisting disabilities who might not qualify for coverage under their new parents' insurance. States may require the subsidy agreement to be approved in writing before adoption (LeMay, 1989).

The Adoption Assistance and Child Welfare Act of 1980 classifies a child as having "special needs" if "there exists with respect to the child a specific factor or condition (such as his ethnic background, age, or membership in a minority or sibling group, or the presence of factors such as medical conditions or physical, mental, or emotional handicaps) because of which it is reasonable to conclude that such a child cannot be placed with adoptive parents without providing assistance" (42 U.S.C.A. sec. 673[c][2]). Children who qualify for the adoption subsidy are entitled to medicaid and Title XX services in the state where they reside, regardless of which state entered into the adoption assistance agreement on their behalf (42 U.S.C.A. sec. 673[b]).

The mental health professional may be called on to evaluate children in foster care to see if they qualify as special needs children. Sometimes, an evaluation may be necessary after the adoptive placement to let the court know of a child's previously undocumented needs.

> *Case study.* A mother adopted a special needs child and received the state and federal adoption subsidy. When the mother became ill and lost her job, she was able to obtain Social Security disability benefits for the child because her own inability to work created a loss of income for the family's support. The state agency terminated her adoption subsidy payment without considering the child's special needs. The court reversed this administrative decision even though the child's disability benefits were in excess of state foster care payments. The court held that termination of adoption subsidy payments must be based on a decision that the actual need for the subsidy no longer exists, the child is ineligible for receiving subsidy payments, or the adoptive parents concur in the termination (*J. P. v. Missouri Department of Social Services,* 1988).

The professional offering preplacement adoption services to the adoptive parents must be fully informative regarding the mental and physical condition of the child being placed. Although adoption annulments are frowned on by statute and by court decision, adoptive parents can sue an agency for monetary damages when that agency knowingly has deceived the parents about the condition of the child.

> *Case study.* An adoption agency deliberately misrepresented information to adoptive parents by describing the 17-month-old boy as perfectly healthy. The agency knew, in fact, that he was the child of a mental patient and that prior to adoption a series of psychological assessments indicated that he was functioning at a low level for his age. Future assessments had been recommended for possible evidence of additional lags in social and emotional development. After the boy developed serious medical and emotional problems that required costly treatment, the adoptive parents sued the adoption agency and were awarded $125,000 (*Burr v. Board of County Commissioners,* 1986).

## Initiating the Process

The adoption agency gives preferential consideration to relatives or foster parents to give the child the continuity of relationships so important in building emotional security. If neither of these alternatives is available, the agency seeks other parents for the child. Recruiting parents requires diligent work, especially for the growing number of special needs children waiting for adoption. Videos of the child, life history books, and statewide adoption registers briefly describe each child in custody who is waiting for placement. In some areas the public library can provide the register to anyone in the community interested in adopting a child. Most persons who want to adopt will apply and be screened at the local adoption agency. In an ideal situation the child will be able to have visits with the prospective parents to help those involved decide whether the placement is suitable. If so, the new permanent home should be available as soon as the child's parental rights are terminated.

Many children are hard to place because of such factors as age; race; sibling group membership; medical, physical, or mental handicap; developmental disability; emotional instability; genetic history; or a history of more than one foster care placement. Some states designate by statute which factors classify a child as "hard-to-place." With that classification, the child can qualify for special adoption assistance funds. It is estimated that placement of 40,700 foster children with special needs into adoptive homes between 1993 and 1997 will save state and federal governments $1.6 billion in administrative costs alone (Westat, Inc., 1993).

## The Mental Health Professional's Role

The mental health professional may be required to provide a report to the court that includes the developmental, emotional, psychological, and educational needs of each child being freed for adoption. The longer the child has remained in foster care and the more moves the child has had from one foster home to another, the more critical are the problems the psychologist is likely to find. A majority of foster children who remained in care in California were relocated a minimum of three times after attempts to reunify with the natural family had failed (Watahara

& Lobdell, 1990). As more infants are entering foster care, many are experiencing multiple placements. In Michigan, newborns in foster care have a 61% chance of finding permanent families within 4 years after their first substitute care placements. They are less likely than any other age group to find permanent families (Abbey & Schwartz, 1992). Each foster care move shatters an attachment to a parent figure. Numerous moves lead to chronic emotional detachment that will have to be resolved before the child truly can feel a part of the adoptive family. A few children will suffer recurrent separation expectation long after they are adopted.

Emotional instability can result also from the trauma the child experienced in the original home. Sorting out emotions resulting from affection for the natural parent and from the breach of trust caused by the abuse or neglect, and the child's confusion and uncertainty about being placed with another family, even though permanent, is a formidable task. The professional will need to evaluate whether the child seems emotionally able to live as part of any family constellation. Can the child establish relationships, or does the child show evidence of severe emotional, mental, or behavioral problems that are likely to create insurmountable barriers to family cohesiveness over a prolonged period? The child also should have the capacity to disengage from his own parents enough to accept parenting from other persons and to form an attachment to those parents (Williams, 1985).

In a study of 800 families who adopted special needs children, a substantial majority of families reported that individual and family therapy was somewhat helpful. Parent support groups and contact with other special needs families were rated as very helpful. Parents reported that they trusted and got along well with their child, felt close, communicated well, and felt respected by their child. Nearly 75% of the families rated the adoption as having had a positive effect on their family (National Resource Center on Family Based Services, 1990).

## Preventing Disruptions

Many children will need to begin therapy to prepare for the move from foster care into an adoptive home. Continuing therapy with the same professional after placement is ideal for the troubled child but often difficult because children can be moved for placement to distant counties or states. The high rate of disrupted adoptions makes a strong case for continuing therapy. *Disruption* is a term used to describe the interruption of an adoptive placement before the court enters its final order of adoption. Typically, an early sense of discomfort within the family not only fails to resolve but intensifies. The escalating conflict can reach crisis proportions before the adoptive parents seek professional help. Ongoing support services to the family during the first year of the adoptive placement help to reduce the possibility of a disruption. A family counselor, teacher, psychiatrist, psychologist, or even a close friend with nonjudgmental, positive attitudes can bolster family strengths by helping to identify and to minimize the sources of conflict.

In one study the adoptive father was found to have a pivotal role in preventing disruption. If he is involved actively in parenting and is able to nurture and support the mother in her role, placements are more likely to be sustained. Finding men committed to that challenging role and providing support to them is crucial for successful permanent placements (Westhaus & Cohen, 1990).

### Long-Term Mental Health Considerations

On reaching adolescence adopted children may face the double burden of working through the identity issues common to all teenagers and resolving their feelings about being separated from their family of origin. Children with a history of multiple placements may not be able to work successfully through the grief that results from a succession of losses. The mental health professional will need to make sure the adoptive parent has dealt with separation and attachment issues openly and sensitively with the child. Such ongoing family stresses as marital instability, midlife crisis, and economic or employment problems can intensify the emotional stress the adopted adolescent already is experiencing. It is easy to deny the importance of these environmental stressors when a parent attempts to focus on a child's alleged mental illness as the primary target for professional attention (Donley & Blechner, 1986).

## Confidentiality of Adoption Records

The question of open adoption records has received much attention in the past decade. For children placed when older, the rationale is weak for confidentiality of adoption records because they usually know the identity of their parents and some members of their extended families. Infants who are placed may need to have genetic medical information that only their natural parents can supply. The Indian Child Welfare Act of 1978 is the only federal legislation controlling adoption records. It allows information to be accessed through tribal councils.

Statewide adoption registries can be used to facilitate contact between adoption participants. Initial contact and reunions can be emotionally draining for all participants, but for many the reward of finding family is worth the experience (Gonyo & Watson, 1988). Others believe that the move toward open adoption records can do more harm than good (Byrd, 1988). In California, the Adoption Information Act of 1983 ensures that complete medical background information is transmitted to the adopting parents and that it is also available to the adoptee when reaching 21 years of age. The act also establishes a procedure whereby birth parents and adult adoptees may discover the identity and location of the other while providing safeguards respecting the right of privacy of all persons (*Michael J. v. Los Angeles County Department of Adoptions*, 1988).

## Guardianship

Alternate legal placements during the age of minority are guardianship and long-term foster care. Legal guardianship provides adult protection to the child who is deprived of the natural guardianship of his parents. Unlike adoption, guardianship does not require termination of parental rights. Parents retain the right to visit, the right to consent to adoption, and the responsibility to provide support. If termination has occurred and the agency has not been able to place the child in an adoptive home, guardianship is a good alternative (Williams, 1985). Although guardianship has been used rarely as an outright placement, its use is growing in acceptance.

## Conclusion

Although statutory time frames are defined clearly for reunification with parents, too many children are left dangling in foster care while reunification efforts continue to meet with failure. These children need a hopeful new beginning before the instability of their young lives robs them of long-range emotional stability. Successful adoption, as early as possible, can give these children the welcoming permanent home they need.

# IV

## Other Areas of
## Legal Involvement for Children

# 13

# Education and Children With Disabilities

*Educating a young person is like writing on a new page.*
"Ethics of the Fathers,"
*The Talmud* 4:25

The San Francisco Unified School District suspended an emotionally disturbed child from school indefinitely and proposed to expel him for violent and disruptive conduct related to his disabilities. John Doe assaulted another student at a school for children with disabilities. One of the goals of his individualized education program (IEP) was to improve his ability to relate to his peers and to cope with frustrating situations without resorting to aggressive acts. John's physical abnormalities, speech difficulties, and his poor grooming habits had made him the target of teasing and ridicule from the beginning of the first grade. When a fellow student taunted him, John choked the student and kicked out a school window while being escorted to the principal's office. He was suspended for 5 days and recommended for expulsion. Until the expulsion recommendation could be acted on by the school board, the principal extended the suspension indefinitely. Does a child with disabilities have any educational rights even when his behavior is threatening?

## U.S. Supreme Court Decisions on Education

The right of every child to have an appropriate education, even children earlier excluded, has evolved gradually through a number of landmark decisions by the U.S. Supreme Court. In *Meyer v. Nebraska* (1923) the court ruled that a state statute cannot prohibit teaching a foreign language in school. In *Pierce v. Society of Sisters* (1925) the court declared unconstitutional an Oregon statute that required children to attend a public school. In *Brown v. Board of Education* (1954) the Supreme Court declared that schools that separated children on the basis of race were inherently unequal and therefore unconstitutional. *Tinker v. Des Moines Independent Community School District* (1969) declared unconstitutional the school board's ban on black arm bands worn to protest the Vietnam War. *Wisconsin v. Yoder* (1972) affirmed the authority of the state to compel school attendance; for Amish who had a strong religious history, attendance could not be required beyond the eighth grade. In *Plyer v. Doe* (1982) the court declared unconstitutional a Texas statute that withheld from school districts any funds for education of undocumented alien children. The court would not allow school districts to deny enrollment to alien children. More recently the U.S. Supreme Court declared that a child with disabilities is guaranteed an adequate education at the expense of the state (*Florence County v. Carter*, 1993).

## U.S. Education

Millions of Americans have used the public schools to lift themselves out of the mire of disadvantage and limited opportunity to attain personally fulfilling and economically secure lives. Yet at the end of this century, far too many children are leaving American schools uneducated and vocationally unprepared for the future. Many children do not enter school ready to learn, nor does every school offer a challenging curriculum, fine-tuned to help each child master needed skills. The nation shows how poorly it values education by failing to allocate sufficient funds to make a difference for many children.

The Economic Policy Institute found that the United States ties for 12th place among 16 industrialized nations for public and private spending on preschool, primary, and secondary education (Rasell & Mishel, 1989). If federal spending on education were restored to its pre-Reagan administration level, 2.5% rather than 2.0% of the budget would go to education (Hewlett, 1991). The spending gap between American public schools and schools in other industrialized nations is especially large for younger children. In the mid-1980s total government spending on public education at the federal, state, and local levels was $264 billion annually for children age 6 years and older, but $1 billion on those age

5 and younger. In this country, Head Start enrolls only one fourth of eligible children. France, Japan, and Italy show a much stronger commitment to early childhood education by providing nearly universal preschool education (Hewlett, 1991).

In 1988 there were 10.2 million children age 3 through 17, or 19.5%, who were reported by their parents to have one or more developmental, learning, or emotional disorder that could interfere with their education (Zill & Schoenborn, 1990). Historically, the notion had long persisted that persons with disabilities were incapable of becoming productive members of society and therefore would be permanently dependent on the charity of others. As a result of such thinking, only a limited right to public education existed for those children with physical or mental disabilities. Ohio was the first state to authorize special classes for children with disabilities; New York followed in 1917 (Ianacone, 1977). Then, early in the 1970s, broad-based changes began that redefined the educational rights of these young Americans who already cope with a variety of physical and mental challenges.

Court action on behalf of the disabled child brought about the passage of the Education for All Handicapped Children Act of 1975. On a national level, section 504 of the 1973 Rehabilitation Act and the more recent Americans With Disabilities Act of 1990 help children by barring discrimination against all persons with disabilities by requiring removal of architectural barriers in public buildings. More recent federal court action gives the severely disabled child who is income-eligible the right to receive a secure monthly income from the Social Security system without having to pass more restrictive tests for disability than those for adults (*Sullivan v. Zebley*, 1990).

## Individuals With
## Disabilities Education Act (IDEA)

All children with disabilities are entitled to receive special services funded by Public Law 94-142, the Individuals With Disabilities Education Act of 1975, formerly known as the Education of the Handicapped Act (EHA). This more comprehensive legislation was passed after several lawsuits were brought in federal court on behalf of disabled children who were being denied public education. The case of *Pennsylvania*

*Association for Retarded Children v. Commonwealth of Pennsylvania* (1972), brought on behalf of mentally retarded children, challenged the constitutionality of the Pennsylvania statute that excluded those children from public education and training. A consent decree enjoined the state from "deny[ing] to any mentally retarded child access to a free public program of education and training" (p. 288). This lawsuit helped establish in law the right to education for all children with disabilities.

The six major principles of IDEA are:

1. *Zero reject.* All children with disabilities must have available to them a free appropriate public education just as it is available to all other children.
2. *Fair evaluation.* No single test may be the sole basis for evaluation, classification as a special child, or placement. All procedures must be culturally and racially fair.
3. *Individualized and appropriate education.* Each special child must have an individualized education program developed and reviewed or revised yearly at a meeting with the parents, the child's teacher, and representative of the educational agency.
4. *Least restrictive placement.* Children with disabilities should be educated in the mainstream with children who do not have disabilities, as much as is appropriate. Placement in a separate program occurs only when the handicap is such that the special child cannot be educated satisfactorily in a regular class even with the use of related services and supplemental aids. The placement is decided annually.
5. *Due process.* Due process procedures are available to parents and schools when there is disagreement regarding the evaluation, placement, or provision of a free appropriate public education. Prior written notice must be given to parents whenever the school proposes a change in the child's IEP.
6. *Parental participation.* Parents must participate in making decisions before evaluation or placement and at yearly reviews. If the child reaches the age of 18 and still desires to be in school, that child also may participate in the IEP and may remain in public school until age 22.

Under IDEA the state must show that it has in effect a policy that ensures all children with disabilities the right to a free appropriate public education. A state receiving federal funds must provide services first to children with disabilities not receiving an education, then to children with the most severe disabilities who are receiving inadequate education, and finally to the maximum extent possible, an appropriate education for all children with disabilities.

## Children With Disabilities

The term *children with disabilities* means children with mental retardation; hearing impairments including deafness, speech, or language impairments; visual impairments including blindness; serious emotional disturbance; orthopedic impairments; autism; traumatic brain injury; other health impairments; or specific learning disabilities, who because of these disabilities need special education and related services.
IDEA further defines *children with specific learning disabilities* to include

those children who have a disorder in one or more of the basic psychological processes involved in understanding or in using language, spoken or written, which disorder may manifest itself in imperfect ability to listen, think, speak, read, write, spell, or do mathematical calculations. The disorders include such conditions as perceptual disabilities, brain injury, minimal brain dysfunction, dyslexia, and developmental aphasia. This category does not include children who have learning problems which result primarily from visual, hearing, or motor disabilities, mental retardation, emotional disturbance, or environmental, cultural, or economic disadvantage. (20 U.S.C.A. sec. 1401 [a][15])

## Related Services

The term *related services* means transportation and such developmental, corrective, and other supportive services including speech pathology and audiology, psychological services, physical and occupational therapy, recreation including therapeutic recreation, social work services, counseling services including rehabilitation counseling, and medical services. Such medical services shall be for diagnostic and evaluation purposes only as may be required to assist a child with a disability to benefit from special education and include the early identification and assessment of disabling conditions in children (IDEA, 1975, 20 U.S.C.A. sec. 1401[a][17]).

Services not directly related to actual instruction may be required if necessary for the child to attend a regular class. In one U.S. Supreme Court case a school was ordered to provide clean intermittent catheterization during the school day, whereas absent this service, a child would be prevented from participating in the regular public school program (*Irving Independent School District v. Tatro*, 1984).

## Preschoolers, Infants, and Toddlers

The term *children with disabilities* for children age 3 to 5 years may, at a state's discretion, include children experiencing developmental delays as defined by the state and as measured by appropriate diagnostic instruments and procedures in one or more of the following areas: physical, cognitive, communication, social or emotional, or adaptive development. Because of these reasons these children need special education and related services. More recently, IDEA has been expanded to include infants and toddlers with special needs. Federal funds were set aside to assist states to develop and implement statewide comprehensive, coordinated, and multidisciplinary interagency programs of early intervention services for infants and toddlers with disabilities and their families. This program, called Part H, is designed to meet the needs of infants or toddlers with a disability in any one or more of the following areas: physical, cognitive, and psychosocial development, language and speech, and self-help skills. Early identification of the infants and toddlers is required by states, together with screening and assessment services, health services necessary to enable the infant or toddler to benefit from the early intervention services, and social work services. Instead of the individualized education program for the child, the infant or toddler has a family service plan. Parents play a major role in designing the plan for their infant or toddler.

## Older Children

For those at the other end of the public education span, the right to attend public school gradually has been extended from the traditional age 18 to the end of the semester following the 22nd birthday for many pupils in special education programs who want to remain in school. In addition, the IEP can specify the right of the pupil to have the extended school year with educational activities continuing through a substantial portion of the usual school vacation periods.

## Individualized Education

IDEA requires a free and appropriate state-provided public education through personalized instruction with sufficient support services to permit the child with disabilities to benefit educationally from instruction provided at public expense. This program must meet the state's educational standards, must approximate grade levels used in the state's regular education, and must comport with the child's IEP. Each child with disabilities must receive a full and individual evaluation based on validated tests tailored to assess specific educational needs in all areas related to the suspected disability. The obvious purpose of this requirement is to assemble individualized information that actually is useful in designing a program for each child.

The IEP for each child must describe the present level of educational performance of the child, the annual goals including short-term objectives, specific educational services to be provided, the extent of the child's integration into the regular education program, the projected date for initiation and duration of service, the appropriate objective criteria and evaluation procedures, and an annual determination as to whether the objectives are being achieved. The parents are involved in developing and revising the IEP with school staff each year. The parents or any aggrieved party can appeal decisions regarding the IEP to a state administrative hearing, any state court, or the U.S. district court.

*Case study.* Amy was a kindergarten child with profound hearing deficits who successfully completed the school year while mainstreamed in a regular classroom. She was an excellent lip reader with a better than average performance in her class. Amy's parents wanted the school to provide a signing interpreter to help her understand everything said in the classroom and to have the same opportunity as her classmates to achieve her full potential. When a signing interpreter was not included in Amy's IEP, the parents appealed to court for a review. The U.S. Supreme Court found that the federal law contains no requirement to maximize the potential of handicapped children nor was the intent of Congress to achieve strict equality of opportunity or services. The federal law requires only that individual services be provided to benefit the child. The court decided that the IEP for each child should be formulated according to the requirements in the federal law and, if the child is in regular class, should be reasonably calculated to enable the child to achieve passing marks and advance to the next grade. How much is sufficient depends on the child's particular needs and abilities (*Board of Education v. Rowley*, 1982).

## Penalties for Inappropriate Placement

Parents may be entitled to reimbursement for private school tuition if public placement is deemed inappropriate for the particular child.

Specifically, the public school authority has three options in providing an education for children with disabilities. The school may provide an adequate education, place the student in an appropriate private setting, or reimburse the parents if they are forced to put the child into an appropriate private setting because the state has failed to provide an adequate education. Thus the school system no longer may place children in inappropriate placements with impunity because of the real out-of-pocket cost resulting from this (*Florence County v. Carter*, 1993; *Town of Burlington v. Department of Education*, 1985). An additional financial penalty to the school system may be the payment of attorney fees to parents who prevail in litigation or due process hearings under the Handicapped Children's Protection Act of 1986 (Public Law 99-372).

## Mainstreaming and the Least Restrictive Environment

IDEA requires that

to the maximum extent appropriate, children with disabilities . . . are educated with children who are not disabled, and that special classes, separate schooling, or other removal of children with disabilities from the regular educational environment occurs only when the nature or severity of the disability is such that education in regular classes with the use of supplementary aids and services cannot be achieved satisfactorily. (20 U.S.C. sec. 1412[5][b])

The regulations implementing this statute require school districts to maintain a continuum of alternative placements to meet the needs of handicapped children for special education and related services as close as possible to the child's home. Unless the IEP necessitates some other arrangement, the child must be educated in the school the child would attend if not handicapped (C.F.R. sec. 300.552[a][3]). The child with disabilities is to be integrated further whenever possible into nonacademic and extracurricular activities. Parental consent is required to participate in a more restrictive placement than a regular classroom. Alternative placements include special classes, special schools, home instruction, and instruction in hospitals and in institutions.

Under the least restrictive environment analysis, there are three basic questions: Does the student's IEP contain the programs and services that will meet the child's needs and will confer reasonable benefit?

Does the IEP provide for the maximum amount of integration, including the supportive services that will allow the child to succeed in that setting? On the basis of the IEP, including the supportive services, what is the least restrictive environment in which the program can be provided?

When a child with the addition of supportive services can receive an appropriate education in an integrated placement such as a regular school, that placement must be chosen over a more restrictive offer from the school district, even if the district's offer is educationally better (*Springdale School District No. 50 of Washington County v. Grace*, 1982).

## Dangerous Behavior: Excluding Emotionally Disabled From School

Suspensions from school often fall more heavily on the child with disabilities. Children with emotional disorders or mental retardation with accompanying behavior disorders are frequently unable to control their behavior. If these children are suspended for violating disciplinary rules and are punished because of their disability-related behavior, suspensions totaling more than 10 days per year are illegal. The determination of whether the child's disability caused the misbehavior should be made by child behavior specialists familiar with disabilities.

The U.S. Supreme Court gave meaning to the "stay-put" provision of IDEA (then known as EHA) in *Honig v. Doe* (1988). This chapter opened with a case of threatened expulsion of an emotionally disturbed child from his school on the grounds that he was dangerous. The U.S. Supreme Court ruled that because of the stay-put provision in the EHA, unless the parents and school agree otherwise, the child must be allowed to remain in the current educational placement whether or not he is dangerous. If his placement is substantially likely to result in injury to the child or others, the school can suspend up to 10 days and seek further relief from the court.

What happens to children with disabilities when they reach adolescence and early adulthood? Of the 40 million Americans age 15 to 24, one tenth are disabled. Of this group 55% complete high school, 62% are unemployed, 18.8% earn under $600 per month, and 11.5% live alone. Those without disabilities compare as follows: 76% complete high school, 77% are employed, 8.3% earn less than $600, and 7.7% live alone (William T. Grant Foundation, 1988).

## Equality and Discrimination

In 1990 a provision of the California Administrative Code required the educational program for children with disabilities to provide equal opportunity for each individual with exceptional needs to achieve his or her full potential (*Pink by Crider v. Mt. Diablo Unified School District,* 1990). In another case a federal court in California ruled that certain mental disability categories employed in California racially discriminated against children by relying on invalidated standardized IQ tests and limited evaluation criteria under the Education for All Handicapped Children Act. Because of the discriminatory effect, the court found a violation resulting from a disparate impact on African American children from the use of IQ tests without a showing of corresponding educational necessity (*Larry P. v. Riles,* 1979).

Greater efforts are needed to prevent an intensification of problems connected with mislabeling of minority children. A higher percentage of minority students continue to be classified for special education than are represented in the general school population. For example, poor African American children are 3.5 times more likely than their White counterparts to be identified by their teacher as mentally retarded. Although African American children represent 12% of elementary and secondary enrollments, they constitute 28% of total enrollments in special education (IDEA, 1975, 20 U.S.C.A. sec. 1409(B)(i-iv), 1990). The federal law now requires that testing and evaluation materials and procedures used for the purposes of evaluation and placement of children with disabilities be selected and administered so as not to be racially or culturally discriminatory (20 U.S.C.A. sec. 1412(5)(C), 1990).

## Other Federal Education Acts

Although the state and local community are responsible for educating the children living in the state, federal funds provide a needed supplement to education. The Soviet Union's launching of *Sputnik I* in 1957 led the U.S. federal government to respond to the educational needs of American children by passing the National Defense Education Act of 1958, which expanded federal funding for teaching science, math, and languages. It also diverted attention from educating the least advantaged students to educating the most promising.

Designed to provide supplemental educational assistance to low-achieving students in schools and districts with high concentrations of poverty, Chapter 1, formerly known as Title I of the Elementary and Secondary Education Act of 1965 (ESEA), funds local school districts for "imaginative new approaches for meeting educational needs of poor children." Allocated to states and school districts roughly on the basis of a poverty count, Chapter 1 funds are to be layered on top of state and local funds to provide students with catch-up services. Although 8 million children theoretically are eligible to receive compensatory education under Chapter 1, fewer than 5 million children are involved (Hewlett, 1991). The National Commission on Excellence in Education (1983) reported that with only one half of all children eligible under ESEA then being served, the school reform movement had had no significant impact on the 30% of students who were low-income minority children.

## Negative Outcome Factors

Other factors affect educational and social outcomes for children. In *A Nation at Risk*, the National Commission on Excellence in Education (1983) found that the most reliable predictors of early childbearing, delinquency, and dropping out were school failure and poor reading performance as early as third grade, truancy, poor achievement and misbehavior in elementary school, and failure to master skills in school. Predisposing factors for negative outcomes included aggressive behaviors; lack of preparation or support for school in the home; and teacher burnout caused by large classes, inadequate assistance from aides, and lack of training in the special needs of disadvantaged children. Another study found that the disadvantaged child will succeed in the first 3 years of school if the teacher is enthusiastic, warm, positively motivating, and cognitively stimulating. By the fourth grade, the child becomes aware of the discrepant values between home and school and the low social and economic status of the home. This leads to a greater divergence in school excellence by class, race, and income level (National Commission on Excellence in Education, 1983). By high school, the dropout rate for minority children in large cities is more than 50% (IDEA, 1975, 20 U.S.C.A. sec. 1409, (B)(vi), 1991).

*Case study.* A pilot program to help prevent elementary school pupils from later becoming dropouts focuses on working with their families. A team consisting of a teacher, parent, probation officer, alcohol and drug counselor, and a mental health social worker meets regularly with at-risk students and family members to forestall academic or social problems. A collaborative work in preventing delinquency in children, the project aims to reconstruct and reconnect the whole family. The program will target initially children age 5 to 9 who are referred by their teachers because they are not performing well in class, need constant discipline, or show signs of neglect and depression. The students and family members meet with the team once a week for 8 weeks, then attend monthly support meetings for 2 years. The principal of the school supports the pilot program because it meets the social needs of students and treats the whole child (Valencia, 1993).

A significant percentage of children who become juvenile delinquents have learning disabilities that often go unidentified (Barnett & Barnett, 1980). The state of Washington found that 76% of the juvenile delinquent population were classified as *seriously emotionally disturbed* (University of Washington, 1988). If these children were identified properly early in their education, under *Honig v. Doe* (1988) schools would be required to provide them with the individualized education each child needs rather than resorting to expulsion when their disabilities result in behaviors that get them into serious trouble.

## Effective Schools

A study commissioned by the William T. Grant Foundation (1988) found that effective schools have several characteristics in common. There is an emphasis on academics. Classroom management maximizes academic learning time and has routines that discourage disorder and disruptions. The school environment is safe, orderly, and disciplined but not rigid. Exercising vigorous instructional leadership, the principal makes clear, consistent, and fair decisions, has a vision of what a good school is, and systematically strives to bring that vision to life. The principal visibly and actively supports a climate of learning and achievement. The teachers have high expectations that all their students can and will learn. Collegiality among teachers supports student achievement. The school has regular and frequent review of student progress and modifies instructional practices in light of information regarding student progress. Public ceremonies are held to honor student achievement. Principals, teachers, students, and parents agree on the goals, methods, and content of schooling and share the belief that each student is capable of making academic progress. They recognize the importance of a coherent curriculum, of promoting a sense of school tradition and pride, and of protecting school time for learning.

## Gifted Children

Federal law does not mandate special education of gifted and talented children, although the Elementary and Secondary Education Amendments of 1969 made some provisions related to gifted and talented children. States were asked to develop their own model program for gifted students, and funds from ESEA were used for that purpose. In 1970 additional federal funds became available for training teachers in gifted education. In 1978 the Gifted and Talented Children Act passed and extended the gifted education provisions contained in ESEA, but the act was repealed by President Reagan in 1981.

During the 1980s local, state, and national supporters of gifted education sought the restoration of a federally funded program. The Jacob Javits Gifted and Talented Students Education Act of 1988 provided federal demonstration and research funds but did not mandate special services. The act emphasized identifying and providing services for gifted and talented children who are disadvantaged and for those who have limited English proficiency.

*Gifted and talented defined.* The Jacob Javits Act of 1988 defines gifted and talented students as children and youth who "give evidence of high performance capability in areas such as intellectual, creative, artistic, or leadership capacity, or in specific academic fields, and who require services or activities not ordinarily provided by the school in order to fully develop such capabilities" (sec. 4103[1]).

All 50 states now recognize the need for gifted and talented education through statutes, board of education policies, or state guidelines. Some states require services for gifted pupils through legislation or action of the state board of education. Mediation and due process hearings resolve most disputes between parents and schools at the local, informal level without recourse to state or federal courts (Karnes & Marquardt, 1991).

## Testing Children
## for Qualification as Disabled or Gifted

When children are classified as children with disabilities or as gifted and talented, the use of appropriate tests and testing procedures is especially important. A qualified professional should administer individual intelligence tests that are normed on a representative group of average children at the same age level. Tests should not be out of date or racially or culturally biased. A full battery of tests is needed to measure the child's abilities and disabilities to lay the foundation for a suitable plan to meet the child's needs.

The professional who evaluates the child should meet with the child, review the child's records and the IEP, and consider what the parent proposes if called on to provide expert testimony at administrative hearings or in state or federal court. The professional should be well versed on the statutory terms used that will qualify or disqualify the child. When the expert witness appears in court, statements made must be absolute and stated in clear language devoid of educational or psychological jargon (Bogin & Goodman, 1985).

## Multidisciplinary On-Site School Services

In 1991 the National Commission on Children recommended that all schools and communities reevaluate the services that they currently offer and design creative, multidisciplinary initiatives to help children with serious and multiple needs reach their academic potential. Adequate funding and flexibility are vital factors in providing quality education. School choice, a comprehensive and interactive curriculum tailored to students' needs, and increased teacher autonomy have helped schools excel in New York City's Harlem Community District No. 4. An alternate program for students who cannot progress in regular schools has been developed in Minnesota with such services as learning centers that provide child care, tutoring, and evening hours for working students and teen parents. In Kansas City the school system has contracted with two privately run alternative schools that offer small classes and intensive one-on-one instruction and counseling (National Commission on Children, 1991).

Other school systems are beginning to provide a range of services for children at the school site. Medical services including immunizations to wellness checkups, vision exams, and emergency care are being offered in elementary and secondary schools. Social services and mental health counseling also are being offered at school sites to give children and families more of the basic services at one site. Even legal services are being integrated into the school consortium to give children legal assistance for problems with guardianships, immigration, and government entitlements.

## Conclusion

Federal, state, and local funding of education must be balanced among the children with disabilities, average children, and those who are gifted and talented. Funding must be available for the most vulnerable: infants, toddlers, and preschoolers with disabilities. Community agencies that coordinate service delivery at the school site will ensure that children with special education needs receive not only quality education but also health, developmental, emotional, rehabilitation, and social services necessary for the well-being of the whole child.

# 14

## Mental Health Issues

*Canst thou not minister to a mind diseased?*
William Shakespeare,
*Macbeth,* ca. 1606

When he was 6 years old, Jimmy was admitted to Central State Regional Hospital. Prior to admission, he had received outpatient treatment at the hospital for over 2 months. His mother then requested the hospital to admit him for an indefinite period. The admitting physician interviewed Jimmy and his parents. He learned that the boy's natural parents had divorced and his mother had remarried. He learned also that Jimmy had been expelled from school because he was "uncontrollable." He accepted the parents' statement that the boy had been extremely aggressive and diagnosed the child as having a "hyperkinetic reaction of childhood."

Jimmy's mother and stepfather agreed to participate in family therapy while their son was hospitalized. When Jimmy was permitted to go home for short trial stays, his behavior at home was erratic. After several months, the parents requested discontinuance of the therapy program. The child was returned to his mother and stepfather on a furlough basis to live at home but to attend school at the hospital. The parents found that they could not control Jimmy. Within 2 months, they requested his readmission to Central State and relinquished their parental rights to the county. Although several hospital employees recommended placement for Jimmy in a special foster home with "a warm, supported, truly involved couple" (*Parham v. J. R.,* 1979, p. 590), the department of family and children services was unable to place him in such a setting. A class action lawsuit was filed on his behalf asking the court to place him in a less restrictive setting more suitable to his needs. The child died before the case reached the U.S. Supreme Court. *Parham v. J. R.* will be discussed later in this chapter.

## Introduction

Committees have been formed, studies have been made, and laws have been passed. Yet throughout the United States today, millions of children with mental disorders remain unidentified as to their urgent need for evaluation and treatment services. And often when children are identified, treatment is unavailable or inappropriate, thus compounding the negative effects of poor mental health service delivery.

This chapter will examine the child population with special mental health needs, particularly the child placed in a restrictive treatment setting. A legal framework will be provided for mental health professionals with clients in need of a restrictive treatment setting. The more restrictive the setting, the more restrictive is the law in requiring custodians to safeguard the basic rights of youth in treatment. After presenting the incidence of mental disorders, the chapter will discuss possible factors that have had an impact on the growth of mental health facilities for adolescents in the past decade. The U.S. Supreme Court decision in *Parham v. J. R.* is the case study in this chapter used to focus on issues involving an individual's commitment to mental health facilities, appropriateness and length of commitment, rights of patients, less restrictive alternatives, and reasons for choosing other restrictive settings such as state training schools and detention centers.

Children and adolescents with mental disorders can receive voluntary evaluation and treatment services through such community agencies as schools, specialized foster or day care settings, and outpatient mental health treatment facilities. Parents are required to provide proper care for their children under the child abuse and neglect statutes discussed in previous chapters. Proper parental care includes the provision of evaluation and treatment for mental disorders. Poor children, especially, should be able to receive mental health screening, diagnosis, and treatment (Omnibus Budget Reconciliation Act of 1989). Youths no longer in parental custody because of delinquency, abuse, or neglect depend on the state to provide them with mental health evaluation and treatment. Professionals who work with youths in state custody have special statutory and constitutional obligations to provide evaluation, care, and treatment to these children who are especially vulnerable to mental disabilities.

## Incidence

At least 12% of children under age 18 in the United States, an estimate of 7.5 million children, suffer mental disorders serious enough to warrant treatment (Institute of Medicine, 1989). Services are available for most children and adolescents with mental health problems if their families can afford individual therapy or psychiatric hospitalization. However, specialized clinics and treatment services are not available in many geographic areas. Some families are excluded from receiving the most effective intervention because they do not have the financial resources to meet the cost. Many mental health practitioners (e.g., psychologists and psychiatrists) in private practice will not see non-paying or medicaid patients, and these, unfortunately, are often from families who require the most intensive assistance (Gadow, 1991).

The lack of adequate community-based outpatient mental health services forces some youngsters into more restrictive settings than they need. For example, boys and girls who could get by very well with day hospital care, staying home at night, may be forced to live in 24-hour residential care settings because day hospital spaces are not available. Between 1983 and 1986 there was a 60% increase in the number of child inpatients under 18 in care in residential treatment centers or in other residential care settings (Select Committee on Children, Youth, and Families, 1990). In 1986 the Office of Technology Assessment estimated the number of children and adolescents receiving some form of mental health treatment as probably in excess of 2.5 million, with approximately 5 million more youth in need of mental health services (U.S. Congress, 1986). One report claimed that mental health treatment is received in California by only 7% of the children who need it (Children Now, 1990).

## Risk Factors

What happens in the lives of some children to place them at high risk for developing a mental disorder? Vulnerable groups of children must be identified before a program of appropriate prevention and intervention can be designed. In its 1989 report the Institute of Medicine summarized research that points to these extrinsic causative factors:

— Parent is mentally ill or substance abusing or both.

— Child has chronic medical illness.

— Child lives in foster care.

— Native American child is from certain tribes (some face a risk of suicide as much as 2.3 times the rate for the U.S. population of the same age).

— Child lives in family on welfare.

— Child is homeless.

— Child is separated from parent for prolonged time with lack of consistent caretaker.

— Child lives in crowded, inner-city neighborhood.

— Child is victim of physical or sexual abuse.

— Child is victim of catastrophic events.

— Child suffers bereavement.

— Child lives in unstable family with marital discord. (Institute of Medicine, 1989)

Many of those children at high risk for mental disorders come to public attention through abuse and neglect reports or through programs for developmentally disabled children. As discussed in previous chapters, service planning provided for these particularly vulnerable children must be sensitive enough to prevent putting the child at even higher risk for developing mental disorders.

## Care Providers

Historically, care for children and adolescents with mental health problems has been left to the child welfare, juvenile justice, and mental health systems. Until the 1960s the mental health system was used rarely for child or adolescent treatment because serious mental illness was believed to be confined to adults. Often when basic services are received they are not related to specific mental health needs of the youth but rather to a label the youth received on becoming known to a public agency. In effect, the child with mental health problems who has been neglected and removed from the home may receive only basic care as a foster child; the adolescent who commits delinquent acts is apt to be placed in a detention center without therapy even if a mental disorder causes the delinquent behavior.

Formerly, runaway and truant children found themselves placed with delinquent children in the juvenile justice system. Now, because federal funding regulations prohibit housing status offenders with delinquents, many teens who have run away from home or are truant from school are being served by the mental health system. Inappropriately, many parents with hard-to-manage children have resorted to using their health insurance to finance institutionalized mental health services to keep those children out of the home.

## Commitment to the Mental Institution

Contrary to what many believe, parents do not have the unrestrained right to commit their children to institutional care. Because the constitutional interest in personal liberty of the individual, even for the small child, is so highly valued, parents seeking commitment of their children must have a physician verify that the child is in need of treatment. In many states an outside expert, a judge in some cases, must approve each admission either before it takes place or soon thereafter. In some states, to protect further the child's individual rights, an attorney is appointed to represent the youth at the commitment hearing. During the 1980s a dramatic increase in the number of commitments brought procedural changes that made the role of a child's attorney difficult. As the number of hearings increased, the limited time available for the hearings resulted in a perfunctory 5- or 10-minute rubber-stamping. During that same period, there was a marked growth in the number of adolescent psychiatric care facilities. This has had both positive and negative effects on youths who need treatment.

### Private Psychiatric Hospitals for Juveniles

A national psychiatric hospital care study found that an increase in the number of private psychiatric hospitals made treatment facilities readily available for those children and adolescents with private funding but not for seriously mentally ill individuals who are dependent on public financing. The study found that private insurance paid for more than 40% of psychiatric patient care overall and more than two thirds of revenues in for-profit specialty hospitals (Dorwart, Schlesinger, Davidson, Epstein, & Hoover, 1991).

In 1971, 6,500 children and teenagers were hospitalized in private psychiatric facilities in the United States. By 1989 this figure had reached approximately 200,000. Although the cause for the increase in psychiatric hospitalization is not clear, several psychological, social, and economic factors must be considered seriously:

— The growth in the number of for-profit juvenile psychiatric care facilities
— An increase in the serious emotional disorders of youth evidenced by an increase in juvenile suicide
— An increase in the need for treatment of substance abuse
— An increase in the number of divorces and single parent homes
— Availability of more child-centered than family-, school-, or community-centered interventions
— The availability of more extensive insurance coverage for inpatient than for outpatient care
— The lack of less restrictive in-home or community-based treatment
— Laws that encourage transinstitutionalization
— Failure to implement Early Periodic Screening, Diagnosis, and Treatment Program (EPSDT)
— The U.S. Supreme Court opinion in *Parham v. J. R.* (1979)

The first nine factors will be discussed briefly before considering the Supreme Court opinion in *Parham.*

*Growth in the number of for-profit juvenile psychiatric facilities.* The first factor contributing to the increased commitment of youth to mental health facilities was the increase in for-profit juvenile psychiatric institutions. This growth was especially pronounced in the 1980s. A restrictive trend in insurance reimbursement policies has led to a decline in building new facilities and the closing of some wards for children and adolescents. The number of private psychiatric hospitals grew from 184 in 1979 to over 450 in 1990 (Dorwart et al., 1991).

Teenage psychiatric hospitalization was a carefully cultivated economic market for big hospital chains. Economist Sylvia Hewlett (1991) described the mushrooming use of mental hospitals for adolescents, which for many U.S. corporations was the fastest growing medical expense, and concluded that the emotional problems of young people had become big business. She suggested that government regulations are needed to safeguard children from the excesses of profit-maximizing entrepreneurs and freewheeling markets.

Parents are attracted to psychiatric hospitals by advertisements that magnify the seriousness of adolescent behavior, stir guilty feelings in the parent for not seeking help, and use the availability of the parents' insurance to make it easier for the parent to decide to commit the child. One hospital pamphlet suggested that teenagers needed hospital evaluation if they showed one or more of the following behaviors: physical violence, stealing or persistent shoplifting, lack of age-appropriate relationships, absence of guilt or remorse, little concern for the welfare of others, absence from school or other daily routines, running away, or persistent lying (Centennial Peaks Hospital, 1989). These advertisements mix symptoms of serious disorders with problems that should be handled readily within the family or through outpatient treatment. Brochures by aggressive entrepreneurial hospitals add to the all-too-familiar television enticements that urge parents to bring their difficult children to the psychiatric hospital before something "really serious" happens.

A University of Michigan study found that 70% of adolescent psychiatric admissions were inappropriate and potentially harmful to the children concerned (Schwartz, 1989). The authors of a national study of psychiatric hospital care concluded that the expansion of proprietary hospitals has increased access for a long-underserved population— children and adolescents. This raises concerns because the young population is at risk for excessive and unnecessary institutionalization (Dorwart et al., 1991).

*Increase in serious emotional disorders of youth.* The second factor to consider when evaluating causes for the expansion of psychiatric hospitalization placements is the increase in serious emotional disorders of youth. The incidence of those disorders can be ambiguous because apparent changes in rates of emotional disorders may partially reflect changes in reporting practices. As an example, the use of suicide rates as a barometer of serious emotional disorders must consider the historical reluctance to report suicide as the cause of death.

In 1960 the suicide rate for teenagers was 3.6 per 100,000 persons. By 1986 the reported rate had climbed to 10.2. In addition, the rate of attempted suicide in 1986 was 10% of teenage boys and 18% of teenage girls (Select Committee on Children, Youth, and Families, 1989). After accidents, suicide is the second leading cause of death among adolescents (Rosenberg, Smith, Davidson, & Conn, 1987). Most suicide victims suffer from depression, substance abuse, or both and come from families with a history of depression and suicide (Institute of Medicine, 1989). The incidence of teen death from accident, homicide, or suicide rose 13% from 62.8 per 100,000 in 1985 to 70.9 per 100,000 teens in 1990 (Center for the Study of Social Policy, 1993).

Common externalizing or undercontrol problems such as fighting and swearing involve insufficient self-control, inhibition, or restraint. These behaviors are on one end of the continuum that leads to violence. Thus, homicide rates could be used as a gauge for the presence of externalizing problems among the youth in our society. Violent behavior results in a homicide rate for African American males at 5.5 times that for White males in the same age group. Among African American youth, homicide is now the leading cause of death (Institute of Medicine, 1989).

*Increase in the need for treatment of substance abuse.* The major impact on children caused by the increase in drug use in the 1980s is reflected both in the numbers of children whose parents use drugs or alcohol and in those preteens and adolescents who abuse substances. For children living in depressed neighborhoods, the presence of drugs adds a pathological element to their lives that was much less prevalent 15 years ago (Schorr & Schorr, 1989). In a survey of state child protective services, almost every state cited substance abuse as a major presenting problem of children in their caseloads. In 1991, 14 states that kept records reported the birth of 9,686 drug-exposed infants (National Committee for Prevention of Child Abuse, 1992). It is estimated that up to 375,000 infants who are prenatally drug exposed are born each year (Toufexis, 1991).

Children with a parent who abuses substances are at high risk of developing a mental disorder (Institute of Medicine, 1989). The state of Washington found that two of three seriously emotionally disturbed children within the state come from a family with a history of drug or alcohol abuse. Despite this serious problem, parent and family support services for dealing with substance abuse were extremely scarce and difficult to obtain (University of Washington, 1988).

As adolescent use of drugs increased rapidly during the 1970s and 1980s, cocaine use reported by high school seniors tripled between 1977 and 1985. In a 1991 survey cited by the American Medical Association, 39% of high school seniors reported getting drunk within the previous 2 weeks (Hewlett, 1991). Even these troubling statistics do not include abusers who have dropped out of school. Their need for treatment is even more pronounced because not only their health but also their education is in jeopardy.

*Increase in the number of divorces and single parent households.* A fourth factor that may influence the increase in psychiatric hospitalization is the rising number of divorces and single parent households. Economic stagnation with the reduction in affordable housing and high unemployment have fueled the recent increase in child poverty and single parent households. Being brought up by a socially isolated single parent is associated often with symptoms of social dysfunction, including early school failure, truancy, fighting in school, dropping out of school and childbearing in early adolescence. Such symptoms are known precursors of mental disorders (Schorr & Schorr, 1989). In a study of children in residential treatment facilities, over 80% of the children were from families in which the biological parents did not live together (Weithorn, 1988).

*Availability of child-centered rather than family-, school-, or community-centered mental health interventions.* Research shows that effective prevention and treatment approaches require attention to the family unit, the school, and the community as key socializing contexts of the developing child (Dryfoos, 1990). Although evidence shows that preventive mental health interventions through these broader entities in the child's life can reduce risk and provide protection from diverse problem behaviors, mental health professionals continue to focus their services on assessment, diagnosis, and treatment of the child as the sole patient (Weissberg, Caplan, & Harwood, 1991).

*The availability of broader insurance coverage for inpatient than for outpatient care.* From medicaid to Blue Cross/Blue Shield, insurance policies have provided coverage for the more costly and more restrictive inpatient care. Physicians working for hospitals have a financial incentive to keep patients hospitalized until insurance coverage is exhausted. Hospital administrators have a similar profit-making interest in keeping hospital beds filled. The popular press has alleged that doctors and administrators in for-profit hospitals are paid bonuses for drumming up business. In the *Chicago Tribune* it was reported that most patients experience a remarkable and full recovery from their disorder just at the time their health insurance benefits run out (Kass, 1989).

Sometimes parents of children with medical insurance prefer to view a troublesome child's problems as an individual mental illness. Thus they hope to avoid coping with the child in the home or becoming involved in community or intensive family therapy. As a useful contrast, a regional mental hospital in Bangalore, India, requires a family member, usually the mother, to live with the mentally ill youth in the hospital. The parent is expected to participate in care and treatment and help bridge the gap between hospital treatment dynamics and life at home. What would happen to the high rate of hospitalization of children if this were a requirement in the United States?

Courts have dealt with the issue of insurance coverage for children and adolescents with differing results. In one case, a father placed his son in a boys' home for treatment of behavioral problems. The court ruled that the placement was not covered because the father's insurance policy defined a covered institution as a hospital providing facilities for diagnosis and surgery (*Woodman Accident and Life Insurance Co. v. Bryant*, 1986).

Compare that with a similar Montana case in which the insurance company was ordered by the state supreme court to pay for breach of contract, bad faith, unfair dealing, and damages for emotional stress to a father and son and punitive damages for failure to cover treatment of the son in a mental health facility (*Tynes v. Bankers Life Co.*, 1987).

*The lack of less restrictive alternatives.* The legal term *least restrictive alternative* requires that treatment be given in the place that exerts the least amount of control over the person's individual freedom as is appropriate for the given mental disorder. More restrictive settings may offer professional staff more control over a patient, but children and adolescents generally would prefer to live in their own homes while participating in outpatient care. In the 1970s many children with mental retardation who were growing up in state mental hospitals were deinstitutionalized. A recent Texas court settlement, begun during the deinstitutionalization of the 1970s, required the state to reduce its state hospital populations and create small group homes for child patients in community settings. A national committee of mental health professionals studied the use of institutionalized mental health services and recommended providing more appropriate community-based mental health services. In 1980, based on this recommendation, an act on mental health systems was passed as a federal effort to discourage inappropriate use of institutional psychiatric facilities; however, just a year later, this model mental health legislation was killed by budget reconciliation legislation. As a result, the consumer may be forced to choose the most restrictive and most expensive type of treatment because hospitalization may be the only funded mental health treatment available.

Acting to stem the tide of juvenile psychiatric facility proliferation, the American Academy of Child and Adolescent Psychiatry released a report (Cohen et al., 1990) that recommended hospitalization only for children with severe problems and when no less restrictive appropriate alternative exists. This professional standard for admission is a model that if adopted by psychiatric hospitals would limit admissions to those who actually require inpatient evaluation or treatment. Proponents of such programs as the Tacoma Homebuilders program, the Child and Adolescent Service System Program (CASSP), and the North Carolina Willie M. program have argued for the effectiveness of in-home or community services that work with the youth in the environment in which the youth lives rather than in the structured, controlled hospital environment in which problems faced in the real world only can be remembered (Stroul & Friedman, 1986). Some research studies conclude that home-based and community-based treatment programs are much better alternatives for most emotionally disturbed and troublesome youth (Weithorn, 1988). If a continuum of care is available, even some short-term hospitalizations can be avoided (Behar, 1990).

*Federal and state laws.* Another major factor that must be considered when evaluating the increase in psychiatric hospitalizations is the effect of federal and state laws on placement decisions for children and adolescents with mental disorders. The Juvenile Justice and Delinquency Prevention Act of 1974 prohibits the allocation of federal funds to states for care of delinquent juveniles if status offenders are housed with delinquents. Nonetheless, the 64% decrease in inappropriate care for status offenders involved with the juvenile justice system has been offset by increases in their admissions to mental hospitals. This ironic development results from federal funding patterns. These juveniles have been called victims of *transinstitutionalization*, the transfer of a population from one institutional system to another as an inadvertent consequence of policies intended to deinstitutionalize the target population.

Studies of juvenile psychiatric hospital populations indicate that two thirds of the inpatients have such symptoms as troublemaking, mild psychological problems, and normal developmental changes (Weithorn, 1988). Medical labels put on these behaviors are conduct disorder, personality disorder, and adjustment disorder. Behavioral symptoms for such psychiatric disorders include chronic misbehavior at home or school, running away, persistent lying, stubbornness, argumentativeness, violation of minor rules, and overreaction to identified social stressors. One legal scholar concluded that most juveniles currently in mental hospitals are not seriously mentally ill and do not require the restraint provided by an inpatient setting (Weithorn, 1988).

The Alcohol, Drug Abuse, and Mental Health Reorganization Act of 1992 established new mental health pilot programs of services for children with serious mental illnesses or emotional disturbances. Entitled "Comprehensive Community Mental Health Services for Children With Serious Emotional Disturbances," the program enables states and communities to establish a broad range of community-based services that include diagnosis and assessment, outpatient care, day treatment, intensive in-home services, respite care for families, therapeutic foster care, and group home services. Each child enrolled in these limited pilot programs will have a case manager and an individualized service plan developed with the participation of the family and the child. Although this program has an extremely low appropriation, it is a good start toward providing the services these children need (Mental Health Law Project, 1993). Chapter 12 discusses Early Intervention for Infants and Toddlers who are developmentally delayed or disabled.

*Failure to implement EPSDT.* A federally funded program for children in low-income families, Early Periodic Screening, Diagnosis, and Treatment covers mental health as well as medical and dental care (see Social Security Act, 42 U.S.C. sec. 1396, 1994). Because most states do not include periodic mental health screening, evaluation, and treatment in their services to poor children, mental illness rarely comes to the attention of professionals until symptoms have become acute, costly to treat, and less promising for successful results.

*The U.S. Supreme Court decision in* Parham v. J. R.   In *Parham v. J. R.* (1979) the U.S. Supreme Court, in reviewing a Georgia district court decision, did not give minors a private interest independent from their parents. By equating the child's interest with the parents', the court decided that if parents possess what a child lacks in maturity, experience, and capacity for judgment required for making life's difficult decisions, and the natural bond of affection causes parents to act in the best interest of the child, commitment of children and adolescents to mental institutions should be left to the parents' decision-making power. The court declined to make states require a process more formal than parental consent with medical approval. One consequence of this decision is to give unbridled discretion to a highly stressed or otherwise desperate parent who seeks respite from an unmanageable or troubled adolescent through hospitalization paid for by health insurance.

In *Parham v. J. R.* the U.S. Supreme Court faced the issue: May parents commit their minor children to public mental hospitals without some form of civil commitment hearing to review the decision as is required before an adult can be committed involuntarily? The Court opinion provides insight into many factors that are significant enough to persuade the Court to balance the scales of justice in favor of parents, children, or the state: the requirement for voluntary admission by parents or custodian to be approved by a mental health professional, the length of hospital stay, the availability of less restrictive community mental health clinics and specialized foster care homes, the emotional and psychic harm caused by institutionalization, whether the parents act in good faith, whether the mental disorder calls for inpatient treatment, the cost in money and professional time for admissions hearings, the need for ongoing review of need to continue hospital placement, and the potential danger that a hearing would pose a significant intrusion into the parent-child relationship.

The Court weighed the factors and found that Georgia's medical fact-finding process gave sufficient protection to the individual rights of a child whose parents want to place the child in a mental institution. The Court considered the facts surrounding the child and concluded by saying:

In defining the respective rights and prerogatives of the child and parent in the voluntary commitment setting, we conclude that . . . the parents retain a substantial, if not the dominant, role in the decision, absent a finding of neglect or abuse, and that the traditional presumption that the parents act in the best interest of their child should apply. We also conclude, however, that the child's rights and the nature of the commitment decision are such that parents cannot always have absolute and unreviewable discretion to decide whether to have a child institutionalized. They, of course, retain plenary authority to seek such care for their children, subject to a physician's independent examination and medical judgment. (*Parham v. J. R.*, 1979, pp. 604, 2505)

In the aftermath of *Parham*, how well are the interests of the child, the parent, and society balanced in clinical practice? One look at the growth of adolescent psychiatric care facilities and the overuse of institutionalization for noncritical illnesses indicates that the child's liberty interest has been outweighed by that of the parent and the state. One commentator has observed that mental health professionals, under the guise of treatment, have allowed and perhaps encouraged "execrable conditions" in their institutions (Silverstein, 1985).

In his dissent in *Parham*, Justice Brennan expressed a concern for the child's liberty interest. He rejected the majority argument that allowed parents and mental health professionals to commit children. Equating hospitalization with incarceration, he wrote:

Children incarcerated in public mental institutions are constitutionally entitled to a fair opportunity to contest the legitimacy of their confinement. They are entitled to some champion who can speak on their behalf and who stands ready to oppose a wrongful commitment. . . . The risk of erroneous commitment is simply too great unless there is some form of adversarial review. And fairness demands that children abandoned by their supposed protectors to the rigors of institutional confinement be given the help of some separate voice. (*Parham v. J. R.*, 1979, pp. 638, 2522)

## Questions Raised by
## the Supreme Court Decision and Dissent

Attention will now be given to some of the questions raised by the Georgia district case and the Supreme Court decision as well as by the dissent of Justice Brennan. These issues will continue to exert major

224 OTHER AREAS OF LEGAL INVOLVEMENT

influence on decisions at all levels in the treatment of severely emotionally disturbed children and adolescents.

## Commitment Hearings

*Legal requirements.* Under the *Parham* decision, states are not constitutionally required to hold commitment hearings for minors but are free
to do so. A majority of states offer few or only moderate protections for
minors in the commitment decision process (Walding, 1990). Some states
require a judge to consider and deem inappropriate less restrictive alternatives before allowing involuntary institutionalization (Weithorn,
1988).

*Values and costs.* Some clinicians believe involuntary treatment runs
counter to fundamental values in society and criticize their colleagues
for undermining the credibility of the mental health profession by
participating. Other clinicians are concerned about the economic costs
of such hearings. Time and energy spent on legal matters no longer is
available for direct care and therapy (Silverstein, 1985).

*Goals.* One critic believes that the ostensible goals of the civil commitment process are subverted routinely in favor of systematic interests
of both the legal and mental health profession. He believes the deeply
held value of the mental health profession to provide treatment takes
precedence over the complex goal of civil commitment. As a disfavored
stepchild in the justice system, civil commitment hearings often are
heard perfunctorily by judges with little training in mental health law
and presented by attorneys who are ill prepared and poorly compen-
sated for their appearances. This results in the mental health professional seeking commitment of persons who do not meet the criteria for
commitment and the justice system that is supposed to provide a check
failing to allocate adequate resources to do so effectively (Appelbaum,
1992).

*Deleterious effects.* Clinicians allege that the adversarial due process
hearings have deleterious effects on treatment: psychotic decompen-
sation of the child or adolescent, further deterioration of the already

troubled relationship between parent and child, damage to the relationship between the patient and therapist as the latter testifies in opposition to the patient's release, assaults on the adolescent's already shaky self-esteem from the disclosure of diagnoses and other evidence of personality appraisal, anxiety and resistance in response to the premature revelation of personality dynamics or unconscious content, reinforcement of pathological defenses among delinquent-prone and narcissistic youths who seek to avoid responsibility for their plights, and a myriad of undesirable effects on the milieux of child and adolescent psychiatric units (Burlingame & Amaya, 1985).

### Reducing Hospitalizations

The mental health profession has not sat by silently as the criticism mounts. In 1990 the *American Society for Adolescent Psychiatry Newsletter* published proposed guidelines for hospitalization and marketing designed to promote appropriate treatment goals and to streamline the treatment process during hospital stays. Motivated by such standards and by managed health care programs attempting to control escalating expenditures, some hospitals have developed short-term psychiatric inpatient programs for adolescents, programs that focus on early diagnosis, efficient identification of medication needs, and timely transition to outpatient medical supervision and parental support.

One hospital developed a 2- to 3-week hospital stay, replacing for many youngsters what had been an average 33-day stay; even that original 33-day arrangement often had turned into a 60-day hospitalization. Goals and objectives of the new short-term program became (a) a completed diagnostic evaluation, (b) crisis management and stabilization, and (c) early liaison with outpatient providers and parents continuing after discharge. Discharge planning was complicated by unavailability of step-down programs for adolescents and by poor response time from social service agencies. Adolescents appropriate for the short-term program included more disturbed patients with supportive families and those who had varied diagnostic indications such as impulsive, minor suicide attempts; adjustment disorders; and previously diagnosed major psychiatric disorders requiring medication adjustment. Excluded from the 2- to 3-week program were patients with a first psychotic episode, those with significant aggressive behavior, and those with severe suicidality and self-injurious behavior and chaotic family dynamics. For those with more severe problems, longer hospitalization was required (Gold, Heller, & Ritorto, 1992).

## Rights of Patients

Within the institution the adolescent has several basic rights. The first is the right to treatment. In *Kent v. United States* (1966), the Supreme Court noted that "[t]here may be grounds for concern that the child receives the worst of both worlds; that he gets neither the protections accorded to adults nor the solicitous care and regenerative treatment postulated for children" (pp. 556, 1054). For children voluntarily committed to mental health facilities by their parents, the provision of treatment is the only justification for denying them due process.

In *Youngberg v. Romeo* (1982), the Supreme Court held that patients in a mental institution have the right to reasonably safe living conditions, freedom from undue bodily restraints, and minimally adequate training related to enhancing their ability to protect themselves. Whether minors have the right to refuse treatment is unclear; this right may be regulated by state statutes. Forcing drugs on a youth who refuses would not be appropriate except in cases of severe behavior disorders such as extreme agitation or hallucination; drug use as a mere control mechanism would be highly questionable as would cruel, demeaning, or dangerous treatment. Depending on the statutes of the state, children and adolescents do have specific rights such as those presented in Table 14.1.

## Appropriateness of Hospitalization

The University of Michigan study that found 70% of adolescent psychiatric admissions to be inappropriate (Schwartz, 1989) supports the conclusion of legal commentator Weithorn (1988) that most juveniles in mental hospitals are not seriously mentally ill and do not require the restraint of an inpatient setting. Weithorn stated that inpatient treatment is typically less effective than focused community-based interventions. She concluded that potential risks present during

**TABLE 14.1** The Rights of Minors While Hospitalized

1. Right to treatment
2. Right to refuse treatment under defined circumstances
3. Posting and explanation of rights on admission
4. Confidential access to counsel and courts
5. Special education and vocational training
6. Participation in play, recreation, physical exercise and outdoor activity on a regular basis
7. Control and use of personal clothing and possessions under appropriate supervision
8. Participation in religious worship
9. Right to make and receive phone calls
10. Right to receive visitors including siblings and friends
11. Access to individual storage space for safekeeping of personal belongings
12. Right to send and receive mail and have access to writing materials (is acceptable to inspect mail for contraband)
13. Right to be free from unreasonable searches of persons and possessions
14. No corporal punishment
15. No use of medication only for institutional control
16. No use of isolation in order to punish a child, only when physically violent and dangerous to self or others and for the shortest possible period of time necessary to restrain and calm the child
17. No coerced work unrelated to similar work minor would perform at home or which is not a part of approved vocational educational program
18. Right to educational services
19. Right to nutrition, housing, sanitation; may not restrict food for disciplinary reasons
20. Confidentiality of hospital records

mental hospitalizations are substantially greater than those present in community-based treatment and may outweigh any benefits of inpatient treatment.

*Race as a factor.* Race may be the determining factor in whether an adolescent with mental disorders and a delinquency record is placed in a mental health facility or in a corrections institution. In a study based in Virginia, the characteristics of children and adolescents in a psychiatric hospital were compared with those held in a corrections facility. Committing a crime was not the determining factor in dispositional placement. Criminal behavior resulted in commitment to a mental health facility for 69% of the youths. Behavioral, emotional, and nonracial demographic characteristics were quite similar in both racial groups. African Americans were overrepresented in corrections despite equivalent scores of total problems of the African American and White youths in the study. Race was the only variable that predicted the site in which the youths were placed (Cohen et al., 1990).

## Length of Hospitalization

The length of stay in a psychiatric hospital is influenced by several factors not always based on the seriousness of the mental illness and the need for hospitalization. These factors include the length of insurance coverage, the scarcity of outpatient community resources, the unavailability of long-term residential treatment facilities, and the lack of funding for long-term care in an out-of-hospital setting. Public funding for adolescents with no personal assets may be available from medicaid if the youth qualifies as a family of one. Because medicaid rules allow payment to private hospitals only for acute care, youths who need more than 15 days of hospitalization must go to public hospitals.

With time frames for hospital treatment programs influenced by limits to public and private insurance coverage, psychiatric hospitals have increased the use of psychopharmacology as a treatment agent and have decreased use of dynamic psychotherapy. The goal of inpatient service in many facilities no longer is long-term therapy but rather diagnosis and acute treatment. The length of time spent on the mental hospital ward can affect the emotional health of the youth. One author concluded that the experience of being confined to a psychiatric ward leaves inappropriately placed adolescents with feelings of powerlessness, helplessness, or rage due to the trauma of exposure to other youths who are seriously emotionally disturbed (Hewlett, 1991).

The hospital is used sometimes as a holding place for children and adolescents with no treatment needs whose case managers cannot find a more appropriate, less restrictive placement (Jemerin & Phillips, 1988). To protect against a prolonged stay, many states allow the minor or someone acting on his or her behalf to request release. In most states this request must be honored unless the hospital moves to retain the patient through another proceeding (Brakel, Parry, & Weiner, 1985). Length of hospitalization can be modified by appropriate programs of aftercare. A national study of psychiatric hospital care found that 46% of the hospitals reported that they followed patients for 1 week or less following discharge. Fifteen percent reported follow-up for up to 1 year (Dorwart et al., 1991).

## Less Restrictive Alternatives

Experts recommend that services for children be centralized to include (a) a full range of mental health and other human services provided in a coordinated fashion; (b) rehabilitative services including residential treatment, specialized foster care, day treatment, and special education; and (c) inpatient care funded for seriously disturbed youth who need hospitalization but are not covered by private insurance (Jemerin & Phillips, 1988).

The concept of the least restrictive alternative refers to the presumption that the commitment cannot be more restrictive than necessary to accomplish the state's purpose. The least restrictive alternative rule requires the state to evaluate the treatment needs of a person and the services available to determine the proper placement for an individual that optimizes both personal liberty and community-based care (Turnbull, 1981). Treatment methods that may adequately address the child's mental health problems should be in the least restrictive setting that is therapeutically most appropriate. Restrictiveness can be defined in terms of limits placed on freedom of movement or choice by the physical facility, rules or requirements, and conditions of entry and departure.

On the basis of ratings by 159 professionals who provide services to children and adolescents, Hawkins, Almeida, Fabry, and Reitz (1992) produced the Restrictiveness of Living Environment Scale, which ranks placements from most restrictive to least restrictive (see Table 14.2).

A few of the residential treatment alternatives listed in Table 14.2 are only for children or adolescents with mental disorders. Others are specifically for children or adolescents with educational or penal needs. Many of the listed settings are available for children who need treatment for mental illness as well as for children with different primary needs. Although these settings were established originally for social or criminal treatment, they are now used by a variety of agencies as treatment alternatives to serve the complex needs of the typical child in any system. If a full spectrum of services is created outside of hospitals, residential treatment is more likely to be utilized only when absolutely necessary (Silverstein, 1980).

**TABLE 14.2** Restrictiveness of Living Environment Scale

1. Jail
2. State mental hospital
3. County detention center
4. Youth correctional center
5. Intensive treatment unit
6. Drug rehabilitation center (inpatient)
7. Medical hospital (inpatient)
8. Wilderness camp (24-hour year-round)
9. Residential treatment center
10. Group emergency shelter
11. Group home
12. Foster family based treatment home
13. Individual home emergency shelter
14. Specialized foster care
15. Regular foster care
16. Supervised independent living
17. Home of a family friend
18. Adoptive home
19. School dormitory
20. Home of natural parents, for a child
21. Home of natural parents, for an 18-year-old
22. Independent living with a friend
23. Independent living by self

SOURCE: From "A Scale to Measure Restrictiveness of Living Environments for Troubled Children and Youths" by R. P. Hawkins, M. C. Almeida, B. Fabry, and A. L. Reitz, 1992, *Hospital and Community Psychiatry, 43*, pp. 54-58. Copyright © 1992, the American Psychiatric Association. Reprinted by permission.

## Service Delivery Needs

A Children's Defense Fund survey of state mental health programs (Knitzer, 1982) revealed inadequacies of inpatient and residential treatment programs, lack of coordination among social systems (child welfare, juvenile justice, mental health, and education), poor tracking of children through any of these systems, and the limitation of services for emotionally disturbed children through the Individuals With Disabilities Education Act of 1975. The problems revealed in the 1982 survey were still evident in a later study of mental health needs of children in the state of Washington (University of Washington, 1988). That study found that almost 7% of the public school population had severe emotional disturbances. Of these youth, 64% had a need for services from two or more distinct service delivery systems. The greatest need the

Washington study found was for nonresidential services. Counseling and mental health centers, the traditional outpatient treatment resources, were more available than other types of nonresidential services but were insufficient to meet the need. Parent and family support services were extremely scarce and difficult for parents of a seriously emotionally disturbed child to obtain. Also unavailable were intensive, long-term, cross-agency case management services. This inadequacy of services led the Washington research team to recommend unification of children's mental health services at the local level through development of local interagency teams responsible for organizing and coordinating services for children and families within their communities.

## Multiagency Model Programs

*Child and Adolescent Service System Project.* Bridging the gaps between child service agencies is the aim of a National Institute of Mental Health funded program that has been introduced in several states, the Child and Adolescent Service System Project. The purpose of this program is to infuse flexibility into the use of funds previously restricted by category and to ensure that limited resources are targeted to the neediest children and adolescents. CASSP provides funding for operating community-based systems of care that emphasize comprehensive and individualized services provided within the least restrictive environment with the full participation of families. Their system of care model, based primarily on child and family needs, relies on the collaboration and coordination of child-serving agencies: mental health, social services, education, health, vocational, recreational, and operational services (case management, self-help and support groups, advocacy, transportation, legal services, and volunteer programs). CASSP aims at galvanizing state mental health authorities to action around coordinated community service delivery. The case manager is the glue that holds the system together by ensuring continuity of services for the child and family. The child- and family-centered focus of CASSP is seen as a commitment to adapt services to the child and family, rather than expecting children and families to conform to preexisting service configurations. This focus can minimize the need for residential treatment (Stroul & Friedman, 1986).

*Ventura County Project.* The state of California established a pilot program in Ventura County to provide home-based mental health services for emotionally disturbed children at risk of out-of-home placement. Mike is an example of the children served to facilitate the goal of allowing the child to remain in the family home while receiving mental health services in the least restrictive and least costly setting. An interagency network was established that included members of the juvenile justice, social welfare, and mental health systems. Mental health services were integrated into the child's home, school, juvenile justice, and social service environments, with a continuum of services that were designed to meet the individual needs of the child and family.

> *Case study.* Mike, 15 years old, had a long history of poor impulse control complicated by a severe learning disability. This was diagnosed when he was in fourth grade, after a history of school failure and poor interpersonal relationships with peers. He lived with his parents who had a very troubled marriage, with the father remaining in the marriage to support Mike and three older siblings. Prior to the intervention of the Ventura Project, Mike had been in a juvenile detention facility for 6 months; this followed earlier placement in two group homes and two psychiatric hospitals. He also had a history of violent altercations with his father and four suicide attempts.
>
> During the brief 6-week period of intervention, the entire family participated in treatment—singly, in dyads, and as a family unit. The parents undertook marriage counseling, and Mike was provided with individual therapy. Unfortunately, he could not be in school during this time because the local school district was unable to decide on a suitable school placement. Although the 6-week intervention program was too brief, Mike made reconnection efforts with family members and learned to take more responsibility for his own behaviors and their consequences. He consciously worked toward more positive goals than he had prior to the intervention. Earlier introduction of such a program might have prevented Mike from the restrictive types of out-of-home placement he experienced during his younger years.

## Developmental Disabilities and Mental Disorders

Children and adolescents with developmental disabilities related to biological disorders may be at higher risk for mental disorders. Services for these especially vulnerable boys and girls are provided through federally funded and state-supported early intervention programs. Services are provided for preschool and school-age children through the Individuals With Disabilities Education Act (IDEA), which is discussed in Chapter 12. IDEA's focus on support for the family with the disabled child and its concentration on interdisciplinary and interagency efforts to plan and carry out services as the infant is developing should help prevent the occurrence of some mental disorders in this high-risk population (Healy, Keesee, & Smith, 1989). Parents of children with developmental disorders compose an active vocal group that has pushed for increased services and case management for their children. Parent involvement is accepted widely and even mandated under IDEA. Parents of children diagnosed with nonbiologically based mental disorders have not been as forceful in their demand for needed services.

## Federal Resources and Protections

*Supplemental Security Income.* SSI is a need-based disability program for children and adults with limited income that provides a monthly income benefit and, in most states, automatic medicaid eligibility. Children with significant emotional, developmental, and behavioral disorders may meet the requirements to qualify. Monthly SSI benefits and automatic medicaid eligibility ease the family's burden of caring for a child or adolescent with special needs, facilitate family reunification for children who have been placed out of the home, and make it easier to obtain therapy, counseling, tutoring, and other needed services. To qualify, the youth must have a medically or psychologically diagnosed condition that causes functional problems; neurological impairments; or speech, language, or other sensory disorders. A child would qualify by showing "marked impairment of age-appropriate functioning" (20 C.F.R. sec. 416.924 [see Social Security Act of 1935, Supplemental Security Income for the Aged, Blind, and Disabled]) in at least two areas of development and functioning: cognitive/communicative functioning; social functioning; personal/behavioral functioning; and concentration, persistence, or pace resulting in completing tasks. The types of disabling conditions include organic mental disorders; schizophrenic, delusional (paranoid), schizoaffective, and other psychotic disorders; mood disorders; mental retardation; anxiety disorders; somatoform, eating, and tic disorders; personality disorders; psychoactive substance dependence disorders; autistic disorder and other pervasive developmental disorders; and attention deficit hyperactivity disorders.

Children with mental disabilities may be categorized as abused or neglected, delinquent, runaway, truant, learning disabled, or mentally ill. Professionals who work with these children must be aware of available resources including SSI disability benefits. Mental health professionals, teachers, social workers, probation officers, CASAs, guardians ad litem, and children's attorneys, as well as parents, need to know how to apply for such valuable benefits and how to provide information to help determine eligibility. In addition to evidence from physicians, psychiatrists, and licensed or certified psychologists, nonmedical evidence and letters of support from therapists, social workers, counselors, probation officers, teachers, coaches, parents, and other caregivers are considered also (Social Security Act of 1935, 20 C.F.R. sec. 416.924).

*Americans With Disabilities Act of 1990.* The ADA protects an individual with a disability defined as a physical or mental impairment that substantially limits one or more of the major life activities of the individual, with a record of such impairment, or being regarded as having such an impairment. Protection under the ADA extends not only to individuals who currently have a disability but also to those who have recovered from such a disability or who have been classified mistakenly as having one (Milstein, Rubenstein, & Cyr, 1991).

## Effectiveness of Mental Health Intervention

How effective are the various methods of treating child mental health problems? Research on the outcomes of psychotherapy has had mixed results. Comprehensive reviews of child psychotherapy research have shown positive therapy effects. For example, Weisz, Weiss, Alicke, and Klotz (1987) examined over 100 controlled studies that included children age 4 to 18. Behavioral therapy was more effective than nonbehavioral techniques. Other reviews (e.g., Casey & Berman, 1985; Kazdin, Bass, Ayers, & Rodgers, 1990) have shown the beneficial effect of therapy with children. However, most of the studies included in these reviews have been experimental, "laboratory-type" tests of therapy and may not accurately represent typical therapy in clinic settings. Thus the findings may not reflect what would be found by studying clinicians working in clinics with spontaneously referred clients.

In the limited research that has been done in clinical settings, most results do not show strongly positive effects of therapy (see Weisz & Weiss, 1993; Weisz, Weiss, & Donenberg, 1992). In general, the findings of outcome research suggest that psychotherapy with children can be very effective when tested in experiments. It may be effective also in many community clinics and hospitals, but there is too little evidence thus far for anyone to be certain. It is important to note that treatment effectiveness is not dependent solely on treatment technique but is influenced by various child, parent, and family factors (Kazdin, 1991). The focus of research needs to turn to more widely used forms of treatment delivery—clinically referred youth seen individually in clinics, mental health agencies, or private practice—and pay greater attention to individual psychotherapy, psychodynamically oriented psychotherapy, family therapy, and eclectic treatment (Kazdin et al., 1990).

# 15

# Delinquency

*We ain't no delinquents, we're misunderstood,*
*Deep down inside of us there's good.*

Leonard Bernstein/Stephen Sondheim,
*West Side Story*, 1957

The sheriff took 15-year-old Gerald and his friend into custody after a woman complained that she had received a lewd prank phone call. Gerald was still on probation for being with another boy who had stolen a wallet from a woman's purse. Gerald was picked up in the morning when both parents were at work and was taken to a detention home. When his mother arrived home, she learned from a neighbor where Gerald had been taken. The officials at the detention home told her that there would be a hearing in juvenile court the following day.

The arresting officer filed a petition alleging that Gerald was under 18 years of age and was a delinquent in need of the protection of the court. It said nothing about the specific incident involving the phone call. The hearing was held in the judge's chambers. The woman who complained about the phone call was not present. An attorney was not appointed to represent Gerald. A week later the judge committed Gerald as a juvenile delinquent to the state industrial school until he reached the age of 21. The penalty for an adult using vulgar language in the presence of a woman was $5 to $50 or imprisonment for not more than 2 months (*In re Gault*, 1967).

## Incidence

Boys such as Gerald Gault and the adolescents involved in drive-by shootings or violent muggings all carry the label "delinquent." The ever burgeoning commission of delinquent acts by children is a major problem in the United States. Each year, almost 1.8 million adolescents are arrested for delinquency, defined as acts done by children or adolescents that if performed by adults would be crimes (Federal Bureau of Investigation, 1989, table 36). A great majority (88%) of these arrests are for nonviolent crimes (U.S. Department of Justice, 1991). Juveniles under age 18 account for roughly one third of all arrests for serious crimes of violence such as forcible rape, aggravated assault, and robbery, as well as serious crimes against property such as burglary, larceny-theft, motor vehicle theft, and arson (Baker, 1991). In 5 years, violent crimes by juveniles increased 48%, from 314 per 100,000 in 1986 to 466 per 100,000 in 1991 (Center for the Study of Social Policy, 1993).

The first juvenile court was established in 1899 in Chicago. Designed to provide a unified jurisdiction and set of procedures for the disorganized methods of providing for children, the Chicago Juvenile Court combined for the first time the functions of a child welfare service agency and a legal adjudicatory body (Rothman, 1991). Delinquent children and adolescents now were to be placed under the juvenile court rather than the criminal court to protect immature minors from criminal prosecution and to foster rehabilitation rather than punishment.

In the 1950s and 1960s confidence in the juvenile courts, then in operation in every state, was low while the number of delinquent children and adolescents continued to skyrocket. Annual arrests of youths under 18 reached over a million and a half by 1950 (Handler & Zatz, 1982). Crimes of violence increased as did crimes against property, creating a growing threat to public safety. Juvenile halls, training schools for delinquents, and jails became seriously overcrowded as juveniles convicted of misdemeanors or minor felonies were mixed in those institutions with violent juvenile offenders. Truants, runaways, and other youths charged with status offenses also were sent to juvenile training schools and to jails for adults.

In 1974 the Juvenile Justice and Delinquency Prevention Act was passed. This act mandated the separation of status offenders from delinquents in both the preadjudication and postdispositional phases. The act also encouraged the use of community-based treatment and rehabilitation to eliminate the need to remove a juvenile from the family and to order confinement except when absolutely necessary. By the mid-1970s there were estimates of nearly half a million juveniles in adult jails and police lockups.

In 1980 the act was amended to require states receiving federal funds to remove all juveniles from adult jails within a 5-year period. By 1986 the number of juveniles in jails had declined to 60,000 (Krisberg & Austin, 1993). Two years later as many as 20 states had not yet met the federal mandate to remove juveniles from adult jails (Steinhart, 1988). Thus in 1990 nearly 60,000 juveniles still were being admitted to adult jails (U.S. Department of Justice, 1991), a number that will probably go even higher as state and federal legislators consider lowering the age for a juvenile to be tried as an adult for certain offenses.

The confinement of juveniles in training schools and detention centers has not been proven effective in helping most of those youths. The head of the federal Office of Juvenile Justice and Delinquency Prevention, Milton Lueger, appearing at a senate hearing on the problem of institutionalizing delinquents, stated, "With the exception of a relatively few youths, it is probably better for all concerned if young delinquents were not detected, apprehended, or institutionalized. Too many of them get worse in our care" (Baker, 1991, p. 32). For this reason several delinquency detention centers are turning to alternative detention programs, such as Ft. Lauderdale's home detention program that keeps many delinquents out of detention centers (Genger, 1994).

## Factors Affecting Delinquency

The National Research Council (1993) report *Losing Generations: Adolescents in High Risk Settings* estimates that 25% of adolescents will engage in high-risk behavior. The council focuses on the societal institutions that are failing the adolescent: the family, neighborhood, schools, health care, and vocational training. Specific factors that affect a child's pathway into delinquency include poverty, substance abuse, racial discrimination, poor school performance, gender, peer pressure, and history of child abuse.

*Poverty.* A Department of Justice survey of inmates of state-operated juvenile institutions revealed that the institutional population closely parallels that of families living in poverty in that three fourths grew up with only one parent; two thirds are from minority groups; over half report at least one close family member who also has been institutionalized; well over half dropped out of school long before even entering high school; and more than 60% used drugs regularly, about half of them having begun before the age of 12 (Baker, 1991). Krisberg and Austin (1993) concluded, "The practices and procedures of juvenile justice agents mirror our society's class and racial prejudices and fall disproportionately on African-American, Latino, and poor people" (p. 109). The increased incarceration of juveniles from low-income families may be accounted for by the lack of adequate community resources such as recreation centers, special school programs for students at high risk of dropping out, family counseling, drug abuse treatment, food, and shelter.

*Substance abuse.* In a study on consequences of adolescent drug use, psychologists Newcomb and Bentler (1988) found that teenage drug use was related significantly to several factors: an increase in criminal activity during adolescence, links with a deviant friendship network, drug crime involvement, and property crime involvement. The use of drugs can be a major determinant in the ultimate placement of the juvenile. Substance abuse by the child or parent was the most important reason for placement outside the home for delinquents included in a study of family treatment. It should be noted that therapy for substance abuse was not one of the main types of therapy offered for those involved in the study (Nelson, 1990). This lack of community-based drug treatment and prevention programs is influential in the steadily increasing numbers of children who use and sell drugs. Judges may order delinquents into state training schools in which there is drug treatment that is not available in the local neighborhood (Krisberg & Austin, 1993).

*Racial discrimination.* In a study of the high rate of incarceration of African American adolescents, Huizinga and Elliott (1987) found that African American adolescents were seven times more likely to be arrested for nonserious crimes than White offenders and twice as likely to be arrested for serious crimes. Although studies on arrest bias have had inconsistent results, African American youths have higher rates of apprehension, detention, charges filed, adjudication, and punishment—but not of self-reported delinquent behavior—than White youths (Henggeler, 1989). In an analysis of the California juvenile court, Krisberg and Austin (1993) found a picture of persistent discriminatory treatment for African American and Latino youth after accounting for factors such as offense and prior record. They concluded that the ethnic disparities in detention and sentencing cannot be explained fully by the juvenile justice attributes of the African American ethnic group.

*School performance.* There is strong evidence that delinquent behavior can be linked to poor school performance and to association with delinquent peers. Students with weak basic academic skills are more than twice as likely to be arrested than students who do well in school. More than 80% of prison inmates are high school dropouts (Committee for Economic Development, 1991). The special burden of minority youth to overcome defeating economic and social conditions hampers educational achievement. Parents who neglect their children at home rarely are motivated to push the school system to provide the special services their children are entitled to receive through special education programs (see Chapter 14). Children with behavior problems may not be identified for special education by school personnel because if they are, the school will not be free to expel them if their disability caused their misbehavior (*Honig v. Doe*, 1988). Latino youth may have language needs that require special attention before further education can be achieved satisfactorily. A consortium of school-site social and medical services being introduced in some school districts may make services needed by vulnerable youth readily available.

One way to help prevent delinquency is by providing universal preschool education for low-income children. A remarkable 24-year study of 123 disadvantaged African American children in Ypsilanti, Michigan, divided the 3- and 4-year-olds into two groups: a control group and one with a culturally enriched early education program. The enriched program included preschool five mornings a week and weekly 90-minute visits by the teacher to the home, where the mother learned parenting skills. The study found that members of the preschool group were less likely to be arrested (31% compared to 51%) and were arrested for the second time less than half as often (Baker, 1991).

*Gender.* Males represent almost 80% of all delinquency apprehensions and are four times more likely to be arrested than females (U.S. Department of Justice, 1990). Although girls have a much lower rate of delinquency than boys, girls often are treated more harshly than boys in the juvenile justice system (Sarri, 1983). A much greater proportion of females than males is arrested, detained, and adjudicated for status offenses (noncriminal offenses such as truancy and running away). Several studies have found that courts are biased against young women for status offenses but lenient with them for delinquent crimes (Bishop & Frazier, 1992; Horowitz & Pottieger, 1991). Official justification for this is the need for the court to intervene to protect the "tender sex" from non-violent behaviors because they are less able to fend for themselves than their male cohorts. In intervening for status offenses, the court often consigns young women to facilities originally designed for male offenders that are not equipped to meet the special medical, mental health, and social service needs of young women (Krisberg & Austin, 1993). The cited survey that found juvenile violent crime arrest rates increased by 48% from 1986 to 1991 also found that the increase for girls had risen 57% (Center for the Study of Social Policy, 1993). Another study found that females who had been abused or neglected were at greater risk for violent crimes during adolescence (Widom, 1991).

*Peer pressure.* Peer pressure must be included in any analysis examining the relationship between crime and drugs. Having a deviant friendship network is associated with performing criminal activities. During adolescence the overlap between self and peer behavior can be associated with damaging property and having aggressive and confrontational friends (Newcomb & Bentler, 1988).

*Child abuse or neglect history.* The majority of children who are abused or neglected do not become delinquents, nor do most delinquents have a history of abuse or neglect. But childhood abuse or neglect has been found to increase a child's risk for arrest as a delinquent by more than 50% (Widom, 1989a).

## Legal Rights of Juveniles

Legal rights of the child and adolescent are spelled out through state statutes and court decisions. A relatively new concept in American jurisprudence is the extension of specific constitutional guarantees to the juvenile offender. Efforts are undertaken currently by the court when framing dispositional alternatives to focus not on the crime alone but also on the needs of the particular juvenile. Recognition of the unique nature and character of the youthful offender has led to more individualized tailoring of justice for juveniles. The U.S. Supreme Court presented reasons for special consideration for juveniles in *Eddings v. Oklahoma* (1982):

> [A]dolescents, particularly in the early and middle teen years, are more vulnerable, more impulsive and less self-disciplined than adults. Crimes committed by youths may be just as harmful to victims as those committed by older persons, but they deserve less punishment because adolescents may have less capacity to control their conduct and to think in long-range terms than adults. Moreover, youth crime as such is not exclusively the offender's fault; offenses by the young also represent a failure of family, school, and the social system, which share responsibility for the development of America's youth. (p. 115, n. 11)

Prior to 1967 the U.S. Supreme Court had emphasized the necessity of satisfying the basic requirements of due process and fairness in juvenile court proceedings (*Kent v. United States*, 1966). The critical turning point in the belated process of ensuring legal rights for children came with the 1967 decision *In re Gault*, which outlined the specific due process requirements applicable to juveniles in court hearings. In earlier years, lawyers rarely had been involved in juvenile court cases because the informality of juvenile court created confusion about their appropriate role; many parents of children involved in the juvenile court process were too poor and unsophisticated to employ legal counsel; and the right of appeal was not always understood (Thomas, 1972). *In re Gault* presented the Supreme Court with the case that ultimately breathed life and meaning into children's rights. The Court decided that juveniles are entitled to the right to notice of the specific charges, the right to counsel, the right of confrontation and cross-examination, the privilege against self-incrimination, the right to a transcript of the proceeding, and the right to appellate review.

The *Gault* decision also laid the groundwork for subsequent decisions that expand and clarify the rights of juveniles. These decisions stipulate that the state must prove beyond a reasonable doubt that a juvenile has committed a delinquent act (*In re Winship*, 1970). This standard is higher than the preponderance of the evidence standard used in civil court. Trial by jury in juvenile court is not a constitutional requirement (*McKeiver v. Pennsylvania*, 1971). The juvenile may be tried by a jury if the case is waived into adult criminal court (*In re Welfare of K.A.A.*, 1986). The juvenile is protected from unreasonable searches and seizures, but school officials do not need a warrant before searching a student who is under their authority if the search under all circumstances is reasonably based (*New Jersey v. T.L.O.*, 1985). A juvenile may be detained in preventive detention on the basis of a finding that a serious risk exists that the juvenile may, before the date of trial, commit another delinquent act. The court reasoned that the juvenile's interest in freedom from restraint must be qualified by the recognition that juveniles are always in some form of custody, juveniles are not assumed to have the capacity to take care of themselves, and juveniles are subject to parental control and, if necessary, to control by the state.

The Juvenile Justice and Delinquency Prevention Act of 1974 contained provisions to reduce the abuses of pretrial detention. By following these provisions, a program in rural Kentucky reduced pretrial detention from 276 of 2,679 arrested juveniles to only 17 of 461 juveniles arrested. They reported no problem with juveniles missing court hearings. Surprisingly, they found recidivism was cut in half when juveniles were not subjected to detention (Baker, 1991).

## Waiver of Juvenile Jurisdiction

A juvenile above a certain age and charged with a serious offense, such as a felony, may be tried as a juvenile in juvenile delinquent proceedings or as an adult in criminal court. The age and requirements for the waiver vary widely from state to state. Generally, the juvenile court has the authority to decide whether to retain jurisdiction or to waive, or transfer, jurisdiction to adult criminal court. Waiver of jurisdiction may have critical repercussions for the youth because of forfeiture of the unique legal protections given to juveniles. For example, the confidentiality of the juvenile court delinquency hearing would give way to the public records of the adult criminal court. Punishment meted out by criminal court could include imprisonment, even capital punishment, whereas a conviction in juvenile court may result only in institutional treatment, community-based care, or probation. Valid exercise of the juvenile court's waiver jurisdiction is subject to satisfaction of the basic requirements of due process and fairness, which include an opportunity for a hearing and representation by an attorney (*Kent v. United States*, 1966).

## Role of the Mental Health Professional

The mental health professional may be asked to provide an evaluation after a preliminary hearing in juvenile court that finds probable cause. The professional must take care to consider whether certain information might prove to be incriminating to the minor at the time of trial. In some states the evaluation can be used only for the transfer hearing to make certain that any self-incriminating statements will not be used later in court. In jurisdictions without this protection, the evaluation can focus only on the psychological aspects of the offense without providing any detailed statements about the offense itself. Criteria for the juvenile court evaluation include the degree of maturity and sophistication of the youth, the seriousness of the offense (not the details), anticipation of any future dangerous acts by the youth, and amenability to available rehabilitation.

Although possible consequences of transfer to adult court could include capital punishment or imprisonment, some youths will prefer a transfer to criminal court because their case dispositions are likely to be less adverse if they are in criminal court for the first time. When waiver jurisdiction occurs, a statement in sufficient detail as to the reasons motivating the juvenile court's order must be produced to allow for meaningful review. Thus the evaluation of the mental health professional should describe clearly the condition of the juvenile and the possibility of successful rehabilitation within a reasonable time.

> *Case study.* A 16-year-old was charged with sexual assault. The prosecution requested a transfer to adult court. Three psychologists and three psychiatrists testified at the waiver hearing that the juvenile was potentially amenable to psychological treatment. Five of the professionals recommended that he remain under the juvenile court jurisdiction because that was his best chance for successful rehabilitation. Despite these recommendations, the court ordered that he be waived into adult court because the evidence did not convince the court that he could be rehabilitated before he reached the age of 20 (*D.E.P. v. State*, 1986).

## Youth and Family History
## as Mitigating Factors in Sentencing

> *Case study.* A 16-year-old runaway, Eddings stood trial as an adult in criminal court and was found guilty of first-degree murder. He was sentenced

to death after the trial court judge refused to consider the boy's immaturity, turbulent family history, parental beatings, and emotional instability. When the U.S. Supreme Court reviewed the case, it found that the trial court should have considered any aspect of the boy's character or record and any mitigating circumstances in his background before imposing the sentence (*Eddings v. Oklahoma, 1982*).

The mental health professional who evaluates the juvenile preparing for sentencing should look for some of the evidence of mitigating factors that the Supreme Court discussed:

Even the normal 16-year-old customarily lacks the maturity of an adult. In this case, Eddings was not a normal 16-year-old; he had been deprived of the care, concern, and parental attention that children deserve. On the contrary, it is not disputed that he was a juvenile with serious emotional problems and had been raised in a neglectful, sometimes even violent, family background. In addition, there was testimony that Eddings' mental and emotional development were at a level several years below his chronological age. All of this does not suggest an absence of responsibility for the crime of murder, deliberately committed in this case. Rather, it is to say that just as the chronological age of a minor is itself a relevant mitigating factor of great weight, so must the background and mental and emotional development of a youthful defendant be duly considered in sentencing. (*Eddings v. Oklahoma, 1982, p. 116*)

## Juvenile Court Disposition

Although the sentences of adult criminal court require imprisonment and/or probation, the disposition in juvenile court aims at rehabilitating the youth. Common dispositions include:

—Payment of fine by the minor

—Compulsory service by minor performed for benefit of community without compensation

—Placement on probation requiring regular meetings with the probation official

—Commitment to a local detention or treatment facility such as a juvenile hall, camp, or ranch

—Commitment to the state training center

—Payment of restitution by the minor and/or responsible parents

—Placement in a residential treatment facility for youths in need of specialized mental health treatment

—Specific orders to attend school regularly with good behavior
—Specific orders to keep curfew hours
—Specific orders to stay away from certain persons or places

## Treatment for Delinquents

Deinstitutionalization became popular in the 1970s when studies found that training schools did not help juveniles to improve their deviant behavior but rather gave them a school for learning criminal behavior. Jerome Miller, as commissioner of the Massachusetts Department of Youth Services (DYS), closed all of the state's large training schools in 1972. As a result, instead of juvenile crime rates soaring, serious juvenile crimes declined (Baker, 1991). DYS assigns each juvenile to a case manager responsible for devising a treatment plan based on clinical and educational evaluations, family history, and severity of current offense. Depending on one's individual profile, the juvenile is placed in a group home, forestry program, day treatment program, outreach and tracking program, or foster care. DYS has only 13 small locked treatment programs with 184 beds. No residential program houses more than 30 youths. Only 15% of the youths are placed initially in a high-security treatment facility, in which they remain for 8 to 12 months before phasing into a less restrictive or nonresidential program. Toward the completion of residential placement, the case manager arranges community services for the juvenile with drug and alcohol treatment or counseling as needed. One goal is to give these juveniles access to normal experiences in school, work, and family settings. DYS estimates that the average annual cost per youth is $23,000, compared with $35,000 to $45,000 spent by many other states (Krisberg & Austin, 1993).

*Delinquents with emotional problems.* Juvenile justice officials have found that approximately two thirds of the children in their system are severely emotionally disturbed. Many children with special needs end up in the delinquency system in which the services they need may not be available (U.S. Congress, 1986). One creative statewide program for juveniles is a model for successful deinstitutionalization of delinquents whose emotional problems cause their aggressive, delinquent behavior. The North Carolina Willie M. program resulted from a federal class

action suit brought on behalf of emotionally disturbed, violent, and assaultive adolescents who were being housed but not treated or educated properly in a state training school (*Willie M. et al. v. Hunt*, 1981). State agencies agreed to work together to develop individualized treatment plans to provide the delinquents with the placements and services each specifically needed rather than placements and services that happened to exist. The multimillion-dollar Willie M. program created a continuum of multidisciplinary services available statewide with a case manager for each youth. Services include inpatient and outpatient individual therapy, outpatient family therapy, day treatment, supervised group living services, supervised independent living services, vocational placement, and specialized foster care.

*Treatment strategies.* Some treatment strategies are preferable for different subgroups of delinquents. According to Henggeler (1989), immature attention deficit offenders might benefit more than socialized-aggressive offenders from cognitive behavioral intervention such as social skills training or self-control training. Family treatment, successfully used for some juvenile offenders, identifies the family rather than the child as the service recipient. Services are short term, intensive, and focused on family-created goals. Comprehensive services delivered through daily or weekly contact include individual therapy, case management, and referral service information. Family therapy is the core service.

## Conclusion

Delinquency, suicide, and mental illness, together with family disintegration, are some of the tragic and often avoidable end-products of a social system that does not put its children—all its children—first. When political ambitions and powerful lobbies determine how and where to spend public funds, often not enough to go around, it is the children with special needs who most often are shortchanged.

Even within that system, professionals who serve children can make a difference. Indeed, there can be a profound difference in outcomes if the many public and private children's agencies can humanize and coordinate their services, if caseloads can be kept within reasonable limits, and if awareness of the legal rights of parents and the best

interests of children is coupled with sensitivity to the unique needs of each family and child in trouble. To help make that difference is to have a positive impact on the lives of the most vulnerable children of this country and thus on the generations to come.

# Références

*ABA Standards*. (1979). Washington, DC: American Bar Association, Juvenile Justice Standards Committee.

Abbey, J. M., & Schwartz, I. M. (1992). *Raising Michigan's children*. Ann Arbor: University of Michigan, School of Social Work, Center for the Study of Youth Policy.

Abel, E. L. (1980). Fetal alcohol syndrome: Behavioral teratology. *Psychological Bulletin, 87*, 29-50.

Adoption Assistance and Child Welfare Act of 1980 (Public Law 96-272), 42 U.S.C.A. § 670 et seq. (1980), 45 C.F.R. § 1357.15 (1991).

Adoption Information Act of 1983 (California).

Alcoff, L., & Gray, L. (1993). Survivor discourse: Transgression or recuperation? *Signs, 18*, 260-291.

Alcohol, Drug Abuse, and Mental Health Reorganization Act of 1992, 42 U.S.C. § 290.

*American Society for Adolescent Psychiatry Newsletter*, 1990.

Americans With Disabilities Act of 1990 (Public Law 101-336), 42 U.S.C. § 12100 et seq. (1990).

Ammerman, R. T., Van Hasselt, V. B., & Hersen, M. (1988). Maltreatment of handicapped children: A critical review. *Journal of Family Violence, 3*, 53-72.

Appelbaum, P. S. (1992). Civil commitment from a systems perspective. *Law and Human Behavior, 16*, 61-74.

Baker, F. (1991). *Saving our kids from delinquency, drugs, and despair*. New York: Harper-Collins.

Barnett, E. R., & Barnett. (1980). Family violence: Intervention strategies. Washington, DC: Department of Health and Human Services, Office of Human Development Services, Administration for Children, Youth, and Families, Children's Bureau.

Barriers to same race placement. (1991). *Adoptalk* [Newsletter of the North American Council on Adoptable Children].

Barth, R. (1991). Adoption of drug-exposed children. *Children and Youth Services Review,* 13, 323-342.

Barth, R., Berrick, J., Courtney, M., & Pizzini, S. (1990). *A snapshot of California's families and children pursuant to the child welfare reforms of the 1980's.* Sacramento, CA: Child Welfare Strategic Planning Commission.

Bassuk, E. L., & Gallagher, E. M. (1990). The impact of homelessness on children. In N. A. Boxill (Ed.), *Homeless children: The watchers and the waiters* (pp. 19-34). Binghamton, NY: Haworth.

Bath, H. J., & Haapala, D. A. (1993). Intensive family preservation services with abused and neglected children: An examination of group differences. *Child Abuse & Neglect,* 17, 213-225.

Bays, J., & Chadwick, D. (1993). Medical diagnosis of the sexually abused child. *Child Abuse & Neglect,* 17, 91-110.

Behar, L. (1990). Financing mental health services for children and adolescents. *Bulletin of the Menninger Clinic,* 54, 127-139.

Belsky, J. (1980). Child maltreatment: An ecological integration. *American Psychologist,* 35, 320-335.

Berlin, F., Malin, H. M., & Dean, S. (1991). Effects of statutes requiring psychiatrists to report suspected sexual abuse of children. *American Journal of Psychiatry,* 148(4), 449-453.

Berson, N., & Herman-Giddens, M. (Eds.). (1986). *Child protection team manual.* Durham, NC: Duke University.

Besharov, D. J. (1990a). *Mandatory reporting of child abuse and research on the effects of prenatal drug exposure.* Unpublished manuscript.

Besharov, D. J. (1990b). *Recognizing child abuse.* New York: Free Press.

Billingsley, A., & Giovannoni, J. M. (1972). *Children of the storm: Black children and American child welfare.* New York: Harcourt Brace Jovanovich.

Binsfield Commission on Adoption. (1992).

Bishop, D., & Frazier, C. E. (1992). Gender bias in juvenile justice processing: Implications of the JJDP Act. *Journal of Criminal Law and Criminology,* 82(4), 1162-1186.

Bjerregaard, B. (1989). Televised testimony as an alternative in child sexual abuse cases. *Criminal Law Bulletin,* 25, 164-175.

Blau, G. M., Whewell, M. C., Gullotta, T. P., & Bloom, M. (1994). The prevention and treatment of child abuse in households of substance abusers: A research demonstration program report. *Child Welfare,* 73, 83-95.

Board of Education of Hendrick Hudson Central School District v. Rowley, 458 U.S. 176, 102 S.Ct. 3034 (1982).

Bogin, M. B., & Goodman, B. (1985). *Representing learning disabled children.* Washington, DC: American Bar Association National Legal Resource Center for Child Advocacy and Protection.

Boland, P. (1990). *Los Angeles Dependency Court Rules.* Los Angeles: Los Angeles County Superior Court.

Bolton, F. G., & Bolton, S. R. (1987). *Working with violent families.* Newbury Park, CA: Sage.

Bolton, F. G., Lane, R. H., & Kane, S. P. (1980). Child maltreatment risk among adolescent mothers: A study of reported cases. *American Journal of Orthopsychiatry,* 50, 489-504.

Bowdry, C. (1990). Toward a treatment-relevant typology of child abuse families. *Child Welfare,* 69, 333-340.

Bowen, J. S. (1988). Cultural convergence and divergence: The nexus between putative Afro-American family values and the best interest of the child. *Journal of Family Law, 26*, 487-544.

Brakel, S. J., Parry, J., & Weiner, B. A. (1985). *The mentally disabled and the law.* Chicago: American Bar Foundation.

Briere, J. N. (1992). *Child abuse trauma.* Newbury Park, CA: Sage.

Briere, J., & Elliott, D. M. (1993). Sexual abuse, family environment, and psychological symptoms: On the validity of statistical control. *Journal of Consulting and Clinical Psychology, 61,* 284-288.

Bross, D. C. (1990). Medical diagnosis and the child welfare system: A brief legal review. In American Bar Association Center on Children and the Law (Ed.), *Lawyers for children* (pp. 158-201). Washington, DC: American Bar Association Center on Children and the Law.

Broughton, D. (1989). Nonorganic failure to thrive. *American Family Physician, 40*(Suppl.), 635-685.

Brown v. Board of Education, 347 U.S. 483, 74 S.Ct. 686 (1954).

Bruce, D. A., & Zimmerman, R. A. (1989). Shaken impact syndrome. *Pediatric Annals, 18*(8), 482-493.

Buchanan, A. E., & Brock, D. W. (1990). *Deciding for others: The ethics of surrogate decision-making.* New York: Cambridge University Press.

Bulkley, J. (1984). *Child sexual abuse and the law.* Washington, DC: American Bar Association Legal Resource Center for Children and the Law.

Burlingame, W., & Amaya, M. (1985). Psychiatric commitment of children and adolescents: Issues, current practices, and clinical input. In D. Shetky & E. Benedek (Eds.), *Emerging issues in child psychiatry and the law.* New York: Brunner/Mazel.

Burr v. Board of County Commissioners, 23 Ohio St.3d 69, 491 N.E.2d 1101 (1986).

Burton, R. V., & Strichartz, A. F. (1991). Children on the stand: The obligation to speak the truth. *Developmental and Behavioral Pediatrics, 12,* 121-128.

Bussiere, A. (1989, September/October). Homeless families and the child welfare system. *Youth Law News,* p. 1.

Byrd, D. (1988). The case for confidential adoption. *Public Welfare, 46,* 20-23.

California. *Civil Code* (Suppl., 1991).

California. *Health and Safety Code.*

California. *Penal Code.*

California Senate Office on Research. (1990). *California's drug-exposed babies.* Sacramento: Author.

California. *Welfare and Institutions Code.*

Canterbury v. Spence, 464 F.2d 772, 786 (D.C. Cir. 1972).

Carter, P. I., & St. Lawrence, J. S. (1985). Adolescents' competency to make informed birth control and pregnancy decisions: An interface for psychology and law. *Behavioral Sciences and the Law, 3,* 309-319.

Casey, R. J., & Berman, J. S. (1985). The outcome of psychotherapy with children. *Psychological Bulletin, 98,* 388-400.

Ceci, S. J., & Bruck, M. (1993). The suggestibility of the child witness. *Psychological Bulletin, 113,* 403-439.

Centennial Peaks Hospital. (1989). *The SOAR program: Shaping oppositional adolescent recovery.* Louisville, CO: Author.

Center for the Study of Social Policy. (1993). *Kids count data book.* Washington, DC: Annie E. Casey Foundation.

Chapsky v. Wood, 26 Kan. 650 (1881).

Chasnoff, I. J., & Schnoll, S. H. (1985). Cocaine use in pregnancy. *New England Journal of Medicine, 313,* 666-669.

Chasnoff, I. J., Landress, H. J., & Barrett, M. E. (1990). The prevalence of illicit drug use during pregnancy and discrepancies in mandatory reporting in Pinellas County, Florida. *New England Journal of Medicine, 322,* 1202-1206.

Chatoor, I., Schaeffer, S. S., Dickson, L., & Egar, J. (1984). Nonorganic failure to thrive. *Pediatric Annals, 13,* 829-842.

Child Abuse Prevention and Treatment Act of 1974, 42 U.S.C. § 5103 (1983).

Child Welfare League of America. (1991). *Homelessness: The impact on child welfare in the 1990s.* Washington, DC: Author.

Children Now. (1990). *California: The state of our children.* Los Angeles: Author.

Cohen, R., Parmelee, D. X., Irwin, L., Weisz, J. R., Howard, P., Purcell, P., & Best, A. M. (1990). Characteristics of children and adolescents in a psychiatric hospital and a corrections facility. *Journal of the American Academy of Child and Adolescent Psychiatry, 29*(6), 909-913.

Cole, C. (1988). [Statement at interim hearings on parental substance abuse and its effects on the fetus and children]. Sacramento: California Legislature, Senate Select Committee on Substance Abuse.

Cole, E. (1983). Advocating for adoption services. In M. Hardin (Ed.), *Foster children in the courts* (pp. 449-487). Boston: Butterworth.

Cole, H. M. (1990). Legal interventions during pregnancy. *Journal of the American Medical Association, 264,* 2663-2670.

Colorado. *Revised Statutes.*

Commission for Children's Services. (1992). *Community plan for family preservation in Los Angeles County.* Los Angeles: Author.

Committee for Economic Development. (1991). *The unfinished agenda: A new vision for child development and education.* New York: Author.

Committee on Early Childhood, Adoption, and Dependent Care, American Academy of Pediatrics. (1993). Developmental issues in foster care for children. *Pediatrics, 91,* 1007-1009.

Committee on Substance Abuse and Committee on Children With Disabilities. (1993). Fetal alcohol syndrome and fetal alcohol effects. *Pediatrics, 91,* 1004-1006.

Council on Scientific Affairs. (1989). *Fetal effects of maternal alcohol abuse.* Chicago: American Medical Association.

Coy v. Iowa, 487 U.S. 1012, 108 S.Ct. 2798 (1988).

Cregler, L. L., & Mark, H. (1986). Medical complications of cocaine abuse. *New England Journal of Medicine, 315,* 1495-1500.

Crittenden, P. M. (1992). The social ecology of treatment: Case study of a service system for maltreated children. *American Journal of Orthopsychiatry, 62,* 22-34.

Curry v. Dempsey, 701 F.2d 580 (1983).

Cynthia D. v. San Diego, 5 Cal. 4th 242, 851 P.2d 1307 (1993).

Daro, D. (1988). *Confronting child abuse.* New York: Free Press.

Davidson, H. (1990). Meaningful new state child protection legislation: 1989-1990. In *Proceedings of ABA Fifth National Conference on Children and the Law* (pp. 15-16). Washington, DC: American Bar Association.

D.C. *Code.* (1981).

Deblinger, E., McLeer, S. V., Atkins, M. S., Ralphe, D. L., & Foa, E. (1989). Post-traumatic stress in sexually abused, physically abused, and nonabused children. *Child Abuse & Neglect, 13,* 313-408.

DeKraai, M. B., & Sales, B. D. (1991). Liability in child therapy and research. *Journal of Consulting and Clinical Psychology, 59*(6), 833-860.

DePanfilis, D., & Jones, W. G. (1990). Interpreting and applying agency risk assessment models in the courtroom: A social work and a legal perspective. In *Proceedings of ABA Fifth National Conference on Children and the Law* (pp. 112-113). Washington, DC: American Bar Association.

DePanfilis, D., & Salus, M. K. (1992). *A coordinated response to child abuse and neglect: A basic manual.* McLean, VA: The Circle, Inc.

D.E.P. v. State, 727 P.2d 800 (Alaska Ct. App. 1986).

DeShaney v. Winnebago, 489 U.S. 189, 109 S.Ct. 998 (1989).

Dixon, S. D. (1989). Effects of transplacental exposure to cocaine and methamphetamine on the neonate. *Western Journal of Medicine, 150,* 436-442.

Donley, K. S., & Blechner, M. H. (1986). *Helping threatened families: Mental health/adoption therapy project reference manual.* Mercer County, PA: Children's Aid Society of Mercer County.

Dorris, M. (1989). *The broken cord.* New York: HarperCollins.

Dorwart, R. A., Schlesinger, M., Davidson, H., Epstein, S., & Hoover, C. (1991). A national study of psychiatric hospital care. *American Journal of Psychiatry, 148*(2), 204-210.

Drotar, D., Malone, C., & Negray, J. (1980). Intellectual assessment of young children with environmentally based failure to thrive. *Child Abuse & Neglect, 4,* 23-31.

Drummond v. Fulton County Department of Family and Children's Services (CA5 Ga.), 547 F.2d 835, on rehg. (CA5 Ga.) 563 F.2d 1200, cert. den. 437 U.S. 910 (1977).

Dryfoos, J. G. (1990). *Adolescents at risk: Prevalence and prevention.* New York: Oxford University Press.

DuBois, W.E.B. (1898). *Some efforts of Negroes for social betterment* (Atlanta University Publication No. 3). Atlanta, GA: Atlanta University Press. (Reprinted by Russell & Russell, 1969)

Dubowitz, H., Feigelman, S., & Zuravin, S. (1993). A profile of kinship care. *Child Welfare, 72,* 153-169.

Duquette, D. (1990). *Advocating for the child in protection proceedings: A handbook for lawyers and court appointed special advocates.* Lexington, MA: D. C. Heath.

Eddings v. Oklahoma, 455 U.S. 104, 102 S.Ct. 869 (1982).

Edelstein, S., & Kropenske, V. (1992). Assessment and psychosocial issues for drug-dependent pregnant women. In M. Jessup (Ed.), *Drug dependency in pregnancy: Managing withdrawal* (pp. 13-35). Sacramento: State of California, Department of General Services.

Edna McConnell Clark Foundation. (1985). *Keeping families together: The case for family preservation.* New York: Author.

Education for All Handicapped Children Act of 1975 (Public Law 94-142), 20 U.S.C.S. § 1401 et seq.

Egeland, B., & Sroufe, L. A. (1981). Developmental sequelae of maltreatment in infancy. *New Directions for Child Development, 11,* 77-92.

Elementary and Secondary Education Amendments of 1969 (Public Law 100-297), 102 Stat. 302, 20 U.S.C.S. § 1201 et seq.

Federal Bureau of Investigation. (1989). *Crime, 1989.* Washington, DC: Government Printing Office.

Feldman, K. W. (1987). Child abuse by burning. In R. E. Helfer & R. S. Kempe (Eds.), *The battered child* (pp. 197-213). Chicago: University of Chicago Press.

Feller, J. N., Davidson, H. A., Hardin, M., & Horowitz, R. M. (1992). *Working with the courts in child protection.* McLean, VA: The Circle, Inc.

Feshbach, N. D. (1980). Corporal punishment in the schools: Some paradoxes, some facts, some possible directions. In G. Gerbner, C. J. Ross, & E. Zigler (Eds.), *Child abuse: An agenda for action* (pp. 204-221). New York: Oxford University Press.

Finkelhor, D. (1979). *Sexually victimized children.* New York: Free Press.

Finkelhor, D., & Browne, A. (1986). Initial and long-term effects: A conceptual framework. In D. Finkelhor (Ed.), *Sourcebook on child sexual abuse* (pp. 180-198). Beverly Hills, CA: Sage.

Finlay v. Finlay, 240 N.Y. 429, 148 N.E. 624 (1925).

Finlayson, L. M., & Koocher, G. P. (1991). Professional judgment and child abuse reporting in sexual abuse cases. *Professional Psychology: Research and Practice, 22,* 464-472.

Fish, A., & Speirs, C. (1990). Biological parents choose adoptive parents: The use of profiles in adoption. *Child Welfare, 69,* 129-139.

Florence County v. Carter, 114 S.Ct. 361, 62 U.S.L.W. 4001 (1993).

Fox, N., Graves, D., & Sanders, S. (1986, February 13). *Definition of a model emergency shelter program.* Paper presented at Child Welfare League of America Group Child Care in North America Conference, Houston, TX.

Freiberg, P. (1991). Panel hears of families victimized by alcoholism. *APA Monitor, 30,* 30.

Furman v. Georgia, 408 U.S. 238, 92 S.Ct. 2726 (1971).

Gadow, K. D. (1991). Clinical issues in child and adolescent psychopharmacology. *Journal of Consulting and Clinical Psychology, 59,* 842-852.

Garbarino, J., & Gilliam, G. (1980). *Understanding abusive families.* Lexington, MA: Lexington.

Genger, V. (1994, January/February). *Youth Today.*

Gifted and Talented Children Act of 1978 (Public Law 95-561), 20 U.S.C.S. § 3311 (1978).

Giovannoni, J. (1985). Child abuse and neglect: An overview. In J. Laird & A. Hartman (Eds.), *A handbook of child welfare* (pp. 193-212). New York: Free Press.

Givelbar, D., Bowers, W., & Blitch, C. (1984). Tarasoff, myth and reality: An empirical study of private law in action. *Wisconsin Law Review,* pp. 443-497.

Glickstein, H. J. (1990). The appellate judge's role in children's issues. In American Bar Association Center on Children and the Law (Ed.), *Lawyers for children* (pp. 362-368). Washington, DC: American Bar Association Center on Children and the Law.

G. L. v. Zumwalt, 564 F. Supp. 1030 (W.D. Mo. 1983).

Gold, I. M., Heller, C., & Ritorto, B. (1992). A short-term psychiatric inpatient program for adolescents. *Hospital and Community Psychiatry, 43,* 58-61.

Golden, D. (1992, December 27). Who guards the children? *The Boston Globe Magazine,* pp. 13, 17, 21-28.

Goldstein, J., Freud, A., & Solnit, A. (1973). *Beyond the best interests of the child.* New York: Free Press.

Goldstein, J., Freud, A., & Solnit, A. (1978). *Before the best interest of the child.* New York: Free Press.

Goldstein, J., Freud, A., Solnit, A., & Goldstein, S. (1986). *In the best interests of the child.* New York: Free Press.

Gonyo, B., & Watson, K. (1988). Searching in adoption. *Public Welfare, 46,* 14-22.

Goodman, G., Pyle-Taub, E., Jones, D.P.H., England, P., Port, L. K., Rudy, L., & Prodo, L. (1989). *Emotional effects of criminal court testimony on child sexual assault victims: Final report.* Washington, DC: National Center on Child Abuse and Neglect.

Goodman, G., & Reed, R. (1986). Age differences in eyewitness testimony. *Law and Human Behavior, 10,* 317-332.

Green, A. H. (1986). True and false allegations of sexual abuse in child custody disputes. *Journal of the American Academy of Child Psychiatry, 25,* 449-456.

Halfon, N., & Klee, L. (1986). *Health care for foster children in California* (Report to the David & Lucille Packard Foundation). Los Altos, CA: David & Lucille Packard Foundation.

Halfon, N., & Klee, L. (1991). Health and development services for children with multiple needs: The child in foster care. *Yale Law and Policy Review, 9,* 71-96.

Handicapped Children's Protection Act of 1986 (Public Law 99-372), 20 U.S.C.S. § 1400 n., 1415, 1415 n. (1986).

Handler, J. F., & Zatz, J. (Eds.). (1982). *Neither angels nor thieves: Studies in deinstitutionalization of status offenders.* Washington, DC: National Academy Press.

Hardin, M. (Ed.). (1983). *Foster children in the courts.* Boston: Butterworth.

Harper, G., & Irwin, E. (1985). Alliance formation with parents: Limit-setting and the effect of mandated reporting. *American Journal of Orthopsychiatry, 55,* 550-560.

Hathaway, P. (1989, May). Failure to thrive: Knowledge for social workers. *Health and Social Work,* pp. 122-126.

Hawkins, R. P., Almeida, M. C., Fabry, B., & Reitz, A. L. (1992). A scale to measure restrictiveness of living environments for troubled children and youths. *Hospital and Community Psychiatry, 43,* 54-58.

Healy, A., Keesee, P. D., Smith, B. S. (1989). *Early services for children with special needs: Transactions for family support.* Baltimore, MD: Brooks.

Helfer, R. E. (1976). Basic issues concerning prediction. In R. E. Helfer & C. H. Kempe (Eds.), *Child abuse and neglect: The family and the community* (pp. 363-371). Cambridge, MA: Ballinger.

Helfer, R. E., & Kempe, R. S. (Eds.). (1987). *The battered child* (4th ed.). Chicago: University of Chicago Press.

Helvey v. Rednour, Ill. App. 3d 154, 408 N.E.2d 17 (1980).

Henggeler, S. W. (1989). *Delinquency in adolescence.* Newbury Park, CA: Sage.

Hewlett, S. A. (1991). *When the bough breaks: The cost of neglecting our children.* New York: Basic Books.

Hillman, P., & Solek-Tefft, J. (1988). *Spiders and flies: Help for the parents of sexually abused children.* Lexington, MA: Lexington.

Honig v. Doe, 484 U.S. 305, 108 S.Ct. 592 (1988).

Horowitz, R., & Davidson, H. (1984). *Legal rights of children.* New York: McGraw-Hill.

Horowitz, R., & Pottieger, A. E. (1991). Gender bias in juvenile justice handling of seriously crime-involved youths. *Journal of Research in Crime and Delinquency, 28,* 75-100.

Howard, J. (1989). Annotation: Cocaine and its effects on the newborn. *Developmental Medicine and Child Neurology, 31,* 255-257.

Howard, J. (1990). Quoted in Berger, C. S., Sorensen, S., Gendler, B., & Fitzsimmons, J., Cocaine and pregnancy: A challenge for healthcare providers. *Health and Social Work, 15,* 310-316.

Howard, J., & Kropenske, V. (1990). A preventive intervention model for chemically dependent parents. In S. Goldston, J. Yager, C. Heinicke, & R. Pynoos (Eds.), *Preventing mental health disturbances in childhood* (pp. 71-84). Washington, DC: American Psychiatric Press.

Howing, P., Wodarski, J., Gaudin, J., & Kurtz, P. (1989). Effective interventions to ameliorate the incidence of child maltreatment: The empirical base. *Social Work, 34,* 330-338.

Huizinga, R., & Elliott, D. S. (1987). Juvenile offenders: Prevalence, offender incident and arrest rates by race. *Crime & Delinquency, 33,* 206-223.

Ianacone, B. P. (1977). Historical overview: From charity to rights. *Temple Law Quarterly, 50,* 953-960.

Idaho v. Wright, 497 U.S. 805, 110 S.Ct. 3139 (1990).

Indian Child Welfare Act of 1978 (Public Law 95-608).

Individuals With Disabilities Education Act of 1975 (Public Law 94-142), 20 U.S.C. § 1400 et seq. (1990); C.F.R. § 300.552(a)(3).

In re Adcock, 69 N.C. App. 222, 316 S.E.2d 347 (1984).

*In re* Angelia P., 28 Cal.3d 908, 623 P.2d 198 (1981).

*In re* Cardo, 41 N.C. App. 503, 255 S.E.2d 440 (1979).

*In re* Devone, 86 N.C. App. 57, 356 S.E.2d 389 (1987), rev. denied and appeal dismissed, 306 N.C. 557, 294 S.E.2d 223 (1984).

*In re* D. K., 245 N.W.2d 644 (1976).

*In re* Gault, 387 U.S. 1, 87 S.Ct. 1428 (1967).

*In re* Gentry, 142 Mich. App. 701, 369 N.W.2d 889 (1985).

*In re* Huber, 57 N.C. App. 453, 291 S.E.2d 916 (1982).

*In re* Hulbert, 186 Mich. App. 600, 465 N.W.2d 36 (1990).

In re Scearce, 81 N.C. App. 531, 345 S.E.2d 404 (1986).

*In re* Scott, 184 A.D.2d 866, 585 N.Y.S.2d 685 (1992).

*In re* Victoria M., 207 Cal.3d 1317, 255 Cal. Rptr. 498 (1989).

*In re* Welfare of K.A.A., 397 N.W.2d 4 (1986).

*In re* Wilkerson, 57 N.C. App. 63, 291 S.E.2d 190 (1982).

*In re* Winship, 397 U.S. 358, 90 S.Ct. 1068 (1970).

In the Interest of Baby Girl W., 728 S.W.2d 545 (Mo. Ct. App. 1987).

In the Interest of S.A.D., 382 Pa.Super. 166, 555 A.2d 123 (1989).

In the Matter of Derek W. Burns, 519 A.2d 638 (1986).

Ingraham v. Wright, 430 U.S. 651, 683, 97 S.Ct. 1401 (1977).

Institute of Medicine. (1989). *Research on children and adolescents with mental, behavioral, and developmental disorders.* Washington, DC: National Academy Press.

Interest of H.R.K., 433 N.W.2d. Iowa (1988).

Irueste-Montes, A., & Montes, F. (1988). Court ordered vs. voluntary treatment of abusive neglectful parents. *Child Abuse & Neglect, 12,* 33-39.

Irving Independent School District v. Tatro, 468 U.S. 883, 104 S.Ct. 3371 (1984).

Jacob Javits Gifted and Talented Students Education Act of 1988, § 4103 (Public Law 100-297), 102 Stat. 237, 20 U.S.C.S. § 3061 (1988).

Jellinek, M. S., Murphy, J. M., Bishop, S., Poitrast, F., & Quinn, D. (1990). Protecting severely abused and neglected children: An unkept promise. *New England Journal of Medicine, 323,* 1628-1630.

Jemerin, J. M., & Phillips, I. (1988). Changes in inpatient child psychiatry: Consequences and recommendations. *Journal of Child and Adolescent Psychiatry, 27,* 397-403.

J. P. v. Missouri Department of Social Services, 752 S.W. 2d 847 (Mo. Ct. App. 1988).

Juvenile Justice and Delinquency Prevention Act of 1974 (Public Law 93-415), 88 Stat. 1109, 18 U.S.C.S. § 4351-4353, 5031-5042, 42 U.S.C.S. § 3701, 3723 (1974).

Kalichman, S. C., Craig, M. E., & Follingstad, D. R. (1990). Professionals' adherence to mandatory child abuse reporting laws: Effects of responsibility attribution, confidence ratings and situational factors. *Child Abuse & Neglect, 14,* 69-77.

Kaplan, J. M. (1990). Children don't always tell the truth. *Journal of Social Issues, 40,* 33-50.

Karnes, F. A., & Marquardt, R. G. (1991). *Gifted children and the law.* Dayton: Ohio Psychology Press.

Kass, J. (1989, May 29). Psychiatrists get rich, but do patients profit? *Chicago Tribune,* p. 5.

Kaufman, J., & Zigler, E. (1987). Do abused children become abusive parents? *American Journal of Orthopsychiatry, 57,* 186-192.

Kawashima, Y. (1982). Adoption in early America. *Journal of Family Law, 20,* 677-696.

Kazdin, A. E. (1991). Effectiveness of psychotherapy with children and adolescents. *Journal of Consulting and Clinical Psychology, 59*, 785-798.

Kazdin, A. E., Bass, D., Ayers, W. A., & Rodgers, A. (1990). Empirical and clinical focus of child and adolescent psychotherapy research. *Journal of Consulting and Clinical Psychology, 58*, 729-740.

Kempe, C. H., Silverman, F. N., Steele, B. F., Droegemuller, W., & Silver, H. K. (1962). The battered child syndrome. *Journal of the American Medical Association, 181*, 107-112.

Kendall-Tackett, K. A., Williams, L., & Finkelhor, D. (1993). The impact of sexual abuse on children: A review and synthesis of recent empirical studies. *Psychological Bulletin, 113*, 164-180.

Kent v. United States, 383 U.S. 541, 86 S.Ct. 1045 (1966).

Kerns, D. L., & Ritter, M. L. (1992). Medical findings in child sexual abuse cases with perpetrator confessions [Abstract]. *American Journal of Diseases of Children, 146*, 494.

Kincannon, M. (1989). The child abuse that doesn't count: General and emotional neglect. *University of California Davis Law Review, 22*, 1039-1071.

Kingsley v. Kingsley, 623 So.2d 780 (Fla. Dist. Ct. App. 1993).

Kirk, J. R. (1989). Effects of crack and cocaine upon infants: A brief review of the literature. *Children's Legal Rights Journal, 10*, 4-10.

Knight v. Deavers (Ark.), 531 S.W.2d 252 (1976).

Knitzer, J. (1982). *Unclaimed children: The failure of public responsibility to children and adolescents in need of mental health services.* Washington, DC: Children's Defense Fund.

Krikorian v. Barry, 196 Cal. App.3d 1211, 242 Cal. Rptr. 312 (1987).

Krisberg, B., & Austin, J. F. (1993). *Reinventing juvenile justice.* Newbury Park, CA: Sage.

Laing, R. D. (1967). The study of family and social contexts in relation to the origin of schizophrenia. In J. Romano (Ed.), *Excerpta medica, s.v. "The origins of schizophrenia."* Amsterdam: N.p.

Laird, J., & Hartman, A. (Eds.). (1985). *A handbook of child welfare.* New York: Free Press.

Landeros v. Flood, 17 Cal.3d 399, 551 P.2d 389 (1976).

Larry P. v. Riles, 495 F. Supp. 926 (N.D. Cal., 1979).

LaShawn A. v. Kelly, 990 F.2d 1319 (D.C. Cir. April 16, 1993).

Lassiter v. Department of Social Services, 452 U.S. 18, 101 S.Ct. 2153 (1981).

Lazarus, W. (1989). *California: The state of our children.* Los Angeles: Children Now.

LeMay, S. K. (1989). The emergence of wrongful adoption as a cause of action. *Journal of Family Law, 27*, 475-488.

Lipscomb v. Simmons, 407 F.2d 114 (1990).

Little, B. B., Snell, L. M., Rosenfeld, C. R., Gilstrap, L. C., III, & Gant, N. (1990). Failure to recognize fetal alcohol syndrome in newborn infants. *American Journal of Diseases of Children, 144*, 1142-1146.

Lloyd, D. W. (1990). *Expert testimony in child sexual abuse cases: What does the expert know?* Washington, DC: American Bar Association National Resource Center on Child Sexual Abuse.

Madden, R. G. (1993). State actions to control fetal abuse: Ramifications for child welfare practice. *Child Welfare, 72*, 129-140.

Madonna, P. G., Van Sroyk, S., & Jones, D.P.H. (1991). Family interactions within incest and nonincest families. *American Journal of Psychiatry, 148*(1), 46-49.

Magura, S., & Moses, B. S. (1984). *The family measurement scales.* New York: Child Welfare League of America.

Maine. *Revised Statutes.* (Suppl. 1988).

Maryland v. Craig, 497 U.S. 836, 110 S.Ct. 3157 (1990).

Massachusetts. *General Laws.*

McCormick, A. T. (1990). Transracial adoption: A critical view of the court's present standards. *Journal of Family Law, 28,* 303-318.

McCurdy, K., & Daro, D. (1993). *Current trends in child abuse reporting and fatalities: The results of the 1992 annual fifty state survey.* Chicago: National Committee for Prevention of Child Abuse.

McKeever, C. (1989). *AFDC grant cut hurts children.* Los Angeles: Western Center on Law and Poverty.

McKeiver v. Pennsylvania, 403 U.S. 528, 91 S.Ct. 1976 (1971).

McKinney Homeless Assistance Act of 1987 (Public Law 100-71), Health and Safety Code § 34077 (1994).

Melton, G., & Limber, S. (1989). Psychologist's involvement in cases of child maltreatment: Limits of role and expertise. *American Psychologist, 44,* 1225-1233.

Melton, G. B., & Pliner, A. G. (1986). Adolescent abortion: A psychological analysis. In G. B. Melton (Ed.), *Adolescent abortion: Psychological and legal issues* (pp. 1-39). Lincoln: University of Nebraska Press.

Mental Health Law Project. (1993). Mental health developments. *Clearinghouse Review, 26,* 1079-1094.

Merz, J. F., & Fischoff, B. (1990). Informed consent does not mean rational consent: Cognitive limitations on decision-making. *Journal of Legal Medicine, 11,* 321-350.

Meyer v. Nebraska, 262 U.S. 390, 43 S.Ct. 625 (1923).

Michael J. v. Los Angeles County Department of Adoptions, 201 Cal. App.3d 859, 247 Cal. Rptr. 504 (1988).

Miller v. Youakim, 440 U.S. 125 (1979).

Mills, J. D., Graubard, B. I., Harley, E. E., Rhoads, G. G., & Berends, H. W. (1984). Maternal alcohol consumption and birth weight: How much drinking in pregnancy is safe? *Journal of the American Medical Association, 252,* 1875-1879.

Milstein, B., Rubenstein, L., & Cyr, R. (1991). The Americans With Disabilities Act: A breathtaking promise for people with mental disabilities. *Clearinghouse Review, 24,* 1240-1249.

Mnookin, R. H. (1973). Foster care: In whose best interest? *Harvard Educational Review, 43,* 599-638.

Monopoli, P. A. (1990). Using the legislative process to improve the legal representation of children. In American Bar Association Center on Children and the Law (Ed.), *Lawyers for children* (pp. 76-93). Washington, DC: American Bar Association Center on Children and the Law.

Moss, K. (1990). Substance abuse during pregnancy. *Harvard Women's Law Journal, 13,* 278-299.

Murphy, J. M., Bishop, S. J., Jellinek, M. S., Quinn, D., Poitrast, F. G. (1992). What happens after the care and protection petition: Reabuse in a court sample. *Child Abuse, 16*(4), 485-493.

Mushlin, M. B., Levitt, L., & Anderson, L. (1986). Court-ordered foster family care reform: A case study. *Child Welfare, 65,* 141-149.

Myers, J.E.B. (1992). *Legal issues in child abuse and neglect.* Newbury Park, CA: Sage.

Nash, M. R., Hulsey, T. L., Sexton, M. C., Harralson, T. L., & Lambert, W. (1993). Long-term sequelae of childhood sexual abuse: Perceived family environment, psychopathology and dissociation. *Journal of Consulting and Clinical Psychology, 61,* 276-283.

National CASA Association. (1991). *Report of the 1991 NCASAA Program Survey.* Seattle, WA: Author.

National Center on Child Abuse and Neglect. (1978). *Interdisciplinary glossary on child abuse and neglect.* Washington, DC: U.S. Department of Education.

National Commission on Children. (1991). *Beyond rhetoric: A new American agenda for children and families* [Final report of the National Commission on Children]. Washington, DC: Government Printing Office.

National Commission on Excellence in Education. (1983). *A nation at risk.* Washington, DC: Author.

National Committee for Prevention of Child Abuse. (1992). *Current trends in child abuse reporting and fatalities: The result of the 1991 annual fifty state survey.* Chicago: Author.

National Council of Juvenile and Family Court Judges. (1992). *Protocol for making reasonable efforts to preserve families in drug-related dependency cases.* Reno, NV: Author.

National Defense Education Act of 1958 (Public Law 85-864), 72 Stat. 1580, 20 U.S.C.S. § 15000 et seq.

National Research Council. (1993). *Losing generations: Adolescents in high risk settings.* Washington, DC: National Academy Press.

National Resource Center on Family Based Services. (1990). *Prevention report.* Iowa City: University of Iowa School of Social Work.

Naylor, B. (1989). Dealing with child sexual assault. *British Journal of Criminology, 29,* 395-407.

Nelson, K. E. (1990). Family-based services for juvenile offenders. *Children and Youth Services Review, 12,* 193-212.

Nelson, K. E., Landsman, M. J., & Deutelbaum, W. (1990). Three models of family-centered placement prevention services. *Child Welfare, 69,* 3-21.

New Jersey Department of Youth and Family Services v. A. W., 103 N.J. 591, 512 A.2d 438 (1986).

New Jersey v. T.L.O., 469 U.S. 325, 105 S.Ct. 733 (1985).

New York Family Court Act. (1983, 1988).

New York State Child Welfare. (1980).

Newcomb, M. D., & Bentler, P. M. (1988). *Consequences of adolescent drug use.* Newbury Park, CA: Sage.

Nicholson v. State, 600 So.2d 1101 (Fla. 1992).

Norfleet v. Arkansas, 796 F. Supp. 1194 (E.D. Ark. 1992).

North Carolina. *General Statutes.*

Northwest Resource Associates. (1986). *Active and reasonable efforts to preserve families.* Seattle, WA: Author.

Note. (1986). *Deprived children: A judicial response.* Reno, NV: National Council of Juvenile and Family Court Judges.

Nuce, G. R. (1990). Child sexual abuse: A new decade for the protection of our children? *Emory Law Journal, 39,* 581-618.

Ohio v. Akron Center for Reproductive Health, 497 U.S. 502, 110 S.Ct. 2972 (1990).

Omnibus Budget Reconciliation Act of 1989 (Public Law 101-239), 103 Stat. 2106.

Omnibus Budget Reconciliation Act of 1993 (Public Law 103-66).

Ornstein, P. A., Gordon, B., & Larus, D. (1992). Children's memory for a personally experienced event: Implications for testimony. *Applied Cognitive Psychology, 6*(1), 49-60.

Oster, J. L. (1965). Custody proceedings: A study of vague and indefinite standards. *Journal of Family Law, 5,* 21-28.

Palmore v. Sidoti, 466 U.S. 429, 104 S.Ct. 1879 (1984).

Parent indiscretional. (1991, April 22). *Newsweek,* p. 64.

Parham v. J. R., 442 U.S. 584, 99 S.Ct. 2493 (1979).

Part H: Early Intervention Program for Infants and Toddlers (Public Law 99-457), 20 U.S.C. § 1400 et seq. (1990).

Pennsylvania Association for Retarded Children v. Commonwealth of Pennsylvania, 334 F. Supp. 1257 (E.D. Pa. 1971), 343 F. Supp. 279 (1972).

*Pennsylvania v. Ritchie:* Criminal defendants' right to child protective service records. (1987). *American Academy of Psychiatry Law Newsletter, 12,* 15-17.

People v. Phillips, 122 Cal. App.3d 87, 175 Cal. Rptr. 703 (1981).

Perry, N. W., & Wrightsman, L. S. (1991). *The child witness: Legal issues and dilemmas.* Newbury Park, CA: Sage.

Peterson, M. S., & Urquiza, A. J. (1993). *The role of mental health professionals in the prevention and treatment of child abuse and neglect.* McLean, VA: The Circle, Inc.

Pierce v. Society of Sisters, 268 U.S. 510, 45 S.Ct. 571 (1925).

Pink by Crider v. Mt. Diablo Unified School District, 738 F. Supp. 345 (N.D. Cal. 1990).

Planned Parenthood v. Casey, 112 S.Ct. 2791 (1992).

Plyer v. Doe, 457 U.S. 202, rehg. denied, 458 U.S. 1131 (1982).

Polansky, N. (1981). *Damaged parents: An anatomy of child neglect.* Chicago: University of Chicago Press.

Pomerantz, P., Pomerantz, D. J., & Colca, L. A. (1990). A case study: Service delivery and parents with disabilities. *Child Welfare, 69,* 65-73.

Popper, C. (1987). Medical unknowns and ethical consent: Prescribing psychotropic medications for children in the face of uncertainty. In C. Popper (Ed.), *Psychiatric pharmacosciences of children and adolescents* (pp. 125-161). Washington, DC: American Psychiatric Press.

Powers, J. L., Eckenrode, J., & Jaktitsch, B. (1990). Maltreatment among runaway and homeless youth. *Child Abuse & Neglect, 14,* 87-98.

President's Commission for the Study of Ethical Problems in Medicine and Biomedical Behavioral Research. (1982). *Making health care decisions* (Vol. 1) [Report]. Washington, DC: Government Printing Office.

Prince v. Massachusetts, 321 U.S. 158, 64 S.Ct. 438 (1944).

Quinn, K. M. (1991, April). Competence to have an abortion: Adolescent issues. *AAPL Newsletter,* p. 19.

Rasell, M. E., & Mishel, L. (1989). *Shortcoming education: How U.S. spending on grades K-12 lags behind other industrial nations* [Briefing paper]. Washington, DC: Economic Policy Institute.

Re Adoption of S.C.P., 364 Pa. Super. 257, 527 A.2d 1052 (1987).

Reece, R. M. (1994). *Child abuse: Medical diagnosis and management.* Philadelphia: Lea & Febiger.

Rehabilitation Act of 1973, 29 U.S.C.A. § 794 (1990).

Rescorla, L., Parker, R., & Stolley, P. (1991). Ability, achievement, and adjustment in homeless children. *American Journal of Orthopsychiatry, 61,* 210-220.

Rindfleisch, N., & Hicho, D. (1987). Institutional child protection: Issues in program development and implementation. *Child Welfare, 66,* 329-342.

Rindfleisch, N., & Rabb, J. (1985). A study to define and assess severity of institutional abuse and neglect. *Child Abuse & Neglect, 9,* 286-287.

Ringwalt, C., & Earp, J. (1988). Attributing responsibility in cases of father-daughter sexual abuse. *Child Abuse & Neglect, 12,* 273-281.

Roark, A. C. (1992, March 18). Most absent parents fail to pay support, study finds. *Los Angeles Times,* pp. A1, A18.

Rodham, H. (1973). Children under the law. *Harvard Educational Review, 43,* 487-514.

Roe v. Wade, 410 U.S. 113 (1973).

Rogeness, G., Amrung, S., Macedo, C., Harris, W., & Fisher, C. (1986). Psychopathology in abused and neglected children. *Journal of the American Academy of Child Psychiatry, 25*, 659-665.

Rosenberg, M. L., Smith, J. C., Davidson, L. E., & Conn, J. M. (1987). The emergence of youth suicide: An epidemiologic and public health perspective. *Annual Review of Public Health, 8*, 417-440.

Rothman, J. (1991). *Runaway and homeless youth*. White Plains, NY: Longman.

Runyan, D., Everson, M., Edelsohn, G., Hunter, W., & Coulter, M. (1988). Impact of legal intervention on sexually abused children. *Journal of Pediatrics, 113*, 647-653.

Russell, D.E.H. (1986). *The secret trauma: Incest in the lives of girls and women*. New York: Basic Books.

Sachs, B. P. (1985). Sharing the cigarette: The effects of smoking in pregnancy. In M. J. Rosenberg (Ed.), *Smoking and reproductive health* (pp. 134-149). Littleton, MA: PSG.

Santosky v. Kramer, 455 U.S. 745, 102 S.Ct. 1388 (1982).

Sarri, R. C. (1983). Gender issues in juvenile justice. *Crime & Delinquency, 29*, 381-397.

Saywitz, K. (1990). The child as witness: Experimental and clinical considerations. In A. LaGreca (Ed.), *Through the eyes of the child* (pp. 329-367). Boston: Allyn & Bacon.

Saywitz, K., Geiselman, R. E., & Bornstein, G. (1992). Effects of cognitive interviewing and practice on children's recall performance. *Journal of Applied Psychology, 77*, 744-756.

Schor, E. L. (1987). A summary of a white paper on the health care of children in foster care: Report of colloquium on health care for children in foster homes. *Children's Legal Rights Journal, 8*, 16-22.

Schorr, L., & Schorr, D. (1989). *Within our reach: Breaking the cycle of disadvantage*. New York: Doubleday.

Schwartz, I. M. (1989). Hospitalization of adolescents for psychiatric and substance abuse treatment: Legal and ethical issues. *Journal of Adolescent Health Care, 10*, 473-478.

Scott v. Prince George's County Department of Social Services, 76 Md. App. 357, 545 A.2d 81, cert. denied, 314 Md. 193, 550 A.2d 381 (1988).

Seagull, E. (1987). The child psychologist's role in family assessment. In R. E. Helfer & R. S. Kempe (Eds.), *The battered child* (4th ed., pp. 152-177). Chicago: University of Chicago Press.

Searcy v. Auerbach, 980 F.2d 609 (9th Cir. 1992).

Select Committee on Children, Youth, and Families. (1989). *U.S. children and their families: Current conditions and recent trends*. Washington, DC: U.S. House of Representatives.

Select Committee on Children, Youth, and Families. (1990). *No place to call home: Discarded children in America*. Washington, DC: U.S. House of Representatives.

Shoecraft v. Catholic Social Services Bureau, Inc., 222 Neb. 574, 385 N.W.2d 448, app. dismd. (U.S.) 107 S.Ct. 49 (1986).

Silverstein, E. M. (1980). Civil commitment of minors: Due and undue process. *North Carolina Law Review, 58*, 1133-1160.

Silverstein, E. M. (1985). Civil commitment of minors: Legal and clinical issues after *Parham v. J. R.* In C. P. Ewing (Ed.), *Psychology, psychiatry, and the law: A clinical and forensic handbook*. Sarasota, FL: Professional Resource Exchange.

Simms, M. D. (1991). Foster children and the foster care system, Part I: History and legal structure. *Current Problems in Pediatrics, 21*, 297-322.

Sloane, M. P., & Meier, J. H. (1983). Typology for parents of abused children. *Child Abuse & Neglect, 7*, 443-450.

Smith, B., Hillenbrand, S., & Goretsky, S. (1991). *The probation response to child sexual abuse offenders: How is it working?* [Free probation report of the ABA]. Chicago: American Bar Association.

Smith, J. C., Benton, R. L., Moore, J., & Runyon, D. (1988). *Understanding the medical diagnosis of child maltreatment: A guide for non-medical professionals.* Raleigh: North Carolina Department of Human Resources.

Smith, S. R., & Meyer, R. G. (1984). Child abuse reporting laws and psychotherapy: A time for reconsideration. *International Journal of Law and Psychiatry, 7*(3-4), 351-366.

Smith v. Organization of Foster Families for Equality and Reform, 431 U.S. 816, 97 S.Ct. 2094 (1977).

Social Security Act of 1935, 42 U.S.C. § 606, 607 (Aid to Families With Dependent Children); 42 U.S.C. § 1396 (Grants to States for Medical Assurance Programs, Appropriations, 1994); 20 C.F.R. 416.924 (Supplemental Security Income for the Aged, Blind, and Disabled).

Soman, L. A., Dunn-Malhotra, E., & Halfon, N. (1993). Perinatal alcohol and drug use: Access to essential services in 12 California counties. *CPS Brief, 5,* 1-8.

Spar, K. (1992, May 20). *Child welfare: State services and federal programs* (455EPW). Washington, DC: Congressional Research Service, Library of Congress.

Springdale School District No. 50 of Washington County v. Grace, 656 F.2d 300 (8th Cir. 1981) reaffd. on remand from U.S. at 693 F.2d 41 (8th Cir. 1982).

State v. Chandler, 324 N.C. 172, 376 S.E.2d 728 (1989).

State v. Lonergan, 505 N.W.2d 349 (Minn. Ct. App. 1993).

Stein, T. J., & Rzepnicki, T. L. (1983). *Decision making at child welfare intake.* New York: Child Welfare League of America.

Steinhart, D. (1988). California legislature ends the jailing of children: The story of a policy reversal. *Crime & Delinquency, 34,* 150-168.

Streissguth, A. P., Martin, D. C., Barr, H. M., Kirchner, G. L., & Darby, D. L. (1984). Intrauterine alcohol and nicotine exposure: Attention and reaction time in 4 yr. old children. *Developmental Psychology, 20,* 533-541.

Stroul, B. A., & Friedman, R. M. (1986). *A system of care for severely emotionally disturbed children and youth.* Washington, DC: Georgetown University Child Development Center, CASSP Technical Assistance Center.

Sullivan v. Zebley, 493 U.S. 521, 110 S.Ct. 885 (1990).

Summit, R. (1983). The child sexual abuse accommodation syndrome. *Child Abuse & Neglect, 7,* 177-193.

Suter v. Artist. M., 112 S.Ct. 1360, 118 L. Ed.2d 1 (1992).

Tarasoff v. Regents of the University of California, 17 Cal.3d 425, 131 Cal. Rptr. 14, 551 P.2d 334 (1976).

Thomas, M. (1972). Juvenile corrections: A brief history. In University of North Carolina, Institute of Government (Ed.), *North Carolina's laws and related cases* (pp. 10-11). Chapel Hill: University of North Carolina, Institute of Government.

Tinker v. Des Moines Independent Community School District, 393 U.S. 503, 89 S.Ct. 733 (1969).

Tjaden, P. G., & Thoennes, N. (1992). Predictors of legal intervention in child maltreatment cases. *Child Abuse & Neglect, 16,* 807-822.

Toth, J. (1992, January 1). Foster care to streets: A beaten path, study finds. *Los Angeles Times,* p. A5.

Toufexis, A. (1991, May 13). Innocent victims. *Time,* pp. 56-63.

Town of Burlington v. Department of Education, 471 U.S. 359 (1985).

Turnbull, H. R. (1981). *The least restrictive alternative: Principles and practices.* Task Force on Least Restriction, American Association on Mental Deficiency, Inc.

Tyler, R. (1992). Prenatal drug exposure: An overview of associated problems and intervention strategies. *Phi Delta Kappan, 73,* 705-708.

Tynes v. Bankers Life Co., 730 P.2d 115 (Mont. Sup. Ct. 1987)

*UCLA Medical Center Protocol.* (1993). Los Angeles: University of California Medical Center.

Ulleland, C. N. (1972). The offspring of alcoholic mothers. *Annals of the New York Academy of Science, 197,* 167-169.

University of Washington. (1988). *Washington State children's mental health system analysis.* Seattle: University of Washington, Division of Community Psychiatry, Department of Psychiatry and Behavioral Sciences.

U.S. Bureau of the Census (1989).

U.S. Code Cong. & Admin. News. (1980).

U.S. Congress, Office of Technology Assessment. (1986). *Children's mental health: Problems and services: A background paper* (OTA-BP-H-33). Washington, DC: Government Printing Office.

U.S. Department of Health and Human Services. (1984). *Report to Congress on Public Law 96-272, The Adoption Assistance and Child Welfare Act of 1980.* Washington, DC: U.S. Department of Health and Human Services, Office of Human Development Services, Administration for Children, Youth, and Families.

U.S. Department of Justice. (1990). *Juvenile court statistics.* Washington, DC: Office of Juvenile Justice and Delinquency Prevention.

U.S. Department of Justice. (1991). *The 1990 annual jail census.* Washington, DC: Bureau of Justice Statistics.

Valencia, C. (1993, May 21). Pilot program seeks to prevent dropouts. *Los Angeles Times* (Valley ed.), p. B-2.

Wald, M. (1975). State intervention on behalf of "neglected" children: A search for realistic standards. *Stanford Law Review, 27,* 985-1018.

Wald, M., Carlsmith, M. M., & Leiderman, P. H. (1988). *Protecting abused and neglected children.* Palo Alto, CA: Stanford University Press.

Wald, M. S., & Wolverton, M. (1990). Risk assessment: The emperor's new clothes. *Child Welfare, 27,* 1340-1347.

Walding, J. K. (1990). What ever happened to *Parham* and institutionalized juveniles: Do minors have procedural rights in the civil commitment area? *Law and Psychology Review, 14,* 281-299.

Watahara, A., & Lobdell, T. (1990). The children nobody knows: California's foster care-dependency system. San Francisco: California Tomorrow.

Waterman, J. (1994, March 17). [Lecture]. Los Angeles: University of California, UCLA School of Law.

Watson, H., & Levine, M. (1989). Psychotherapy and mandated reporting of child abuse. *American Journal of Orthopsychiatry, 59,* 246-256.

Waxman, L. D., & Reyes, L. M. (1987). *A status report on homeless families in America's cities.* Washington, DC: U.S. Congress of Mayors.

Weissberg, R. P., Caplan, M., & Harwood, R. L. (1991). Promoting competent young people in competence-enhancing environments: A systems-based perspective on primary prevention. *Journal of Consulting and Clinical Psychology, 59,* 830-841.

Weisz, J. R., & Weiss, B. (1993). *Effects of psychotherapy with children and adolescents.* Newbury Park, CA: Sage.

Weisz, J. R., Weiss, B., Alicke, M. D., & Klotz, M. L. (1987). Effectiveness of psychotherapy with children and adolescents: Meta-analysis findings for clinicians. *Journal of Consulting and Clinical Psychology, 55,* 542-549.

Weisz, J. R., Weiss, B., Donenberg, G. R. (1992). The lab versus the clinic: Effects of child and adolescent psychotherapy. *American Psychologist, 47,* 1578-1585.

Weisz, V. (1978). Viewpoint: Preventive programs unconstitutional? *Human Ecology Forum, 8,* 19-20.

Weisz, V. (Ed.). (1987). *Legal proceedings involving children: Abuse and neglect cases* (3rd ed.). Raleigh, NC: Administrative Office of the Courts.

Weisz, V. (1990). Building a legitimate best interest of the child standard through the guardian ad litem. In American Bar Association Center on Children and the Law (Ed.), *Lawyers for children* (pp. 68-75). Washington, DC: American Bar Association Center on Children and the Law.

Weisz, V. (1992). Child abuse reports aid patient healing. *The Psychiatric Times, 9,* 4, 29.

Weithorn, L. A. (1988). Mental hospitalization of troublesome youth: An analysis of skyrocketing admission rates. *Stanford Law Review, 40,* 773-838.

Wessow, L. S. (1990). *Child advocacy for the clinician: An approach to child abuse and neglect.* Baltimore, MD: Williams & Wilkins.

Westat, Inc. (1993). *Study of adoption assistance impact and outcomes: Final report.* Chicago: Westat, Inc.

Westhaus, A., & Cohen, J. S. (1990). Preventing disruption of special-needs adoptions. *Child Welfare, 69,* 141-155.

White v. Illinois, 112 S.Ct. 736, 116 L.Ed.2d 848 (1992).

White v. North Carolina State Board of Examiners of Practicing Psychologists, 97 N.C. App. 144, 388 S.E.2d 148 (1990).

Widom, C. S. (1989a). Child abuse, neglect and violent criminal behavior. *Criminology, 27,* 251-271.

Widom, C. S. (1989b). Does violence beget violence? *Psychological Bulletin, 106,* 3-28.

Widom, C. S. (1991). Childhood victimization and adolescent problem behaviors. In M. E. Lamb & R. Ketterlinus (Eds.), *Adolescent problem behaviors.* New York: Lawrence Erlbaum.

Wilder v. Bernstein, 848 F.2d 1338 (CA2 N.Y. 1988).

Wilker, S. (1990). Child abuse, substance abuse, and the role of the dependency court. *Harvard Blackletter Journal, 7,* 1-32.

William T. Grant Foundation Commission on Work, Family and Citizenship. (1988). *The forgotten half: Pathways to success for America's youth and young families.* Washington, DC: William T. Grant Foundation.

Williams, C. (1985). *Dispositional alternatives: Examining the options for permanence.* In proceedings of conference on Children Need Permanent Families. Raleigh, NC: Administrative Office of the Courts.

Willie M. et al. v. Hunt., No. CC-79-0294 (W.D.N.C. filed December 7, 1981). See also 657 F.2d (4th Cir. 1981).

Wisconsin v. Yoder, 406 U.S. 205, 92 S.Ct. 1526 (1972).

Wolfe, D. A. (1987). *Child abuse: Implications for child development and psychopathology.* Newbury Park, CA: Sage.

Wood, D. (1990). [Lecture]. Los Angeles: University of California, UCLA Medical School Grand Rounds.

Woodman Accident and Life Insurance Co. v. Bryant, 784 F.2d 1052 (10th Cir. 1986).

Woolf, G. D. (1990). An outlook for foster care in the United States. *Child Welfare, 69,* 75-81.

Yates, A. (1987). Should young children testify in cases of sexual abuse. *American Journal of Psychiatry, 144,* 476-480.

Youngberg v. Romeo, 457 U.S. 307, 102 S.Ct. 2452 (1982).

Zellman, G. L. (1991). Reducing underresponding: Improving system response to mandated reporters. *Journal of Interpersonal Violence, 6,* 115-118.

Zill, N., & Schoenborn, C. A. (1990). *Developmental, learning, and emotional problems: Health of our nation's children, United States, 1988* (Advance Data from Vital and Health Statistics, No. 190). Hyattsville, MD: U.S. Department of Health and Human Services, National Center for Health Statistics.

# Index

# About the Author

Virginia G. (Jenny) Weisz is the Directing Attorney of the Children's Rights Project at Public Counsel, a public interest law firm in Los Angeles. She is the author of numerous publications on children and the law. She teaches and directs legal internships for law students at the University of California at Los Angeles (UCLA) and the University of Southern California (USC) and has been Visiting Professor in the Department of Psychology at UCLA. From 1983 to 1990 she implemented and directed the Office of Guardian ad Litem Services for the state of North Carolina. Before beginning her career as an advocate for children, she taught school in the Peace Corps in Nairobi, Kenya. She earned her law degree from Cornell Law School and her undergraduate degree from Blue Mountain College in Mississippi. She is the mother of two daughters, Dawn and Allison, and lives with her husband, John, in Los Angeles.